DATE DUE

MY 5 '98			
JE 10 '00			

DEMCO 38-296

Endangered Mexico

Endangered Mexico

An Environment on the Edge

Joel Simon

SIERRA CLUB BOOKS • *San Francisco*

The Sierra Club, founded in 1892 by John Muir, has devoted itself to the study and protection of the Earth's scenic and ecological resources—mountains, wetlands, woodlands, wild shores and rivers, deserts and plains. The publishing program of the Sierra Club offers books to the public as a non-profit educational service in the hope that they may enlarge the public's understanding of the Club's basic concerns. The point of view expressed in each book, however, does not necessarily represent that of the Club. The Sierra Club has some sixty chapters coast to coast, in Canada, Hawaii, and Alaska. For information about how you may participate in its programs to preserve wilderness and the quality of life, please address inquiries to Sierra Club, 85 Second Street, San Francisco, CA 94105.

http://sierraclub.org/books

Library of Congress Cataloging-in-Publication Data
Simon, Joel.
    Endangered Mexico : an environment on the edge / Joel Simon.
        p.   cm.
    Includes bibliographical references and index.
    ISBN: 0-87156-351-7 (alk. paper)
        1. Environmental degradation—Mexico. 2. Environmental policy—
    Mexico
    GE160.M6S55   1997
    363.7'00972—dc20   96-43720

Production by Susan Ristow • Jacket design by Amy Evans
Book design by Amy Evans • Map by Hilda Chen

Printed in the United States on acid-free paper containing a minimum of 50% recovered waste paper, of which at least 10% of the fiber content is post-consumer waste.

10 9 8 7 6 5 4 3 2 1

To My Grandmother

Contents

Acknowledgments

This book would not have been possible without the support of the Center for Latin America Studies at Stanford University, where I was a media fellow in 1995. Special thanks to the staff and faculty there; Terry Karl, the director of the Center; and also Jutta Mohr and Liz Jusino.

I received consistent support from Mexico's environmental community and U.S. environmentalists who follow Mexico. I have acknowledged most of them in my chapter notes, but a few people deserve special mention: Dick Kamp, Mary Kelly, Homero and Betty Aridjis, Edwin Bustillos, Gustavo Alanis, Korina Esquinca, Barbara MacKinnon Montes, and Luis Manuel Guerra. Obviously, their views and opinions helped shape this book; but the conclusions—as well as any errors—are my own.

Two grants from the Dick Goldensohn Fund in New York helped fund part of the research for this book. In 1992 I was awarded a grant to travel along the United States–Mexico border to investigate the environmental consequences of the North American Free Trade Agreement. In 1994 I received a second grant to look at Indian communities in the wake of the Chiapas uprising.

Working with Sandy Close, executive editor of Pacific News Service, for seven years has most shaped my style and approach to reporting. Irene Schneider at *Condé Nast Traveler,* Mark Abel at the *San Francisco Chronicle,* and Marcelo Rodríguez during his tenure at *SF Weekly* also supported my environmental reporting in Mexico.

Various people read drafts of chapters and contributed immensely to improving this manuscript. They are: Judith Barish, Henry Tricks, Dudley Althaus, Paige Bierma, Jan de Vos, Ingrid Abramovitch, and Mary Kelly. Above all I would like to thank Nancy Nusser and Mauricio Tenorio, both of whom went well beyond the call of duty in providing detailed criticism. Thanks also to Barbara, Alissa, Jerrold and Marcia Simon, Colum Lynch, Mark Fineman, Jonathan Lethem, Michelle Quinn, Andy Blauvelt, Paul Catasus, Mike McIntosh, Irv Muchnick, and Dirk Vandersypen for their support and encouragement.

My agent, Richard Parks, helped me turn a half-baked idea into a proposal and a proposal into a finished book. I would also like to thank Sierra Club Books—Peter Beren, the publisher, and Barbara Ras, my editor, who read the manuscript with both rigor and enthusiasm. Also, special thanks to Danny Moses, who took over the project after Barbara's premature departure.

A book of this nature requires the collaboration of dozens of people, many of them strangers. It was often those who had the least who offered the most: a place to sleep, food to eat, a late-night meeting at the end of a long day. Joaquín Sánchez in San Juan Mixtepec, Miguel Alvarez Montalvo in Tototepec, Petronilo Bustillos in Aboreachi, and Kinbor in Lacanjá are a few who come to mind. Most of the people who helped me in this manner will never see this book; some do not read, fewer still read in English. It is to them, therefore, that I owe my most profound gratitude.

When we saw all those cities and villages built in the water, and other great towns on dry land, and that straight and level causeway leading to Mexico, we were astounded. These great towns and cues [temples] and buildings rising from the water, all made of stone, seemed like an enchanted vision . . . It was so wonderful that I do not know how to describe this first glimpse of things never heard of, seen or dreamed before . . . I was never tired of noticing the diversity of trees and the various scents given off by each, and the paths choked with roses and other flowers, and the many local fruit trees and rose bushes, and the pond of fresh water . . . But today all that I then saw is overthrown and destroyed; nothing is left standing.

Bernal Díaz del Castillo,

The Conquest of New Spain, circa 1568

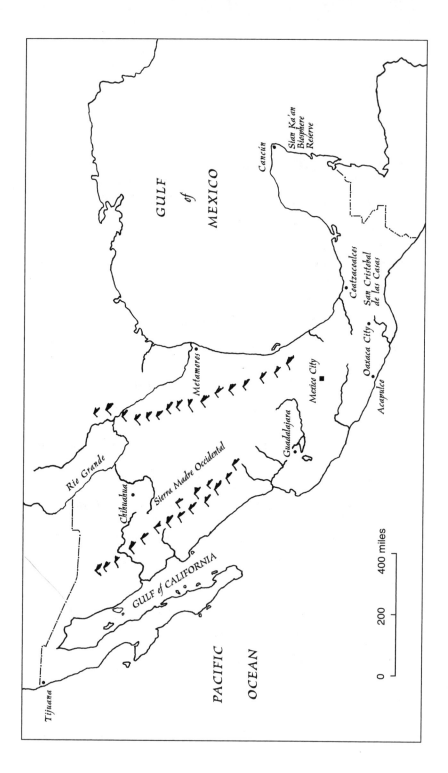

PACIFIC

OCEAN

GULF of CALIFORNIA

Tijuana

Rio Grande

Chihuahua

Sierra Madre Occidental

Guadalajara

Matamoros

GULF

of

MEXICO

Mexico City

Cancún

Sian Ka'an
Biósphere
Reserve

Coatzacoalcos

San Cristóbal
de las Casas

Oaxaca City

Acapulco

0   200   400 miles

Introduction

I did not go looking for Mexico's environmental crisis. One morning it found me. On March 7, 1991, I woke up in Mexico City with a sore throat, red eyes, a stuffed nose, a powerful headache, and the distinct impression that I had drunk an entire bottle of cheap tequila the night before. Twenty million *chilangos,* as the denizens of Mexico City are called, climbed out of bed with a similar array of symptoms. The collective hangover—certainly the largest in history—was not the result of a massive citywide celebration. We had all been poisoned. The night before, the wind had stopped blowing and a brown cloud containing more than ten thousand tons of toxic gunk had stalled over the city. There is something viscerally terrifying about trying to breathe polluted air. It feels as if a stranger has slipped his hand around your throat.

Mexico City's air—the world's worst—it is the country's best-known environmental problem. And yet in the course of my research I have come to see air pollution largely as symptomatic of a much more generalized crisis. I used to struggle to figure out why most Mexicans dismiss the air pollution with a shrug. Now I realize they do it because they can. For the most part, you can make a decision to live with it. The same cannot be said of the country's other environmental threats—a lack of water, eroding farmland, and a massive depletion of natural resources. Even in Mexico City water is a more pressing problem than air. The underground aquifer that supplies 70 percent of the city's water may run dry in a matter of decades.

Environmental destruction in Mexico has global implications because Mexico is the third most biologically diverse nation on the planet. It has more than 30,000 species of plants, 50 to 60 percent of which are found nowhere else on earth. It has 1,000 species of ferns, more than 135 species of oak, forty-nine species of pines—half of all the pine species in the world. Then there are the animals. There are 285 species of amphibians, 449 mammals, 694 species of reptiles, more than 1,000 kinds of birds, 2,000 kinds of fish, and 100,000 insects, many of which have not been catalogued. Many of the world's most important domesticated plants—corn and tomatoes to name but two—are native to Mexico. The climatic extremes—from snow-capped volcanoes to sweltering jungles, from alpine lakes to coastal mangroves—give Mexico one of the most dramatic landscapes in all the world.

That preserving this enormous biological wealth is crucial for the whole planet is the implicit assumption rather than the specific focus of this book. This is largely a book about people—people and their place in the natural world.

I first began to explore Mexico's environmental crisis in a systematic way in 1992, when the relative merits of the North American Free Trade Agreement (NAFTA) were being debated by the American public. Environmentalists in the United States who opposed the treaty argued that its passage would encourage U.S. factories to cross the border into Mexico in order to take advantage of cheap labor and lax environmental enforcement. The result would be a dramatic loss of well-paying factory jobs in the United States and a rapid deterioration of the continentwide environment. The process, environmentalists argued, was already well advanced along the border, where a free-trade zone had attracted nearly two thousand foreign-owned factories and created a binational environmental disaster.

That summer, I traveled from Tijuana to Matamoros visiting industrial parks and shantytowns. I talked to mayors, business people, factory workers, and academics. In the end I came to a conclusion that surprised me. It was not that the environmentalists were wrong—the factories and the hundreds of thousands of workers they had attracted had indeed turned parts of the border into an environmental wasteland. But the reasons went far beyond anything being considered by those negotiating the free-trade agreement.

It was Mexico's economic crisis (which had driven down the cost of labor) combined with the globalization of the U.S. economy that had brought the factories to the border. It was a failed development strategy emphasizing rapid industrial development that had brought the workers. Compared with these weighty processes, NAFTA seemed almost beside the point. The uproar directed against the treaty was really a response to enormous forces of global change, which, among other things, linked the United States and Mexico more intimately than ever before.

The point at which U.S. and Mexican interests converge is often expressed in negative terms—runaway immigration, drug trafficking, political and financial instability, pollution along the border. In fact, by 1990, even before NAFTA was under discussion, Mexico's total trade with the United States had topped $58 billion, making it the United States' third largest trading partner behind Canada and Japan (by 1995, trade with Mexico had nearly doubled, to $108 billion). The U.S. economy is dependent on Mexican natural resources, especially oil, and on cheap Mexican labor, provided both by immigrants and, increasingly, by Mexican workers in U.S. factories on the Mexican side of the border. Mexico's dependence on the United States is even greater. The Mexican economy would collapse without the U.S. market, which accounts for more than 70 percent of its exports. The vast majority of foreign investment in Mexico is from the United States. Meanwhile, immigration to the United States is both a social escape valve and an economic boost, since billions of dollars are sent home to Mexico each year.

In fact, politicians in Washington came rather late to a conclusion that was already obvious to anyone who lives in Houston, Los Angeles, Fresno, Chicago, Michoacán, or Oaxaca—the cultural and economic melding of the United States and Mexico is well under way. More than NAFTA itself, the $48 billion bailout orchestrated by the Clinton administration to stave off Mexico's economic collapse in 1995 was an explicit acknowledgment that the two countries' economic and strategic interests have converged.

Once we recognize that integration is inevitable, it seems that U.S. policy should focus not only on reacting to periods of instability in Mexico but also on understanding their basic causes. Over and over, as I traveled across Mexico, I saw the destruction of the country's environment at the root of many seemingly unrelated problems.

Since 1989 I have divided my time between Mexico City and San Francisco. I originally came to know Mexico as the correspondent for Pacific News Service. In 1990 I visited Michoacán to write a story on federal agents who had gunned down peasants growing marijuana. There I learned how the eroding land and dependence on fertilizers had pushed peasants into a cycle of debt that made growing drugs seem like the only way out. In 1994, when I began covering the Zapatista rebellion in Chiapas, it quickly became clear to me that the rebellion had an environmental basis. The Zapatistas have risen up not only against the government but also against the thin jungle soils that will no longer support their corn crop. Meanwhile, one of the primary causes of Mexican migration to the United States is the ecological decline of the countryside.

Even Mexico's newest guerrilla group—the Revolutionary Army of the Poor, or EPR—has exploited discontent over environmental problems to garner support. The EPR first made its appearance on June 28, 1996, and, at the time of this writing, the group's ideology, goals, and tactics remain too obscure to draw any definitive conclusions. But one thing was immediately clear: access to fertilizers, pesticides, herbicides, and the whole technological package essential to making degraded farmland produce is a key demand of the group's supporters.

In the fall of 1994, I spent several months at Stanford University compiling an environmental history of Mexico. Given the enormous amount of scholarship on Mexico, I was surprised by how little looked at historical environmental change. In 1972 biohistorian Alfred Crosby published a groundbreaking book on the environmental consequences of the Spanish Conquest called *The Columbian Exchange*. More than twenty years later, Elinor G. K. Melville's *A Plague of Sheep* provided the first well-documented study of the ecological upheaval caused by the introduction of grazing animals in the Mexican highlands. In fact, the Spanish Conquest may have precipitated the greatest environmental catastrophe in human history. A century after the conquest, European plants and animals had completely transformed the Mexican landscape while disease wiped out as much as nine-tenths of the human population.

The conquest also represented a violent rupture in the way that land was both conceived of and managed in Mexico. In colonial society two competing land ethics coexisted—the Indians saw access to land as a basic right, while the Spaniards saw land as private property. The conflict was played out in the 1910 Mexican Revolution and partially resolved through a massive agrarian reform program begun in the 1930s. The agrarian reform, however, was always intended as a means of fomenting the country's industrial development, and by the 1950s one of the world's great rural to urban movements was under way. Often the impetus for leaving the farm was the environmental deterioration of the countryside, caused by intensive cultivation of marginal land and a growing dependence on expensive fertilizers.

Mexico's size alone (it is the world's fourteenth largest country) makes it impossible to cover the entire environmental crisis in a single book. I have tried to cover a variety of regions and ecosystems, to balance urban and rural problems, and to emphasize what I believe are the country's most pressing concerns. I have also sought out stories that dramatically illustrate particular problems. In writing this book, I spent more time talking to the people affected by environmental problems than I did to experts who study them. I often traveled by second-class bus, slept on people's floors, and ate their food. In doing so, I developed friendships and obligations that took me beyond journalistic objectivity. Without the generosity of dozens of strangers who shared their time and their often meager resources, I could not have written this book. To a large extent, wittingly or unwittingly, I have adopted their concerns—clean water, basic sanitation, a piece of productive farmland. The challenge of meeting basic human needs in a depleted environment is my central theme.

I do rely on academic and scientific studies to frame my discussions and support my arguments. But one of the reasons I feel this story must be told anecdotally is that scientific research is often inadequate. For example, there is no scientific study that correlates the air pollution in Mexico City with long-term health problems. There are no comprehensive studies looking at the long-term water supply in Mexico City; none on oil-related pollution in Tabasco; none of pesticide use in Sinaloa.

From the 1940s to the 1970s, Mexico's fantastic economic growth made it a model for developing countries around the world. Today, the country's environmental crisis should serve as a warning about the long-term costs of such a strategy. More significant, at a time when even the concept of managing the environment has come under attack in the

United States, Mexico is a clear example that taking nature's resilience for granted has real economic and social costs.

As I traveled from one end of the country to the other, it began to occur to me that Mexico, for all its grandeur, is a fragile land. The blazing deserts of the north, the volcanic chain that stretches across its broad waist, the jungles and swamps that crowd the southern reaches, all give the appearance of solidity. But the land itself is in constant flux—moving, shifting, cracking. The Aztecs saw this instability as proof that Mexico would one day be destroyed in an environmental cataclysm. I do not feel that such a fate is imminent. But five hundred years after the Aztecs were crushed by the conquering Spaniards, it is a not a prophecy I can easily dismiss.

one

Environmental Conquests

In the beginning, the Aztecs believed, the sun had been stillborn, lifeless. It had hung motionless in the sky. Then Cihuacoatl, the demonous earth-mother, had pulled an obsidian knife from her loins and cast it upon the earth. Humans used the knife to give their blood to the sun, and only then did the orb begin its slow journey across the heavens. The sun was sustained by offerings of human hearts. Without them it would stall again and the earth would perish.

The Aztecs believed that their world was created in violence, that it was a fragile place in which their existence was precarious. They believed that nature could not be depended upon to function without their guidance and assistance. It was an awesome responsibility—and one that their conquerors never assumed.

The Aztecs always expressed their vast knowledge of nature and natural forces in mythical terms. They may not have known the scientific details about the origins of their world, but they were right to believe that it was born in cataclysm. Fifty million years ago an enormous tectonic trench collapsed off the Pacific coast and volcanoes sprouted from the shaking earth. These explosions raised the swampy lowlands into a plateau seven thousand feet high. Lava spread across the land and became mountains; it sealed off valleys and turned rivers into lakes. The process is still not completed. In 1943 the Paricutín volcano erupted from the earth and swallowed the village of San Juan Parangaricutiro, leaving nothing but the church spire protruding from the lava. In late

1994, Popocatepetl, the volcano the Aztecs called "the smoking mountain," sent a plume of ash and steam billowing into the air. Hundreds of earthquakes shake the land each year.

The Aztecs had no idea that the same great tectonic forces that raised the land from the sea also created the mountains. But they understood the role the mountains played in their lives, and they built pyramids that emulated and reflected their image. Just one day's walk from the Aztec capital of Tenochtitlan, pines and firs grew on the slopes of the snow-capped volcanoes of Popocatepetl and Iztaccihuatl; north of the city lay a scrub desert where shade was at a premium. There was virtually no place in the enormous Aztec realm where one could stand and not see a ridgeline in the distance.

The Aztecs knew nothing about high-pressure systems or tropical depressions or prevailing westerlies. They knew that the water god, Tlaloc, was at times benevolent, at times fickle. Tlaloc would sometimes send the rains in June and sometimes in July; sometimes he stopped them in September and sometimes he let them continue until November. Some years he was angry and would send no rain at all; other years he sent terrible storms that flooded the crops in the field. The Aztecs had never heard of aquifers but believed that the mountains were hollow and full of water.

The Aztecs did not know that the first big-game hunters were Asiatic people who had crossed the Bering Strait and arrived in Mexico twenty thousand years earlier. They had no idea that seven thousand years before the founding of their empire, the growing human population had hunted the big game—the mastodons, mammoths, horses, sloths, and camels that once roamed Mesoamerica—to extinction. Their history said nothing about how humans had survived on small game until two thousand years ago when it too became scarce. The Aztecs did not know that around that time the hunter-gatherers had learned to cultivate wild plants like maize (corn), squash, amaranth (a grain), and manioc, and had built villages that later became cities.

And yet their own myths perfectly reflected this history. They believed that there was a time in the past when food was plentiful. Their ancient homeland of Aztlan ("the place of the white heron") was a watery Eden full of fish, deer, and birds. Then the game suddenly disappeared. The

Aztecs wandered in the desert eating prickly pears and hunting scarce game. Huitzilopochtli, or Hummingbird-on-the-Left, had led them to the Valley of Mexico and pointed them to the long-awaited sign—an eagle perched on a cactus eating a snake. They named the island Tenochtitlan, "Place of the Cactus Fruit," and it was there they settled, learned to grow corn, and built their great city. Mexico City was built on its remains.

The Aztecs knew nothing of La Venta, the capital of the Olmec civilization, which thrived for four centuries until 800 B.C. on the spectacularly rainy delta of the Coatzacoalcos River. Perhaps through Toltec myths the Aztecs knew something of the Maya. They may have known that a great civilization had grown out of the jungle, built enormous pyramids, and then vanished without a trace.

The Aztecs, however, were acutely aware of living in a land dotted with ruins, where great civilizations had simply vanished, and this knowledge fueled their sense of collective doom. In the northern part of the valley they discovered two enormous pyramids covered with moss and scrub. They named these ruins Teotihuacan—meaning "Place of the Gods" in their native Nahuatl. They believed that the pyramids had been created by the gods at the same time they created the sun and the moon.

The Aztecs were also familiar with the Toltecs, whose capital city of Tula had lain in ruins for two centuries by the time the Aztecs rose to prominence. They imagined that Tula was once a cultural mecca governed by enlightened rulers and surrounded by a paradisiacal landscape where cotton grew in different colors.

It has taken five centuries for archaeologists, geologists, and meteorologists to fill in the gaps in the Aztecs' understanding of their world and their history. Yet the new knowledge has done nothing to alter the Aztecs' quite rational conclusion: they lived in a world on the brink. Earthquakes, volcanic eruptions, droughts, hurricanes, floods, and enormous forest fires were known to all in the course of a lifetime.

The Aztecs did not know anything about the environmental basis for the Mayan collapse; they did not know that both Tula and the Zapotec capital of Monte Alban had been destroyed by droughts. They did not know that the residents of Teotihuacan had cut down so many trees that the underground springs that fed their cornfields had run dry. Like all great imperial civilizations, the Aztecs' past was often consciously mythologized.Yet a fear of environmental collapse emerges as a persistent theme in their understanding of their world and their place in it. The Aztecs explained their ultimate demise in ecological terms.They believed that they lived under the fifth sun, which would be destroyed by earthquakes, just as the first sun had been destroyed by wild animals, the second by wind, the third in a raging fire, and the fourth in a terrible flood.

The only way to stave off the fate that awaited them, the Aztecs believed, was through worship and devotion. What greater way to express it than to offer up their own hearts, their own blood, to the forces that would one day destroy them?

The Aztecs believed that time was cyclical, that events repeated themselves at regular intervals. When they looked north at the ruins of Tula they saw a reflection of their own eventual demise. Quetzalcoatl, the Plumed Serpent, the Precious Twin, the god of wind and air, and the ruler of the Toltecs, had one day destroyed Tula's temples of gold and coral, driven off the birds, and turned the cacao trees into mesquite bushes. Then he traveled eastward across the land to the sea where he wove a raft out of snakes. He rode off on the waves, vowing to return one day to reclaim his ancient realm.

I

The Aztecs' religion of imminent ecological doom did not prevent them from constructing a massive infrastructure that transformed the natural habitat and brought remarkable stability to an unstable world. In fact, there was a natural coincidence—since the Aztecs fully expected their capricious gods to send wind or rain or earthquakes or wild animals at any moment, they took measures to protect themselves.

The Aztecs had an enormous advantage. The Valley of Mexico was not Aztlan, but it was still an ecological marvel. Two million years ago, during a period of intense volcanic activity, lava sealed off the valley's natural drainage, and the waters that had formerly flowed south to the sea spread out into a series of five interconnected lakes. The valley's geology fostered a series of microclimates—marshes and dry scrub, subtropical plains and alpine forests, and fresh- and saltwater lakes—which shared a small and clearly defined area.

Within half a century of their arrival in the Valley of Mexico, the Aztecs had given up the life of hunter-gatherers and taken up farming. Since they had settled on an island in the middle of Lake Texcoco, they had to create farmland artificially. They dredged mud from the shallow lake bottom and piled it along the shores, a technique borrowed from other tribes that had already settled in the valley. These artificial fields, called *chinampas* or "floating gardens," were astonishingly productive, producing 100 million pounds a year of maize alone. Water seeped up through the mud, keeping the soil moist, allowing plants to germinate before the rainy season began and protecting the crop from drought. As the population of Tenochtitlan expanded, the *chinampas* were appropriated for urban settlement while food production was shifted to the southern part of the valley. Tenochtitlan emerged as a city of thousands of small islands divided by canals—the Venice of the New World.

The canals formed the basis of a transportation revolution. A fleet of 200,000 canoes brought the valley's products to the city's doorstep. Squash, chiles, and tomatoes came from the *chinampas* of Xochimilco. Corn, beans, and amaranth, which were grown along the lakeshore in small irrigated plots and in terraced fields that climbed the mountain slopes, arrived daily in enormous canoes.

Aztec engineers set to work constructing an urban infrastructure that amazed the first European visitors. Despite a large population of perhaps 500,000—as much as ten times the size of the largest Spanish city of the time—Tenochtitlan had an ingenious transportation system that made getting around easy. Each street was half roadway and half canal. Canoes went everywhere in the city, including directly into the emperor's palace. The city was connected to the shore by a series of well-defended causeways. Fresh water, meanwhile, was brought in through an enormous stone aqueduct that spanned the lake. Around 1440, Nezahual-coyótl, poet-king of the neighboring city of Texcoco, was commissioned to construct a ten-mile-long dike, which divided Lake Texcoco and helped alleviate damage from the perennial floods.

In their urban design the Aztecs tried to replicate the paradisiacal realm of the water god, Tlaloc. The streets of the city were lined with flowers, and nearly every house had a rooftop garden. Moctezuma II, the Aztec emperor at the time of the Spanish Conquest, kept an aviary full of quetzals, macaws, ducks, and other rare birds, as well as a zoo with pumas and jaguars. The streets were spotless, there were no beggars, and unlike the European cities of the time, which reeked of sewage, the Aztecs had found a highly effective and efficient way to get rid of human waste. Small outhouses at the end of each street emptied directly into canoes, which were poled each day across the lake to the farmland, where the cargo was used as fertilizer.

The Aztecs' ability to expand their dominion over all of Mesoamerica was based on their good fortune in settling in such an ecologically advantageous location. The interconnected lake system allowed them to use canoes to exploit the diverse products of the ecosystem. This was an enormous breakthrough in a country that had no domesticated animals (the decline of game had been so complete during the era of the big-game hunters seven thousand years earlier that Mesoamerica had been left without any large animals from which to breed domestic livestock).

Given the topography of Mexico (the mountain terrain had prevented the formation of any major navigable rivers in the highlands) and the technology of the time, no culture outside the valley could hope to generate the same level of production. By the sixteenth century, the Aztec empire extended from the Atlantic to the Pacific.

Still the Aztecs believed that the end was near. While the canals, aqueducts, canoes, *chinampas,* and dikes had helped Tenochtitlan achieve a remarkable ecological stability, by the middle of the fifteenth century the city was confronting some serious environmental problems. Drought, flood, frost, and famine became increasingly common. To the Aztecs, then, the most important project of their environmental infrastructure was the enormous pyramid that towered above Tenochtitlan's central plaza. The pyramid offered a way for the Aztecs to petition the gods who controlled the natural forces. When the rains were late or when the lake waters rose quickly, the Aztecs offered human sacrifices to Tlaloc, the god of water.

Each victim, who was usually a prisoner captured in battle, was led up the 114 steps of the great pyramid, where priests bent him back over the sacrificial stone, plunged an obsidian knife into his taut stomach, and then reached under the rib cage to extract the beating heart. The heart was placed in a basin while the body, representing the setting sun, was tumbled down the steps of the pyramid. At the bottom, other priests made quick work of dismembering the body. The arms and legs were cooked with chiles and tomatoes and served at a ceremonial feast, while the torso was fed to the beasts in Moctezuma's zoo. The head was placed on a wooden rack at the base of the pyramid which, according to one of Hernán Cortés's men, contained more than one hundred thousand skulls.

Although the Aztec practice of human sacrifice horrified the Spaniards and helped to justify their toppling of the empire, to the Aztecs it was merely an expression of their belief that the world was constantly threatened with environmental calamity. The Aztecs were extremely devout and extremely apprehensive. Throughout Mesoamerica, human sacrifice was a widely accepted and institutionalized form of showing devotion and subservience to the gods. "[It] was inspired by neither cruelty nor hatred," wrote Jacques Soustelle in his classic *Daily Life of the Aztecs.* "It was their response, and the only response they could conceive of, to the instability of a continually threatened world."

Indeed the Aztec world, their carefully constructed and maintained universe, was doomed. But the source of the danger was unimaginable. In 1502 vague and unsettling rumors reached Moctezuma about a new race of men who came from the east. Then, in the summer of 1518, some Indians near Tabasco saw a mountain range bobbing off the coast. When they paddled out to explore, they realized that these were ships carrying strange white men with beards. After a bit of barter, the ships sailed up the coast, fighting a brief battle with other Indians near present-day Veracruz, before turning eastward, dipping below the horizon, and sailing back into the oblivion from which they had come.

II

The Spanish galleon returned to Cuba bearing rumors of its own: westward across the sea was a rich land, a new world populated not by naked savages but by wealthy lords who possessed vast treasures of gold and jewels. That was enough information for a small-time lord and big-time adventurer named Hernán Cortés. Within a year, he had cobbled together a small fleet and sailed west from Havana. He had no idea what he would find—all he knew was that he would conquer it.

Nearly five hundred years after Cortés's short voyage, it is hard to fathom how different the New World was from the Old in 1519. They were separated not merely by history and culture but by the vastness of time. Roughly 200 million years ago, Europe, Africa, and North America were part of the same land mass, an enormous supercontinent called Pangaea. By the middle of the Jurassic period, the continents began pulling apart. Africa detached from North America, creating what would become the Gulf of Mexico, and slowly, over the next 50 million years, wiggled loose from South America to form what would become the Atlantic Ocean. This means that although many of earth's life forms have a common origin, the plants and animals of North America evolved for 200 million years in relative isolation. Animals, plants, and humans had all crossed the temporary land bridge that connected the continents across the Bering Strait, but the biological differences between the two worlds were staggering. Almost none of the plants or animals were familiar to Europeans. They had never seen a hummingbird or a rattlesnake or tasted corn, or tomatoes, or chiles. Americans, on the other hand, had never seen a horse or a cow and had never eaten oranges or wheat.

It is remarkable that two worlds separated by forces so powerful should be reconnected by one so slight. Cortés's fleet of ragtag adventurers not only conquered the people of the New World; the flora and fauna they brought with them conquered the land. A century after the conquest, the American landscape was utterly transformed. But even more significant from a human standpoint was what this continental isolation had meant in terms of the development of pathogens—the microorganisms that cause disease. The only human diseases in the New World were the ones brought by the migrants who crossed the Bering Strait beginning thirty thousand years ago. The new settlers lived for generations in small groups spread out across a cold climate, not very favorable conditions for the pathogens. By the time the ice age ended and the Bering Strait was resubmerged, relatively few pathogens had colonized the New World. Hepatitis, polio, intestinal parasites, and perhaps syphilis were there. But smallpox, mumps, measles, bubonic plague—the killers of Europe—were unknown.

Europe, meanwhile, had been a veritable petri dish for a host of devastating epidemic illnesses. The difference was precisely its lack of isolation. For thousands of years, European traders had brought back spices from Asia and slaves from Africa, as well as new pathogens. These diseases spread across Europe, which had few natural barriers. By the fifteenth century, Europeans had been exposed to hundreds of terrible epidemics, and the surviving population had developed immunities. Europeans were therefore the perfect vessels in which to transport a host of new diseases to America, Australia, New Zealand, and the Pacific Islands. Smallpox is a good example. It was a widespread and often fatal childhood disease in Europe in the sixteenth century, but those who survived its ravages into adulthood developed a resistance.

When Cortés sailed from Havana in February 1519, he provisioned his fleet of eleven ships with an array of steel weapons. He procured sixteen horses, which were rare in Cuba and more expensive than slaves. But the most important weapon in the Spanish arsenal was not even aboard Cortés's ships. It was brought later by a single African slave who landed on the shore of Veracruz in 1520. The slave was infected with the smallpox virus. He was well enough, however, to march to Tenochtitlan, where he introduced smallpox among the Aztecs.

The nature of epidemic disease was poorly understood until very recently. Both the Spaniards and the Aztecs attributed the terrible plague to divine forces. William Prescott's famous history of the conquest written in 1843 has exactly one mention of smallpox, and even more recent accounts analyze the victory of the Spaniards over the Aztecs in terms of technological superiority, military strategy, cultural misunderstanding, and Moctezuma's unwillingness to attack the Spanish force immediately. Each of these played a role in the early campaign, but Cortés would not have been able to conquer the Aztecs without the aid of European disease.

In the early stages Spanish armor, cannons, and crossbows allowed Cortés and his forces to defeat the large armies that attacked them soon after they landed at Veracruz. Horses in particular terrified the Indians. They had never seen an animal that big and initially thought that man and beast were a single beast. The Spaniards' easy victories strengthened their belief that they had been sent on a divine mission against the forces of evil. The final proof that the Indians were waiting to be liberated was the fact that many joined their campaign. By promising relief from Aztec tyranny, Cortés fomented a rebellion and recruited Indian allies to his side.

Moctezuma heard of the alliance between the Spaniards and his old enemies and became nervous. Legend has it that Moctezuma at first believed that Cortés was Quetzalcoatl returned from the east as he had once promised. But even if that story were true, Moctezuma also never doubted that his vast armies could defeat the Spaniards. He knew, too, that it would be a costly campaign and so, in the best Aztec tradition, decided to try and cut a deal. Moctezuma offered Cortés an annual gift of gold and jewels, believing the Spaniard would accept, sail away, and let the Aztec emperor return to the business of government. With this proposal on the table, Cortés and his men entered Tenochtitlan as Moctezuma's guests.

The Spaniards immediately betrayed Moctezuma's trust, taking the Aztec emperor captive. Several months later the Aztecs rose up and drove the invaders from Tenochtitlan. But while the Spaniards themselves were driven out, they had left behind a time bomb. Within months, Tenochtitlan was ravaged by smallpox. In the tightly packed city the disease spread with terrible swiftness, striking down commoners and rulers without distinction. In the general carnage of the conquest no one bothered to tabulate who died of smallpox and who died of other causes, but given Tenochtitlan's close quarters and the way that the disease is known to spread in similar environments, it is not inconceivable that it could have killed 50 percent of the population within a few months.

In December 1520, with the smallpox epidemic at its peak, the Spaniards began to lay siege to the Aztec capital. Soon neither food nor water was reaching the population. On August 13, 1521, the Spaniards broke through the last Aztec defenses and marched into the ruined city. "We found the houses full of corpses and some poor Mexicans were still in them who could not move away," recalled Spanish soldier Bernal Díaz in his account of the conquest. "The city looked as if it had been ploughed up. The roots of every edible greenery had been dug out, boiled and eaten, and they had even cooked the barks of the trees. There was no fresh water to be found; all of it was brackish."

"The sky was crushed," recalled an Aztec poet. "The sun did not follow its course."

III

In the century following the Spanish Conquest, a host of European diseases from measles to chicken pox ravaged the New World. Smallpox raged like a firestorm across a drought-stricken land. Within decades, it had spread from the Great Lakes to the tip of South America, reaching the Incas before the Spanish conquistadors. It devastated the Amerindian population on the eastern seaboard and along the Mississippi River, a population that, because its settlements were made of wood rather than stone, disappeared with hardly a trace. Across the Great Plains, the disease opened up new areas for the buffalo herds, which expanded into once heavily populated areas. The nomadic existence of the Plains Indians who followed the buffalo was an adaptation to an environmental transformation that had taken place only a few centuries earlier.

In Mexico, especially across the urbanized heartland, the diseases were devastating. There is too much debate about the size of the population at the time of the conquest to cite any reliable figure—estimates for Tenochtitlan range from about 60,000 to 1 million, for the valley itself from 1 to 3 million, and for what is present-day Mexico from 6 to 25 million. What is certain is that millions were killed in the epidemic. Data confirm that many individual towns lost 90 percent of their population.

The population collapse also changed the shape of the land itself. Over the course of a century, the Aztecs' highly regulated system of environmental management, which supported an extremely dense population, gave way to a much more haphazard exploitation of resources. Essentially, disease opened an ecological niche for the Spaniards to occupy. Actually it was not the Spaniards themselves who moved in—they were not much for farming—but their animals. Pigs were in the vanguard; conquering Spanish expeditions drove herds of swine in front of their advance so that they would be provided with food. Many pigs that escaped the ensuing hunt went feral; within a few generations in the wild they had sprouted tusks and lost their pudge. The Arkansas razorbacks are their descendants. Pigs flourished along riverbanks and in lowland forests; they also did well across the highlands. A decade after the arrival of the first pigs, the beasts were so numerous that raising them was no longer a profitable enterprise.

Luckily for the Spaniards, cattle took hold in the next decade. Mexico's vast plains extending north to points unknown had not been grazed in ten thousand years, since the New World horse and the mastodon had died out. The cow's-eye view must have been overwhelming; the tufts of thick, tall grass were the bovine equivalent of a Roman banquet. As the herds grew, the price of beef plummeted, until by 1542 meat was so cheap that butcher shops opened in Indian villages. Before the conquest, only warriors who participated in the cannibal feasts ate meat regularly.

Herds of cattle were soon traipsing through Indian fields, often before the corn could be harvested. In the Valley of Mexico, Indians built fences, dug trenches, killed invading cows, and burned pasture to ward off the hungry beasts. The marauding cattle could not be contained. They ate the Indians' food and poisoned their water supply, the creeks and springs, with their manure. Soon, whole villages picked up and moved to avoid the ravenous herds. Because unplanted land was considered open pasture, the abandoned plots often fell into Spanish hands.

The cattle not only chased the Indians off; overgrazing in the central highlands led to long-term and even permanent degradation of the land itself. The herds left hillsides bare, and the exposed soil was washed away in the next rain. Cows were often introduced into areas that had been recently deforested for Spanish construction or cleared for grazing or mining; in these areas the soil tended to be even more unstable. Hillside erosion was accelerated by animal-drawn plows, which replaced the Indian digging sticks. Finally, as disease wiped out the Indians, many hillside plots were abandoned; when their stone terraces collapsed, the rains washed away the uncontained top soil. Fifty years after the conquest, once-cultivated hillsides were pocked gullies of hard yellow earth. Whole areas were permanently lost to production. The prevalence of the phenomenon is suggested by the fact that *tepetate,* the Nahuatl (Aztec) word for exposed hardpan, was quickly incorporated into the New World Spanish vocabulary.

The Spanish authorities did take some steps to protect the Indians' corn supply, which in the first century after the conquest also fed the Spaniards. By the 1530s, most of the large herds had been driven north into the grasslands region now known as the Bajío, which was then occupied by nomadic Indians. There, amidst the lush waving grasses interspersed with cacti, prickly pears, and scrub, the cattle population exploded. By the time a mining strike at Zacatecas in 1546 drew Spanish settlers into the region, herds of twenty thousand animals were not uncommon.

The damage caused by grazing was compounded by the fact that the hillsides around the mining centers were quickly deforested. The mines consumed huge amounts of timber for the construction of shafts and the production of the charcoal used for smelting. In 1543, Indians around Taxco in present-day Guerrero complained that the mines had not left a tree standing. The same was true around the sugar plantations developed in the upland valleys of Veracruz and the interior lowlands of Morelos. Extensive stands of highland tropical forests were cleared to make way for the cane; timber was also needed to power the mills that ground the cane into sugar. The cattle swarmed over the denuded hills, preventing the forest from regenerating. Widespread desertification was the result.

By 1570, as the mining boom continued, the Bajío was turned over to wheat production, and the cattle were driven further north into the sparsely populated grasslands of Coahuila, Durango, and Sinaloa. For twenty years or so, cattle herds doubled every fifteen months; the largest herds had 150,000 animals. Then, suddenly, the cattle started to die off. The rate of reproduction slowed; herds thinned. The Spaniards could not understand what malady had befallen them. They blamed the shrinking herds on packs of wild dogs and Indian nomads. But in fact, the cows were eating the pasture more quickly than it could reproduce. A mere sixty years after the first cow was brought from Cuba, the vast country—from the rugged mountains of the south to the grass-covered northern reaches—was so crowded with cattle that the land had reached its carrying capacity. Some grazing areas, like the Sinaloa plains where scrub replaced the grasslands, were damaged beyond repair.

If cattle were a blight on the land, sheep were an absolute pestilence. Like cattle, the sheep herds exploded across the landscape, grazing hillsides bare. Sheep crop grass much more closely than cattle; they also graze in steep and rocky terrain, which is especially vulnerable to erosion. In the Mezquital Valley north of the Valley of Mexico sheep "transformed . . . a complex and densely populated agricultural mosaic into a sparsely populated mesquite desert." That's the conclusion of Elinor G. K. Melville in *A Plague of Sheep*.

When the first Spaniards came upon the Mezquital Valley, it was densely populated by Otomi farmers who were under the sway of the Aztec empire. The hillsides were covered with pine-oak forests, and creeks ran clear down from the mountains. The valley floor was heavily irrigated; terraced fields climbed the hillsides. To the Spanish eye, the valley seemed ideal for pastoralism. The Spaniards could not possibly have understood the underlying fragility of a region that appeared so fertile; nor could they have imagined the destructive potential of sheep, animals that after millennia of grazing in Europe had reached an accommodation with the Old World environment.

The first sheep were introduced in the Mezquital Valley in the 1530s and 1540s. By the late 1550s there were 421,200 of them. Fifteen years later there were over 2 million. The growth of herds coincided with the demise of the human population as the waves of plagues wreaked their usual havoc.

Then in the 1580s the sheep suddenly began to die off. The Spanish pastoralists were at a loss to explain it; the animals were not fattening and breeding was slowing. An explanation for this strange phenomenon would have to wait nearly four centuries until scientists came up with a model called "ungulate irruption." Scientists discovered that when ungulates—sheep, deer, goats, pigs, horses, bison, or any herbivores with hard, horny hooves—are introduced into virgin grasslands the animals reproduce at a frenetic rate until the growing herds have eaten every bit of grass down to the nub. Then the population crashes as the animals die in droves. The decline in the population allows the flora to recover. When the grass returns, the herds grow slowly, rising and falling until they reach an accommodation with the available resources. Scientists who have studied the cycle by introducing ungulates onto isolated islands have found that the whole process takes only thirty-five to forty years.

By the 1590s the sheep herds in the Mezquital Valley had been reduced by half. The cycle had come to an end. After three decades of being picked over by millions of sheep, the Mezquital Valley was too degraded to recover. Springs dried up and the torrential summer rains eroded the exposed hillsides. By the beginning of the seventeenth century the hillsides showed extensive sheet erosion and deep gullies. The topsoil was carried away, leaving only *tepetate.*

One final ingredient transformed the American environment once disease and grazing animals had done their damage—weeds. A new era of biological competition ensued in the degraded environment as New World and Old World plants competed for the same ecological niche. A great many New World food crops made it to Europe and beyond— corn, potatoes, and tomatoes are three important examples. But European weeds won the battle in the New World. Most arrived accidentally, in animal dung or stuck to clothing. By 1600, entire meadows were largely devoid of New World plants. Dandelions, nettles, a host of grasses, and European clover annihilated their New World rivals. Thousands of plant species were wiped out within the first century after the conquest.

Why did European weeds have an advantage over the New World varieties? Biohistorian Alfred Crosby calls weeds "the Red Cross of the plant world"; their evolutionary niche is to recolonize land that has been destroyed in floods, fires, and other natural disasters. Their specialization, however, is also their vulnerability. Once the emergency is over, weeds generally give way as the original ecosystem reestablishes itself.

These hardy plants did so well in the New World precisely because it was suffering an ecological calamity of historic proportions. The population crash meant that plowed fields were never planted, and European weeds quickly rooted in the exposed soil. An overgrazed and eroded hillside is a propitious environment for a weed. The weeds wiped out hundreds of native plants, but they also stabilized eroding hills—essentially cauterizing an open wound. In the Mezquital Valley, for example, grazing sheep had so damaged the environment that the original ecosystem could not regenerate. Forests of pine and oak and native grasses gave way to European weeds and drought-tolerant plants like maguey, yucca, thorn scrub, and mesquite. The Spaniards began to disparage the once-fertile valley as a blasted badlands marginally suitable as sheep pasture.

This unprecedented ecological transformation was utterly lost on contemporaries. The Spaniards were unequipped to notice or understand what was going on. It happened with such rapidity that they had no reference point. Even if they had noticed, they would not have been concerned that familiar weeds were thriving in the new land. The Indians must have been aware of the process, but in most cases we are not privy to their observations. All we know for sure is that if Moctezuma had returned in 1600 he would not have recognized the place.

IV

Before the Spanish Conquest, the Aztec religion stressed man's vulnerability and frailty against the forces of nature. The Spaniards, on the other hand, believed just the opposite: that nature had been created by God to serve man. In the Garden of Eden, sixteenth-century theologians argued, nature was so abundant that Adam and Eve lived a life of leisure, plucking the bountiful fruit that God had provided. Once they were expelled, God provided them with the raw materials but stipulated that they would have to work to bring forth the fruits of the earth. "Be fruitful and multiply and replenish the earth and subdue it," he had commanded. "Have dominion over the fish of the sea, and over the fowl of the air, and over every living thing that moveth upon the earth."

To transform the environment and put it at the service of man was therefore to do God's will. It was impossible to live a Christian life in the wilderness—forests, deserts, and jungle were the refuge of the devil. This thesis was proven time and again, whenever Spanish Christians fell into Indians' hands. Gonzalo Guerrero, a Spanish soldier who had been shipwrecked in the Yucatán in 1504, pierced his ears and lower lip, tattooed his body, and became a pagan. When Cortés landed in the Yucatán in 1519, Guerrero led the Indians in an attack on the Spanish invaders. During the Cabeza de Vaca expedition, a shipwrecked crew had sunk to the abominable depths of cannibalism. Even today, few Mexicans venture into the woods unless they have some business there—corralling a stray cow, hauling firewood, growing drugs, fighting a guerrilla war.

The Latin word for city—*civitas*—is the root of the word "civilization," and for the Spaniards the equation was literal. Cortés barely mentioned the Mexican landscape, but he was enthralled by Tenochtitlan. He marveled at its wide streets, its flowering gardens, its sense of order. "The Indians," Cortés declared, "live almost as we do in Spain."

In the first century of the colonial era the Spanish vision of nature triumphed. Land was so abundant that the Indians could have their plots of land and their villages as long as they surrendered part of their labor. Because a city was the ultimate example of man's dominion over nature, the Spaniards sought to Christianize the Mexican landscape by urbanizing it. The friars gathered the Indians in villages, while Cortés built his imperial capital on the ruins of Tenochtitlan.

By the early part of seventeenth century, some semblance of ecological equilibrium had been restored. As the surviving Indians developed immunities, the plagues became less frequent and less devastating. By 1650 the Indian population began its slow recovery. Grazing animals as well had reached an accommodation with their new environment. The cattle herds stabilized between 1570 and 1590; sheep a bit later. Throughout most of the highlands, European plants had completed their colonization.

The collapse of the Indian population, combined with the opening of the northern frontier to cattle ranching, transformed a country that was living at the limits of its environmental capacity into one in which the natural resources seemed vast and inexhaustible. This temporary abundance meant that the trauma of environmental upheaval and demographic collapse was not reflected in the social order. Just the opposite—the colonial era was one of the most stable periods in Mexican history. But the underlying conditions that produced the stability were fleeting.

One of the Crown's goals in Mexico—now christened New Spain—was to avoid the kind of reckless exploitation that had destroyed the Indies. The key was to create two separate societies—the Republic of Indians and the Republic of Spaniards. In 1542 laws were established to protect the Indian communities from slavery, servitude, and plunder.

Spanish society in the sixteenth century was highly legalistic and the conquest precipitated a half-century-long debate among theologians and lawyers: who were the Indians and what responsibility did the Spaniards have toward them? The first argument, invoked by backers of the slave trade, cited Aristotle's theory of "natural slavery." Indians, it was argued, lived no differently from the beasts—they survived, as does a monkey or a deer, from what nature offered them. The inability to transform nature—to grow crops and build cities—was a sign that the Indians were not fully developed human beings.

But the discovery of the Aztecs' great cities and later those of the Incas raised new questions about this conclusion. A new theory emerged that was to find its champion in Chiapas Bishop Bartolomé de Las

Casas, who argued that the Indians were spiritual children, whose deficiencies were the result not of any innate qualities but of their hostile environment. They needed to be separated from nature, put into towns, and evangelized. Inspired by the enthusiasm with which the Indians accepted the gospel, the friars spread across the New World at a rate that rivaled the spread of cattle.

Throughout the century, Indians were gathered into towns built in a grid pattern, with a central plaza dominated by a church and town hall. According to royal decree, each Indian was to cultivate sixty fathoms and own six hens and a rooster; royal "chicken officials" made the rounds to ensure that Indians were keeping the proper number of poultry. At the behest of the friars, many farmers abandoned their terraced plots for land in the valleys, turning the hillsides over to the sheep. Domestic animals allowed the Indians to diversify their economy, introducing meat, milk, and wool production. But their grazing of unstable hillsides accelerated erosion and desertification. Abandoned farmland was confiscated for grazing by both Spaniards and Indian leaders, dubbed *principales* or *caciques* by the Spaniards. Nature and the friars conspired to wipe out indigenous systems of land use.

In the Spanish realm of Mexico—the *República de Españoles*—an entirely different perception of the new land took hold. While the Indian universe was the village, the Spaniards were rubbing their eyes and trying to take in the vast new horizon. They perceived Mexico almost as if they were seeing it from an airplane—the new land was endless, almost unknowable. The conquerors who wandered for years through the country had not found its limits. Resources—from timber to silver to pasture—were enormous in a land where they had never been exploited. The Spanish settlers saw no reason to manage an environment that was this bountiful; the Indians were silly and sentimental to grow corn in little mountain plots while vast plains were left uncultivated in the north. Spanish colonists cobbled together royal grazing permits called *estancias* into enormous estates, which would evolve into the eighteenth-century haciendas.

The boom fueled by a massive and reckless consumption of vast and unexploited resources lasted until the middle of the seventeenth century. By then livestock, having devoured ten millennia worth of grass in less than a century, were in decline, while most of the easily prospected mines had been picked clean. New World agricultural exports—sugar, cotton, cochineal, indigo, and cacao—bottomed out as Spain entered a prolonged recession. Writing about the Valley of Mexico, historian Charles Gibson noted: "The colonial population, while it fell and rose sharply, always did so within the environment's declining potential." The same can be said for the colony as a whole. Ironically, however, it was Mexico's economic stagnation that partly accounted for the social peace. The lack of markets had turned agricultural production inward, emphasizing self-sufficiency. Most peasants had some land to farm, either in a village or on a large estate.

But the social peace collapsed with the beginning of a second mining boom in the eighteenth century. New techniques made it possible to extract silver from the previously discarded ore. Mine owners sank their profits into refurbishing the decrepit haciendas. Many of the estates were retooled, switching over from cattle ranching to wheat cultivation in order to meet the demand in Mexico's growing cities. As the haciendas expanded wheat production, they pushed their cattle onto the marginal land that had been farmed by villages and tenant farmers—land that the friars and the Crown had promised the Indians in perpetuity. Even in the north, land was no longer so plentiful that it could simply be occupied without conflict. The demographic recovery of the Indian population meant that it had become a zero-sum game—when the haciendas took land they stepped on the villagers' toes, and vice versa.

The colonial era had left a legacy of two competing and even contradictory land ethics. Within the confines of the *República de Indios,* and at a time when land was abundant, the Crown had instituted a series of laws to protect Indian land holdings from Spanish encroachment. While it was never realized, the colonial ideal, articulated by the friars and the Crown, was that a small piece of land—enough to grow a subsistence crop of corn and beans—was the right of every Indian. The state had a responsibility to provide it.

That ideal clashed with the Spanish settlers' concept of private property. Under Spanish law, land and all other natural resources belonged to the sovereign, who granted titles that were theoretically revocable. The estate owners, or *hacendados,* saw their land as inviolable private property, which, like capital itself, could be used at the absolute discretion of its owner. The growth of mining and cattle ranching and the decline of the Indian population had fostered the development of a parallel economy that was centered around the large estates and tied to international markets.

These two competing land ethics have been a source of constant and still unresolved conflict. Both ideals—land as private property and land as a birth right—have roots in the colonial era and in Spanish law. But they had been applied within the two separate realms of colonial society—the former to Spaniards, and the latter to Indians. By the late eighteenth century Indian villagers, mestizo ranchers, small farmers, and agricultural laborers, despite their different cultures, languages, and circumstances, often found themselves with the same grievance: their land was being usurped.

V

During three centuries of uneasy peace, the struggle over land simmered just below the surface. Then in 1808 the heat got turned up—Spain fell to Napoleon, leaving the colonies on their own. As muted grievances suddenly boiled over, land hunger swept the new nation. The environmental cost of the colonial policy was thus paid in the first century of independence.

The cause of the social unrest was not merely that two societies began fighting over an increasingly scarce resource. The problem was also that a third and unrecognized society had been created. Throughout the colonial era, Spanish officials had tried to get the Indians and the Spaniards to mate with their own kind. They did not try too hard, however, and by the eighteenth century all they could do was acknowledge that miscegenation was a fact of life and develop an elaborate legalistic nomenclature to describe the progeny of every possible coupling. The child of a Spaniard and Indian was officially a mestizo; the child of a Spanish woman and a black was a mulatto; a Spaniard and a mulatta produced a morisco; and so on. No one paid the slightest bit of attention to such classifications. By the time independence rolled around, anyone who was not white or Indian went by a single name—mestizo. But to whom did these bastard children owe their allegiance—their Spanish fathers or their Indian mothers?

Mestizos—who ran the gamut from dirt-poor tenant farmers to hacienda owners—shared a common sense of alienation from the land in which they been born. The Indians were bound to the land because it had once belonged to them; the Spanish by virtue of the conquest. But what tied the mestizo to Mexico? Neither officially recognized society accepted him—he was invisible, rootless. Mestizos filled the margins of the new society, becoming mule skinners, miners, tenant farmers, and outlaws. Even the *criollos* (Creoles), native-born Mexicans of Spanish descent, were uncertain about their place in colonial society. They were outraged by the legal privileges granted to Spanish-born *peninsulares*.

Miguel Hidalgo, the copper-skinned Creole parish priest who is exalted as the father of Mexican independence, was obsessed with this system of legal discrimination. He felt that his status as a Creole had thwarted his advancement in the church. Hidalgo's initial plan was to organize a broad Creole revolt against the *peninsulares,* but when his conspiracy was exposed he was forced to turn to his secret weapon—the poor. The festering anger over land meant that aggrieved peasants were easily enlisted in national struggles, and Hidalgo's status as a parish priest in the town of Dolores, Guanajuato, allowed him to wield unusual authority over the Bajío's poor mestizos. "Will you be free?" he asked his parishioners on September 16, 1810. "Will you make the effort to recover from the hated Spaniards the lands stolen from your forefathers three hundred years ago?"

Hidalgo developed an incipient Mexican nationalism that united *criollos,* mestizos, and Indians and tied them all to the land. All three groups, Hidalgo pointed out, were born in America and were therefore the heirs to the Mexican nation that had been extinguished by Cortés and the Spanish conquerors. While the *peninsulares* identified implicitly with the conquerors, the *criollo* insurgents claimed descent from the friars. They revived the Black Legend of Spanish atrocities and extolled Las Casas as their spiritual father. The Mexican nation had been destroyed by the conquest—now it would be reclaimed.

Despite Hidalgo's efforts, most *criollos* in the colony came to the quite rational conclusion that whatever privileges were denied them under the Spanish regime, it was still preferable to mob rule. The insurgency met its match against the well-disciplined royalist forces outside Mexico

City. Hidalgo was captured six months later in northern Mexico. Like almost all Mexican national heroes, he met a gory end. He was defrocked, executed, and decapitated. His head was displayed in a cage in the state capital of Guanajuato for a decade.

With the peasant rebellion put down, the Creole elite ended its marriage of convenience with the Spaniards and mounted a conservative coup against the royalist forces. In 1821, Agustín Iturbide was crowned Agustín I, the first monarch of the newly independent nation of Mexico.

In the half century that followed independence, the vestiges of the colonial elite retreated to Mexico City. As central authority collapsed, the countryside reverted to lawlessness, boss rule, and banditry. Old feuds between the estates and villages—once mediated by the friars and the Spanish authorities—were settled by force. The haciendas enlisted private militias that eventually went on the offensive, usurping village lands for their *patrón*. The villages turned to local strongmen for protection. Juan Alvarez who ran the state of Guerrero from 1820 to 1862 was the quintessential caudillo of the era. A former soldier in the rebel army, Alvarez parlayed his defense of village lands into a regional power base. With the central government in decline, it was caudillos like Alvarez, ensconced in their mountain strongholds, who ran the show for most of the century. Not surprisingly, banditry thrived in this environment. Coaches traveling from Veracruz to Mexico City were robbed so frequently and so thoroughly that passengers sometimes arrived at their destination without a stitch of clothing.

At a time when the onset of the Industrial Revolution in Europe and the United States was producing an idealization of rural life, the demise of rural authority strengthened the equation in the minds of Mexico City's battered elite between the countryside and lawlessness. The city had reverted to the function it served during the early years of the colony: a bastion of civilization in the midst of rural backwardness.

Throughout the war-filled century, as different factions, cliques, and ideologues battled for power, the nation experimented with ways of melding the hispanicized city with the Indian and mestizo countryside. The most formidable effort came from Benito Juárez. Juárez, a Zapotec Indian from Oaxaca who remains Mexico's only indigenous president, put forth a new agrarian ideal. The cornerstone of the new nation would be the development of a class of small farmers whose toil in the fields would bring moderate prosperity and tie them both to their community and, in the Jeffersonian sense, to the nation. Indians were not explicitly part of the program, however. The liberals hoped this kind of agrarianism would produce rapid assimilation.

The plan failed because the central government was too weak to impose the kind of sweeping changes that Juárez envisioned. The strongest forces in rural life—the Indian villages, the church, and the large estates—all resisted the reforms.

As in the colonial era, the underlying agrarian instability was brought to a head by a wave of unprecedented economic growth. Under Porfirio Díaz, who ruled Mexico from 1876 to 1911 with only one brief interruption, the Mexican economy grew an amazing 350 percent. The key was stability—achieved largely by repression—and a boom in foreign investment. In the north, foreigners bought up the mines and controlled enormous estates. In the south, Díaz gave away "wilderness" lands to anyone who would agree to survey them.

The boom in commercial agriculture was made possible by the development of the railroads, which covered twelve thousand miles by 1910. The tracks were like rivers of steel flowing across the arid north, through thick jungles, and over rugged mountains, linking a landscape that had been divided 50 million years ago by geologic upheaval. Like the Aztecs' use of canoes on the lakes in the Valley of Mexico, this transportation revolution allowed the effective exploitation of Mexico's remarkably diverse ecosystems.

This transformation of the rural economy brought enormous economic growth and enormous suffering to the peasant farmers it displaced. The villagers' outrage at seeing their lands taken was compounded by a sense of historical entitlement. Nowhere was this conflict more acute than in Morelos, the interior lowland valley just south of the capital city. Since the conquest, when Cortés had introduced sugar production into the region, the villagers had been fighting a losing battle with the estates that claimed their lands, their water, and their timber. Each time the national economy grew, the estates looked for more land to increase production; each time the villagers dug in. In the 1870s, innovations in sugar production, plus the expanding railway system, opened new markets. Estate owners made new claims on village lands and water, and began restricting access to the woodlands on which many villages depended for charcoal production. Displaced peasant farmers gathered in long lines outside the hacienda gates hoping for work. Meanwhile, wages and conditions continued to deteriorate.

Almost every one of the hundred towns in Morelos was feuding with some nearby hacienda over land, water, or timber rights. Village councils elected delegates, filed petitions, and hired lawyers, but to no avail. The Porfirian regime, the courts, and the state government invariably sided with the haciendas. José Merino, who had been representing the town of Anenecuilco in its battle with an encroaching hacienda, had traveled to Cuernavaca and Mexico City to make his case. In the summer of 1909, Merino convened a village meeting in Anenecuilco at which he said that at seventy years of age he was too tired to continue the fight. The two hundred men in Anenecuilco—hired hands, small farmers, and merchants for the most part—elected a thirty-year-old part-time mule skinner, small farmer, and share cropper to represent them. His name was Emiliano Zapata.

VI

The revolutionary battle cry was "Land to those who work it!" This was exactly what the friars had promised the Indians three centuries earlier —and never delivered. Porfirio Díaz had forgotten that the Crown had kept the peace by at least paying lip service to that ideal, by mediating between the estates and the villages. In Díaz's view, Indians and peasants had little to offer the nation except their labor. Through a precise formula of repression, cooperation, and charisma, Díaz brought both social peace and sustained economic growth for thirty-five years. Progress and modernity, the Porfirians argued, would eventually wipe out the vestiges of the dying Indian culture.

In fact, at precisely the moment that Zapata was named the representative of Anenecuilco, Mexico City was preparing for a massive celebration. The occasion was the centennial of Hidalgo's *grito de independencia,* the triumph of the city over the countryside, and Mexico City was getting a spit shine. The Porfirian elite had inherited the colonial prejudice for urban life. Enormous amounts of money had been poured into improving Mexico City's infrastructure: streets had been widened and paved to accommodate electrical trolleys and automobiles; theaters, hospitals, and sanitariums had been built; electricity became commonplace in the good neighborhoods. The rural population, meanwhile, had sunk deeper into poverty. Only 2 percent of Mexicans owned land, and nearly half worked as peons on the haciendas. Much of the countryside was not even hispanicized. Half the population still spoke only their Indian dialect.

But for the elite who were celebrating the 1910 centennial this was not necessarily bad news; they saw the dominance of the city as the triumph of civilization over the wilderness. In the Valley of Mexico the subjugation of the countryside to the needs of the city was literal. As Mexico City expanded, reaching a population of 500,000 by the turn of the century, it absorbed outlying haciendas, displacing campesinos and tenant farmers who were absorbed into the growing *colonias*—the poor neighborhoods on the periphery.

But the reign of the city was ephemeral; soon the countryside would descend upon it and swallow it up. Nine months after ringing in the centennial celebration, a revolt led by liberal reformer Francisco Madero toppled the regime, and Porfirio Díaz sailed to exile in Paris where he died four years later.

By late 1914, however, the reformist revolt had mutated into a terrible civil war. On November 24 of that year, a regiment of ragtag soldiers led by Emiliano Zapata clambered over the mountains from Morelos to occupy the city and team up with Pancho Villa, who had come from the north. The Zapatista soldiers, with their tattered clothes and muddy sandals, camped in the plazas and wandered around the city begging for food while Zapata himself set up shop in a rundown hotel near the railroad station. In December, Zapata and Villa held a brief and awkward meeting in the southern suburb of Xochimilco. The two men quickly found they had little in common either personally or politically. Zapata was a drinker, Villa a teetotaler. Zapata was formal and restrained; Villa was ebullient and ruthless. Zapata, an Indian, was fighting for a piece of land and a return to an idealized past. Villa, a mestizo, was fighting for something very different—a place in a nation that had never accepted him.

But neither Villa nor Zapata triumphed in the revolutionary fratricide. It was Venustino Carranza, a planter and member of the Sonoran aristocracy, who emerged from the fracas sitting in the presidential chair. Carranza's army dispatched Villa on the plains outside Celaya in 1915, but Zapata proved more nettlesome. Zapata kept the federal forces on the run for a year before he was assassinated by an ambush in April 1917 outside the gates of the Chinameca hacienda in Morelos.

Even though the Zapatistas were defeated, their revolt, and the hundred years of rural instability that had preceded it, made one thing abundantly clear—there would be no peace in Mexico without some sort of resolution of what is commonly called "the agrarian question." Carranza, who had never been a big fan of agrarian reform, was forced to ratify a liberal constitution, which left the door open for the major land reform program of the 1930s.

Agrarian reform is usually seen as a political response to Zapatismo. By the same token, the rise of a culture of *mestizaje,* or race mixture, could be seen as a response to Villismo. In the 1920s, Mexican intellectuals began talking about *la raza cósmica*—a fusion of the European and Indian. The new regime tried to create a national myth that incorporated two marginalized groups: Indians, who were so tied to the land that they had no need for the nation; and mestizos, whose sense of rootlessness had produced a similar effect.

VII

After the Mexican Revolution, Mexico remained a vast and largely unexploited land. The population of 15 million may have been smaller than at the time of the conquest. The Porfirian regime had begun to develop some of the country's resources—primarily mining and commercial agriculture. But whole stretches of Mexico—forests, jungles, and coasts—remained unpopulated and undeveloped. Under the new revolutionary government, these resources were put at the service of the nation—not merely the elite who had dominated Mexico's economic life since the colonial era.

The concept of the nation, in fact, was redefined. Peasants were elevated to the symbol of the enduring bond between humans and the land. In the postrevolutionary version of history, Cortés was excoriated as the great destroyer. Diego Rivera, the court artist of the Mexican Revolution, painted enormous frescoes in the National Palace showing Indians living in natural harmony, sowing corn, swimming in clear rivers, hunting deer, making pots. Their reverie was broken by the arrival of Cortés, who is portrayed as a sickly hunchback. He stands counting gold while a priest looks on; the foreground is crowded with pigs, sheep, and horses. In the background, a Spanish soldier oversees Indians cutting down the forest.

The 1917 constitution provided the legal justification for an ambitious land reform program carried out largely in the 1930s. The document presented a vision of the responsibility of the state, which owed much to the country's colonial period. Article 27 declared:

> Ownership of the lands and water within the boundaries of the national territory is vested originally in the Nation, which has had, and has, the right to transmit thereof to private persons, thereby constituting private property.... The Nation shall at all times have the right to impose on private property such limitation as the public interest may demand, as well as the right to regulate the utilization of natural resource which are susceptible to appropriation, in order to conserve them and to ensure a more equitable distribution of wealth.

This constitutional directive to use the state's resources as a mechanism for social welfare has been the guiding principle of modern Mexican political culture. Article 27 provided the basis for both agrarian reform and the nationalization of the oil industry. The state's responsibility was not to protect resources and preserve wilderness; it was to use them to propel Mexico into the modern era. The campesino quickly become as much of an icon as the cowboy—the only problem was that he refused to totally disappear.

The revolution transformed Mexico, but what created the modern nation was a force even more profound—the twentieth century. The two decades of violence left virtually no village untouched; land was usurped, infrastructure was destroyed, social relations were decimated, and lawlessness prevailed. The years of conflict turned like an enormous plow over the fertile Mexican earth. The modern world quickly took root. Mexico industrialized at a phenomenal rate—in less than half a century. But it made no effort to manage this growth or to consider its side effects. No romantic or even practical vision of wilderness or nature had taken hold in the Mexican national consciousness.

—two—

Crisis in El Campo

Before the conquest, the Mixteco Indians called their forest-covered home in the mountains of Oaxaca *Nudzavuiñuhu,* which means "heavenly and esteemed land." Today, all that is left of the forest are a few stands of pines on the ridges. The earth itself is deeply scarred. Enormous fissures cut through the landscape; hillsides have been eroded down to the bedrock. According to a United Nations report, the mountains of Oaxaca are the most eroded landscape on the planet.

The Mixtecos, who for centuries clung to their culture of corn, have been slowly giving up, leaving their villages for the slums of Mexico City, the tomato fields of Sinaloa, California's Central Valley, and farms from Virginia to Saskatchewan. Anthropologists, sociologists, and economists have offered myriad reasons for the exodus: the collapse of village authority, growing social networks linking villages to the United States, the expansion of international capitalism. But the Mixtecos have their own explanation. Time after time I heard the same refrain: *"porque la tierra ya no da,"* because the earth no longer gives. The exact reasons why the land suddenly gave out are complicated, a combination of the long history of erosion and more recent changes in agricultural techniques. The final blow to the Mixtecos' precarious existence was the advent of the "Green Revolution" and the introduction of chemical fertilizers.

Whatever the causes, the Mixtecos understand their exodus primarily in ecological terms. "When I was a child, there were avocado trees, and bananas and papayas," recalled one seventy-year-old farmer I met in the town of San Juan Mixtepec. "The corn grew green and strong, and the rains watered the pastures. We had many animals—goats and cows. Then a plague wiped out the avocado trees and the skies dried up. The rain that does fall washes away the earth, until there is nothing but rock. Today, we are poorer than ever. What choice do we have but to leave?"

It would be easy to attribute such ruminations to nostalgia if scientific research had not confirmed that the Mixteco region, like much of the Mexican countryside, is confronting ecological ruin. Nearly a third of the country's 50 million acres (20 million hectares) of farmland have been severely eroded; 86 percent is suffering erosion of some degree. The worst damage is on the marginal land farmed by Mexico's rural poor. In the state of Tlaxcala, half of the land has already been destroyed by erosion, and researchers predict that the state could become a desert by the year 2010 unless measures are taken. In Oaxaca, 70 percent of the once-arable land in the Mixteco region is ruined.

The demise of the Mexican countryside is at the root of the country's environmental crisis. Erosion, deforestation, and desertification threaten not only the land itself but also Mexico's ancient culture of corn. The decline in agricultural productivity has spawned more intensive uses of the land, from logging to overfarming. As yields have declined and populations increased, poor farmers have inundated cities, creating an insurmountable infrastructure backlog. They have colonized marginal lands from lowland jungles to pine forests, fueling the highest rate of deforestation in the world. Because corn farming has been Mexico's social safety net for centuries, the collapse of the rural economy has continent-wide implications. It is Mexico's rural refugees who man the factories in Tijuana, pick the crops that fill supermarket shelves from Boston to San Francisco, clean offices and homes in Phoenix, build the new suburban subdivisions in southern California's Orange County, and keep gardens green in Los Angeles.

There is a strong correlation across the Mexican countryside between erosion and migration. Michoacán, Hidalgo, and Jalisco are some of the country's most eroded regions and the source of the bulk of migrants to the United States. The mountains of Oaxaca are Mexico's most devastated landscape; many of the towns are being rapidly depopulated. The view of the Mixteco region taken from space shows why. Satellite photos show the ancient forest as a smudge of white earth, a devastated landscape of scrub and gullied hillsides. The picture is not much prettier up close. From a ridge overlooking the Mixteco village of San Juan Mixtepec, I saw six-foot gullies carved into the red earth. The barren hills to the west were stripped nearly bare of soil. Between 80 and 90 percent of the men have worked or are working in the United States.

The back-and-forth migration has created a bizarre cultural fusion. Satellite dishes sprout above adobe huts. New model pickup trucks with license plates from Oregon, California, and Virginia prowl the dusty streets. Illiterate peasants in the villages communicate with their relatives in the states by sending messages on videocassette recordings. Carlos Salazar, the village grocer, is a news junkie and keeps CNN on in his store. Basketball, not soccer, is the favorite sport in town, and a Chicago Bulls T-shirt and a pair of fake Nikes are high fashion.

The contrast between traditional agriculture and the modern world also gets played out in cornfields, and it is this dependence, I soon learned, that provoked the original exodus from San Juan Mixtepec and countless other villages. Beginning in the 1950s, Mexican government officials began touting chemical fertilizers and improved hybrid seeds as the means of ending rural poverty. Sometime between 1975 and 1978—no one I talked to could remember the exact year—the Green Revolution arrived in San Juan Mixtepec. Government officials triumphantly donated several bags of chemical fertilizers to each farmer in town. The fertilizers worked—the corn stalks grew larger and more quickly—and farmers soon began to depend on them. A few years later, however, the government program ended and the fertilizer was no longer free. Instead, a government bank called Banrural offered credit. Everyone took out a loan; in a few years the whole town was in serious debt.

Then people began to notice something strange. Three years after they first began to use fertilizers, corn yields had dropped to their original levels. Not only that, if farmers did not add fertilizers the corn would not grow at all.

By the early 1980s, with their debt continuing to grow, the people of San Juan Mixtepec were caught up in a cycle of dependence. More and more were going to the United States to earn money to pay off their debts. By the end of the decade, the situation had deteriorated to the point where the cost of the fertilizers required to produce a marginal corn crop often exceeded the value of the corn itself. Wage labor, which had begun as a means of earning a bit of extra cash or paying off a debt, had become an annual necessity because raising an acre of corn required several hundred dollars in fertilizers. The economic logic of their culture of subsistence had been undermined—it became cheaper for the Mixtecos to buy corn than to grow it.

Joaquín Sánchez, San Juan Mixtepec's mayor, has done the math. Yet he continues to grow corn because that is what his father and grandfather did before him. The difference is that Sánchez has had to leave the village in order to subsidize his cornfield. Of course, after working everywhere from San Diego to Brooklyn, he also acquired a taste for luxuries uncommon at home. In the United States he drove a motorcycle. "I liked to dress well and eat well," he told me. "I liked to go to Tijuana and go out dancing and go to the horse track." That life seemed far away as we sat in his modest house. Outside the night was dark as pitch, but the living room glowed with the light from a color television. Sánchez barked orders in Mixteco to his two children, who sat transfixed by Mighty Morphin' Power Rangers captured on a satellite dish. "Sometimes I think it is crazy that our lives depend on chemicals," he said to me in Spanish. "But the truth is that without fertilizers we can no longer survive."

I

What has happened in San Juan Mixtepec has happened to some degree throughout the Mexican countryside: intensive farming on marginal lands has devastated whole regions of the country. The roots of Mexico's rural crisis can be traced directly to the land reform implemented by President Lázaro Cárdenas. The irony is that Cárdenas, who governed the country between 1934 and 1940, is revered as the savior of the Mexican countryside. He took a special interest in the Mixteco region, targeting it for development. His visit by helicopter a decade after his presidency ended was one of the high points in the town's history.

But while Cárdenas is responsible for the greatest land reform program in Latin American history, and to some extent for Mexico's fragile social peace, his utopia was never rural. His goal was to reorganize the country-side to serve the city. Cárdenas's industrial policy represented a rupture with the postrevolutionary order—and he needed the peasants on his side. Venustiano Carranaza, Alvaro Obregón, and Plutarco Elías Calles, the triumvirate of generals who ruled Mexico from 1917 to 1930, all saw large-scale plantation agriculture and development of the country's natural resources as the key to Mexico's economic future. All three also owned large estates. The postrevolutionary economy, like the Porfirian one, was geared toward the export of nonfood products like cotton, sugar cane, and coffee grown on massive plantations.

But the Wall Street stock market crash and the ensuing world depression destroyed the generals' plans for an export-driven economy. The market for agricultural goods disappeared almost overnight as the U.S. economy withered. In 1933 the government shifted gears and announced a six-year plan to foment industrialization. Calles selected Lázaro Cárdenas to be the next president and the man who would carry out the ambitious program.

With Calles's backing, Cárdenas's victory was a foregone conclusion. Yet Cárdenas mounted a strenuous campaign—crisscrossing the country by train, car, and mule to promise the peasants who crowded the muddy plazas that he would give them land and justice. After he became president, Cárdenas continued to travel the country's back roads. The journalists who accompanied him wired back stories of Indian hamlets tucked into forgotten valleys, steamy jungles, vast deserts, mountains, plains, and sleepy fishing villages. For the insular residents of Mexico City, Cárdenas's trips expanded their vision of the nation. Mexico shifted in the popular imagination from a country of barbarous regional warlords into a true nation of diverse people and still untapped resources. Not since the friars traveled the same routes centuries earlier had the center made such a concerted effort to acculturate the hinterland.

Cárdenas's tool was not the cross but the land title. Land reform goaded the peasants to recognize federal authority, and this created the modern, centralized nation. In his first year in office Cárdenas handed out 7.4 million acres (3 million hectares) of land. In 1937 he gave out 12.4 million acres (5 million hectares). He became the peasants' patron and they his loyal clients.

The legal basis for the land reform was Article 27, which declared the land and natural resources to be the property of the state. The nation reserved the right to redistribute them in order to ensure "a more equitable distribution of wealth." Land titles were granted not to individuals but directly to the villages in collective holdings called *ejidos*. For the next fifty years, until land reform was abolished by President Carlos Salinas de Gortari in 1992, Mexican presidents used the promise of land titles to garner political support for the government. San Juan Mixtepec was granted its definitive land title by President Gustavo Díaz Ordaz in 1967.

Under the agrarian reform law, individuals who received a plot had the right to farm the land and to leave it as an inheritance. They could not mortgage, sell, or rent it. Technically the state remained the owner of a peasant's land, and it could be confiscated and redistributed for a variety of reasons, including failure to plant it. Cárdenas organized the *ejidatarios* into the National Confederation of Peasants and told them that if they had any problems they should come to him. Thus the federal bureaucracy, rather than state or village authorities, assumed responsibility for the welfare of the peasantry. Cárdenas himself often traveled to villages to iron out disputes.

The ejido system proved the ideal mechanism for Cárdenas to achieve his twin goals of bringing the peasants into the national economy and at the same time maintaining political control over them. By becoming the benefactor of Mexico's rural masses, Cárdenas was able to exercise unprecedented control over agricultural production and thereby reshape the national economy. With the international market in the dumps, the government used loans, credits, and price regulation to shift rural production toward basic foodstuffs. The motor for the new economy, however, was the cities. The peasants' role in the national economy was to grow cheap food for the urban workers.

Cárdenas perfected the Mexican political model of corporatism, mediation, and government control. Everyone depended on the government for something—the peasants for their piece of land, the workers for their cheap food, the factory owners for the protectionist policies that allowed them to reap obscene profits. In 1938 Cárdenas founded the Mexican Revolutionary Party, which eight years later became the Institutional Revolutionary Party (PRI). Largely owing to support in the countryside, the PRI has monopolized power for more than six decades.

Cárdenas is often remembered for having the political courage to redistribute some of the nation's most productive farmland—the cotton-growing region of Coahuila, the hot country of Michoacán, the Mexicali Valley just over the border from California. But, in fact, the vast majority of the land distributed was not pieces of haciendas, but small plots of marginal land not even suitable for farming. Only 23 percent of the land given out before 1945 was classified as farmland, and only 2 percent was irrigated. Eighteen percent was forests and 44 percent pasture. A survey completed in 1940 at the end of the Cárdenas administration determined that 54.4 percent of the ejidos were growing just enough corn for bare subsistence; 31.4 percent were below subsistence.

When Cárdenas left office in 1940, he named the more conservative Manuel Avila Camacho as his successor. Avila Camacho is often described as having abandoned Cárdenas's agrarian reform program in favor of industrial development. Industrialization, in fact, was part of Cárdenas's original plan, and what brought it about was not a change in government policy but the outbreak of World War II. When the export economy picked up, the economic infrastructure was in place to launch three decades of phenomenal industrial growth. Cheap food policies meant that, as the urban economy took off, workers had more income to spend on manufactured goods, feeding the cycle of growth.

The growth of the urban economy combined with the recovery of agricultural exports also spawned a three-decade boom. Yet even as the rural economy was growing by leaps and bounds, the millions of peasants who had received marginal lands found their circumstances more and more precarious. Because corn prices were kept low, poorer peasants simply dropped back out of the economy and grew corn for subsistence. Without access to the national market, the poorest peasants tried to wrench enough corn out of their land to survive. They abandoned fallowing or moved onto the dry plains or cut down the forest lands that had been part of the original ejido grant. When the land finally gave out, the peasants abandoned their plots for the cities, fueling an unchecked wave of urban growth.

II

In 1953, halfway through the twenty-year economic explosion known as the "Mexican miracle," writer Juan Rulfo captured the pain of those who had been left behind. In his collection of short stories called *El llano en llamas (The Burning Plain),* Rulfo wrote of the campesinos who inhabited the badlands of his native southern Jalisco. His stories are filled with lonely marches across the plains, murder, death, and epic battles against hopelessness and despair. In "They Gave Us the Land," four campesinos trek across the desolate plain that has just been given to their village as part of the agrarian reform program.

"No, the plain is no good for anything. There're no rabbits or birds. There's nothing. Except for a few scrawny huizache trees and a patch or two of grass with the blades curled up; if it weren't for them, there wouldn't be anything. . . ."

They told us, "From the town up to here belongs to you."

We asked, "The Plain?"

"Yes, the plain. All the Big Plain."

We opened our mouths to say that we didn't want the plain, that we wanted what was by the river. From the river up to where, through the meadows, the trees called casuarinas are, and the pastures and the good land. Not this rough cow hide they call the Plain.

But they didn't let us say these things. The official hadn't come to converse with us. He put the papers in our hands and told us, "Don't be afraid to have so much land just for yourselves."

"But the Plain, sir?"

"There are thousands and thousands of plots of land."

"But there's no water. There's not even a mouthful of water."

"How about the rainy season? Nobody told you you'd get irrigated land. As soon as it rains out there, the corn will spring up as if you were pulling it."

"But, sir, the earth is all washed away and hard. We don't think the plow will cut into the earth of the Plain that's like a rock quarry. You'd have to make holes with a pick-axe to plant the seed, and even then you can't be sure that anything will come up; no corn or anything else will come up."

"You can state that in writing. And now you can go. You should be attacking the large estate owners and not the government that is giving you the land."

"Wait, sir. We haven't said anything against the Center. It's all against the Plain."

Across the country peasants in thousands of villages felt the same way. What they knew was corn. Regardless of what kind of land they had been given—no matter how worthless and marginal—they planted corn and beans. In Jalisco and Guanajuato they planted it in the desert and prayed for rain. In Michoacán, the ejidatarios contracted with logging companies to chop down the forests and then moved in and planted their cornfields. When the topsoil eroded away and the land would not produce, they asked the government for more land. The Mixtecos of Oaxaca and Guerrero climbed further up the mountains, planting slopes too steep to stand on.

This kind of overfarming had a terrible effect on the land itself. Millions of acres were eroded away; steep slopes were planted without terracing; forests and jungles were cleared to make way for the expanding population. Exactly how much land was destroyed is hard to calculate because no one kept track. But today 85 percent of the country's 28,000 ejidos rely on agriculture, while only 12 percent of their land is considered arable. The government officially classifies 2 million small farmers who cultivate 10.6 million acres (4.3 million hectares) as marginal; their attachment to their corn plot and to the culture of corn itself means that they will fight to stay on that land and farm it until one day it simply gives out. Then they will turn their backs on it and head to the city—a Mexican or a U.S. one. Today, the route is established. Many Mexican towns have a sister city in the United States. The migrants from Aguililla, Michoacán, go to Redwood City, California, just south of San Francisco; those from Napízaro along the eroding slopes of Lake Patzcauro go to North Hollywood in southern California; the migrants of Puebla have shown a strong affinity for Brooklyn, while the Zapotecs from Oaxaca seem to congregate in California's San Fernando Valley. In fact the Zapotec town of Yatzachi El Bajo in Oaxaca is completely abandoned because the entire town is working in Los Angeles. "Nothing but grandmothers there and the one man who takes care of the church," said resident Joel Aquino Maldonado. "But it fills up once a year when everyone comes home from California for the town's fiesta."

While millions have gone to the United States, many more have chosen Mexico City. Between 1950 and 1990 the city grew from about 3 million to about 18 million. The exodus of the countryside has made Mexico an urban society: only 25 percent of the population today is rural; 65 percent lived in rural areas at the time of the revolution. The rural population has grown in absolute terms—nearly doubling, from 14 million to 22.5 million in the same period. Large families remain the norm in the countryside, although they are much smaller than even a few decades ago. Overall, Mexico's birthrate has dropped from 3.5 percent in 1965 to 1.8 percent today.

Given the improvements in agricultural technology in the past half-century, 8 million new residents in the Mexican countryside is not as overwhelming as it sounds. Land pressure, however, became acute in many regions where the plots were small and the land was already marginal. It is technically illegal to subdivide ejido land, but everyone does it, giving tiny pieces of land to all their children. As any second-grade graduate knows, you cannot divide by zero. The postage stamp–sized plots cannot support a family, and so campesinos have had to look for part-time work off the farm. Today, there are four hundred thousand farmers in Mexico who farm less than twelve acres (five hectares).

The strategy of spending half the year in the village and the other half working in the United States began with the outbreak of World War II. With American men being shipped off to war, Mexicans were invited north to pick the crops. Four thousand Mexican farm workers were invited to the United States in 1942 under the Bracero, or guest-worker, program. In San Juan Mixtepec, Eliseo Vega was one of a handful of Mixtecos who went to the United States to work the following year. Between 1943 and 1950, he spent the summers working in Salinas, California; San Benito, Texas; Michigan; Georgia; Arkansas; and Arizona. He picked cotton mostly, but also vegetables.

By the time the Bracero program was ended in 1964, 5 million Mexicans had made the trip to the United States. And the program established a pattern of permanent dependence that ran both ways; across Jalisco, Michoacán, Hidalgo, Oaxaca, and Guanajuato thousands of men planted their corn and then headed north for a few months. They left the weeding to the women and children and returned in time for the harvest. Meanwhile, U.S. farmers became dependent on low wages and U.S. consumers accustomed to cheap food. As in Mexico, the availability of cheap food freed up resources for U.S. industrial growth, as consumers spent an increasingly larger percentage of their income on manufactured goods. In that sense, U.S. industrialization depended on the availability of cheap Mexican labor.

The U.S. war economy also transformed production around the world. An international labor shortage and intensive industrial research linked to the war effort brought new technologies and increased automation into the factories. Agriculture went through a similar transformation when farmers were called on to increase production as quickly as possible. In Switzerland, the firm Ciba-Geigy discovered that a chemical it had developed practically wiped out insect pests. It named the chemical DDT. Parathion, another powerful insecticide, also came out of World War II defense research. To give some idea of its potency, parathion was originally developed as a nerve gas.

These technological breakthroughs spawned a second revolution in Mexico—only this time it was green. The man responsible for introducing these new agricultural techniques into the country was U.S. Vice President Henry C. Wallace. After spending several weeks in Mexico following Manuel Avila Camacho's inauguration in 1940, Wallace decided that the country's salvation lay in improving its agriculture. The following year, Wallace convened members of the Rockefeller Foundation and told them to get to work on the problem. Several weeks later a team of researchers visited Mexico. After traveling through the countryside for several months accompanied by an interpreter, the U.S. scientists concluded that many of the plots distributed under the agrarian reform program were too small to sustain the farmers. The problem, the team believed, was neither social nor economic—it was technological. The commission recommended new varieties of crops, better control of pests, and improved soil management. Through a program of grants to Mexican agricultural students and funding for national institutions, the new thinking was disseminated throughout the country with the enthusiastic backing of the Mexican government.

Today, more than three decades after the publication of Rachel Carson's *Silent Spring,* and at a time when pesticides have been linked to cancer and disease, it is difficult to imagine the optimism created by these agricultural breakthroughs. A 1945 issue of *National Geographic* shows children happily riding their bicycles through a DDT haze while a caption triumphantly declares that the new pesticide would eliminate the mosquito infestation at New York's Jones Beach. The new hybrid plant varieties, fertilizers, pesticides, soil management, and irrigation led to dramatically higher yields. As the Green Revolution spread from Mexico to the rest of the developing world, scientists and politicians boldly declared an imminent end to world hunger.

The most dramatic transformation was in the lowland tropics, where crop-devouring insects had previously prevented the development of a viable commercial agriculture. Now the pests vanished in a cloud of insecticides as the savannah was transformed into neat rows of corn, tomatoes, chiles, onions, lettuce, and fruit orchards of every type. The Mexican government invested billions in infrastructure projects to develop these new areas—in the coastal plains of Sinaloa, Sonora, and Tamaulipas, rivers were dammed, artesian wells were sunk, roads were built, and production skyrocketed. Inspired by the success of the Tennessee Valley Authority dam project, Mexico dammed every river in sight, built hydroelectric plants, and diverted the water for agriculture. Today a quarter of Mexico's farmland is irrigated—one of the highest proportions in the world—and large-scale commercial farms cultivate about half of Mexico's farmland.

During the two decades of impressive growth—agriculture expanded an average of 6.6 percent annually between 1945 and 1965—ejidos participated in the boom by growing most of the nation's corn. But the years of growth widened the gap between the ejidos that had productive land and the millions of farmers who were trying to farm rocky hillsides and desert plains.

The productive farms benefited most from the Green Revolution technologies, but government promoters also ensured that the new seed varieties, fertilizers, and pesticides trickled down to the peasants. Government technicians, the evangelists of the Green Revolution, traveled the highways and byways of Mexico preaching the new gospel. In the late 1960s, agricultural graduate students working with a government program called Plan Puebla began visiting Mixteco communities. By the mid-1970s, when free fertilizers were distributed in San Juan Mixtepec, the entire Mixteco region had been hooked on the Green Revolution. The government-owned fertilizer company Fertimex made the new technologies available to poor farmers at subsidized prices, and federal agencies also provided low-cost credit. Today, fertilizer use is virtually universal, and many communities also use chemical herbicides to clear their land and pesticides to battle the increase in infestations. Peasants regularly spend hours hiking the trails around San Juan Mixtepec carrying bags of fertilizer.

The new techniques raised yields on even the least productive lands, but at a terrible cost. The traditional strategy of growing corns, beans, and squash in the same field relies on highly refined environmental adaptation. Corn varieties were honed over centuries to the conditions of the region—altitude, soil conditions, rain—which changed dramatically from one valley to the next. Growing corn together with beans and squash in the same field is one example of how the ecological balance was maintained. While corn depletes nitrogen from the soil, beans replace it. Certainly, erosion, plagues, and crop failure had not been unknown, but the fact that fields continued to produce after thousands of years of intensive cultivation is compelling evidence of the sustainability of traditional Mesoamerican agriculture.

Fertilizers transformed traditional agriculture across the nation. In Emiliano Zapata's old stomping ground in Morelos, peasants adopted the fertilizers and gave up fallowing, the practice of periodically leaving a field unplanted to allow nutrients to be restored to the soil. For the first few years everything was fine. Then the problems started. The fertilizers made the corn ripen three weeks earlier than usual, and new pests invaded the region. Now the campesinos also needed pesticides and the bank credit to buy them. As their debts mounted, they farmed the land more intensively in a futile effort to catch up. Within a few years, yields on the exhausted fields had dropped by 25 to 40 percent despite the use of fertilizers. Peasants were working twice as much land in order to produce the same amount of corn. With the land depleted and their debts mounting, the Green Revolution practices became a Faustian bargain. Once the peasants adopted the new techniques there was no going back.

This growing dependence on agrochemicals and credit gave new strength to the Mexican agrarian bureaucracy, which became so complex it would have confused Kafka. "No claim was ever entirely resolved," wrote Arturo Warman in *We Come to Object,* his scathing critique of Mexican agrarian reform. "All the petitions or demands were lost from sight. They passed from hand to hand and climbed the hierarchical ladder until they were lost in the heights and descended again, not infrequently in some other direction; the apparatus swallowed them. It was necessary to wait, to apply again and go on waiting, to get support and influence, to seek out circuitous routes, and again, to wait."

Whatever lingering good will remained between the campesinos and the federal government began to dissipate in the early 1970s when an economic recession forced the government to keep the lid on its guaranteed price of corn while inflation carried the price of fertilizers into the stratosphere. Between 1965 and 1975, 5 million acres (2 million hectares) of farmland were abandoned and converted to pasture as, during the colonial period, intensive agriculture was replaced by extensive grazing. Even as production of basic foodstuffs slacked off, Mexico's growing middle class demanded beef. Cornfields were turned over to pasture or were planted in sorghum, an animal feed that can be grown with little water. The beef went to the cities and the United States, while malnutrition grew in the countryside. In response to a government survey conducted in the 1980s, 25 percent of Mexicans reported they never eat meat.

Meanwhile, the fact that Mexican peasants had become dependent on costly chemical fertilizers and pesticides to produce a marginal corn crop on degraded land was not of particular concern to the Mexican government. Just the opposite—it had the peasants just where it wanted them.

III

The way in which the Mexican government has translated the enviromental deterioration of the Mexican countryside into a mechanism for political control became apparent to me when I watched the election day voting in the Mixteco town of Tototepec in 1994. Tototepec is less than fifty miles from San Juan Mixtepec, but it lies on the other side of a series of rugged canyons in the neighboring state of Guerrero. Both communities speak Mixteco, but the dialect is so different that it is not mutually intelligible.

Like San Juan Mixtepec, and much of the Mexican countryside, Tototepec is confronting terrible erosion, a legacy of the conquest. But erosion and deforestation were problems long before the arrival of the Spaniards, and traditional Mixteco farmers had developed methods to control its effects. They had terraced the hillsides and built small dams along the creekbeds to limit flooding and recapture the topsoil washed away by the rains. They cleared small plots to plant corn but left stands of trees in place to stabilize the hillsides.

After 1519, European disease and forced labor caused Mixteco villages to abandon the maintenance of the terraces and dams. The forests were cut down for construction of the new towns, and cows and goats were turned loose on the hillsides. The torrential rains that soaked the bone-dry earth each June carried the fertile mountain topsoil away to the sea. By the beginning of the eighteenth century, the oak forests had been turned into deserts and the Mixteco culture was deeply impoverished. Activities were geared entirely toward subsistence; the Mixtecos abandoned goldsmithing, jewelry making, and the elaborate weaving that had so impressed the Aztec emperors. Today, Tototepec is a desperately poor place with nothing more than a few dozen dirt-floor huts scattered through the hills and some adobe buildings arranged around the muddy field that passes for a plaza.

On August 21, 1994, as a light rain fell over the village, residents prepared to cast their votes in the presidential elections. For the previous six years, since the last presidential election, Tototepec had been utterly and completely ignored. But because the PRI's ability to hold on to power in 1994 depended in good measure on the rural vote, suddenly miserable, forgotten hamlets took on strategic importance. In 1988 the PRI presidential candidate, Carlos Salinas de Gortari, had been forced to resort to fraud in order to ensure victory. Cuauhtémoc Cárdenas, who had left the PRI to run for president as the head of center-left coalition, had stolen the PRI's thunder by claiming that he, not Salinas, was the true heir to the agrarian populism promulgated by his father Lázaro.

By 1994, Cárdenas's support had softened and, according to opinion polls published before the elections, he had no chance of winning. The PRI's only concern was that Cárdenas's Party of the Democratic Revolution (PRD) would split the vote in the countryside, giving an edge to the conservative National Action Party (PAN), which had strong support among the urban middle class. To make matters a bit more complicated, the PRI knew it would have to take it easy on the ballot stuffing and other tricks that had usually put it over the top. With the implementation of the North American Free Trade Agreement (NAFTA) earlier that year, the world media were paying unusually close attention to the Mexican elections. National and international election observers were monitoring the voting for the first time. In addition, the PRI candidate, Ernesto Zedillo, was a dull technocrat who had spent his whole life in Mexico City and had virtually no name recognition in the countryside. He had been chosen as a last-minute stand-in for Luis Donaldo Colosio, who was assassinated at a campaign rally in March 1994.

I got a primer on Tototepec politics from the town's schoolteacher, Miguel Alvarez Montalvo.

"I've lived here all my life," said Alvarez, "and I don't like it that the people are fighting like a couple of stray dogs." He described the division of the town into two camps. PRD supporters had organized themselves into the ominous-sounding Emiliano Zapata Revolutionary Agrarian League of the South. They had packed the schoolhouse and were keeping a wary eye on the voting. PRI backers gathered under a tree and glared back.

Alvarez supported the PRD but was planning to stay out of the fray. "What difference does it make?" he asked. "The PRI always wins. The PRI is going to win here today." Then he launched into a tirade against the government. In the previous six years President Salinas had destroyed the campesino. Everyone in the town hated the government. Prices for everything were going up. There was no credit to buy seeds and fertilizers. "Ernesto Zedillo is exactly the same," said Alvarez. "He doesn't respect the campesino."

"But the problem is that without the PRI the land does not give," he explained. As in San Juan Mixtepec, the land will not produce without fertilizers, and the only place to get them is from the government. "Without fertilizers we starve," said Alvarez.

In May the government had delivered tons of fertilizers to the PRIista mayor in the regional capital of Tlapa. He in turn had sent trucks full of fertilizers out to his henchmen in the villages. Geronimo Maldonado, the delegate in Tototepec, had handed out the bags of fertilizer in Tototepec with a stern warning. "He told the people that if they don't vote for the PRI, there will be no more fertilizer," Alvarez recalled. "He said, 'We won't charge you now, but you remember this the day of the elections.'"

I watched the voting in Tototepec over the shoulder of Jaime Margarito Campos, a Mixteco Indian who had been trained by a national voting rights group called Civic Alliance to keep an eye out for irregularities. There was no fraud in Tototepec. It was not necessary. While the voting was going on I wandered into the town hall. Stacked up neatly against the wall were hundreds of bags of fertilizer. The vote in Tototepec went to the PRI—a victory that was repeated throughout the countryside and across the nation as a whole. The final tally nationwide: 50.17 percent for the PRI, 26.69 for the PAN, and only 17.08 for the PRD.

It was not the Mexican government's intention to destroy the rural environment, but since the destruction translated into greater dependence and greater political control, there was no incentive to halt it. And in many communities it is too late. When the peasants finally abandon their plots, they leave behind devastated landscapes of eroded soils, clear-cut forests, and depleted wildlife. What has already been lost includes not only the land itself, but millennia of highly refined biological and natural knowledge—Mexico's natural heritage. The environmental destruction is fomenting a social crisis.

On the coast of Guerrero, for example, across the Sierra Madre del Sur from Tototepec and just an hour up the coast from the tourist trap of Acapulco, the Campesino Organization of the Southern Sierra (OCSS) had been noisily advocating for greater access to fertilizers and pesticides. In fact, at a meeting on May 3, 1995, then-governor Rubén Figueroa promised to donate fertilizers to the group.

Nearly two months later the fertilizers had not arrived, and so on June 28 members of the OCSS left their tiny hamlets in the mountains and headed to the municipal capital of Atoyac to protest. Near the town of Aguas Blancas their convoy was ambushed by Guerrero State Judicial Police. A videotape, which somehow made it into the hands of the media, shows that the police opened fire without provocation and then calmly walked among the dying as they lay groaning in agony. Seventeen campesinos were killed in the attack.

A year later, at a solemn event held to commemorate the attack, about 80 armed men, wearing masks and carrying AK-47 assault rifles, interrupted the meeting, reading a brief manifesto before disappearing back into the bush. This was the first appearance of the Popular Revolutionary Army (EPR), the second guerrilla force to emerge in Mexico since 1994, when the Zapatista Army of Liberation rose up in the southern state of Chiapas.

Over the next few months, the EPR launched a series of attacks against military and police targets, including a coordinated strike on August 28 that hit seven towns in three states. That attack left at least 14 dead.

While the goals, strategies, and strength of the EPR are unclear at the time of this writing, access to fertilizers is a key demand among their supporters in the states of Guerrero, Oaxaca, and Hidalgo. During the coordinated strike on August 28, a column of around 50 EPR guerrillas attacked the town hall in the Tlaxiaco, the regional capital of the Mixteco region, deep in the mountains of Oaxaca. They left behind three dead—two policemen and one civilian caught in the crossfire—before commandeering a truck and heading off down the dirt road to San Juan Mixtepec. According to the residents of the town with whom I spoke soon after the attack, the rebels never arrived there, apparently abandoning the vehicle along the way and disappearing into the forest that remains on the ridges outside town.

Of course, only a handful of peasants will pick up a gun in response to environmental deterioration. The much more common response is simply to leave. That is certainly what most of the people of San Juan Mixtepec have done. According to the 1990 census report, there are thirty thousand Mixtecos living permanently in Mexico City, ten thousand in Sinaloa, and ten thousand in Baja California. There are perhaps fifty thousand more in the United States—thirty thousand in California alone. Of the approximately three hundred thousand left in Oaxaca and Guerrero, the majority work outside the village at least part of the year, many in the United States.

I have run into Mixtecos in every place in Mexico where misery congregates. I met José Ramírez, for example, begging with his family on a Mexico City street corner. He was wearing ragged clothes and sandals. He told me he had left his village the week before and moved with his wife and three young children to Pantitlan, a growing slum. "I have land but it no longer gives," he said, uttering the now familiar refrain.

I have run into Mixtecos harvesting cotton in Mexicali, tomatoes in Sinaloa, lettuce in Salinas, California. In San Quintín, a fertile valley on the coast of Baja California where Mixtecos have worked for two decades harvesting vegetables for the U.S. market, I met José López, a refugee from San Juan Mixtepec. He sat outside his cinderblock home wearing camouflage fatigues and cradling his newborn baby. "I have only two hectares of land in my village, and it is all rocks," he said. "I want to go back there, but there is no work."

José López's experience shows how the managed decay of the Mexican rural environment feeds the labor pool, in both Mexico and the United States. Since the 1940s, when a handful of Mixtecos began to migrate to work harvesting crops in the United States and cutting sugar cane on plantations in Veracruz, the Mixtecos have played a crucial role in North American agribusiness. By the early 1980s, Mixteco farm workers were absolutely essential to California agriculture. Mixtecos were willing to work for less than the traditonal mestizo migrants who came largely from places like Michoacán and Jalisco. And because they often did not speak Spanish they were less likely to organize.

For a while the system seemed perfectly calibrated. The Mixtecos planted their corn crop, took off for four months and found ready work in California, and then came back home with a pocket full of dollars and a field full of ripe corn. For agribusiness, the Mixtecos were a godsend. For centuries, plantation agriculture had employed all sorts of strategies to ensure a large seasonal labor supply—from slavery to sharecropping. Now they had a nearly foolproof system—hunger pushed the Mixtecos out when the crop needed picking, and their corn crop called them home once the labor was done. Consumers in Mexico and the United States thus began to depend on the environmental destruction of the Mixteco homeland to put cheap food on their tables.

By the early 1980s, the delicate balance began to tip against the Mixtecos. The economic crisis that hit Mexico in the 1980s sent millions across the border into the United States. Finding a job took much longer—often weeks or months. They lived in the fields and squatted in caves near San Diego in southern California. Often they ran up huge debts with the Mixteco loan sharks, who charged as much as 100 percent interest a month. By the end of the decade, crisis-driven immigration from Mexico had saturated the U.S. labor market for unskilled labor. For example, San Juan Mixtepec mayor Joaquín Sánchez used to earn as much as $150 a day as a farm worker in the mid-1980s. By 1990 work had become sporadic and the best workers made around $50.

In the early 1990s, when the U.S. economy stalled, policy makers in Washington blamed illegal Mexican immigrants and increased enforcement along the border. Slipping into the United States—once a minor hassle—became an enormous expense. Often the migrants had to spend a week in Tijuana paying for a hotel and food before they could get across. Having invested more money to get into the United States, they were less likely to leave once they got there. Today, many Mixtecos spend years at a time in the States, and many are not planting their cornfields at all.

What one could call the Mixtecoization of the Mexican countryside—the evolution from subsistence farmer to part-time wage laborer, to agricultural, full-time worker—is a process that has been going on for most of this century and that is expected to accelerate. In fact, with a few brief interludes, the Mexican policy toward the campesino has been remarkably consistent for the past quarter century. The strategy has been to get rid of them—but slowly, in order to minimize the social disruption. The policy reached new heights under Salinas. Since the peasants were dependent on the government for fertilizers and pesticides, Salinas slowly squeezed them by tightening credit. Price supports for corn were replaced by direct payments; under a program called Procampo peasants receive a cash payment for each hectare of land they own (the program was dubbed PRI-campo by government opponents, who claim the checks were handed out right before the elections). In fact, the economic reforms implemented under NAFTA are expected to force millions more off their land as all price supports are phased out by the year 2010. From 5 to 15 million farmers are expected to abandon the countryside in the first decade of the twenty-first century. NAFTA boosters argued that many rural migrants would be absorbed by the industry that would flock to Mexico after the treaty was approved. But the financial crisis that began in late 1994 and soon became a recession has dashed any such hopes for the immediate future.

But because prospects are so bleak in the countryside, rural migrants continue to head for the cities. Mexico City is not the only city growing out of control. Guadalajara, Monterrey, Tijuana, Matamoros, and provincial capitals like Morelia in Michoacán and Tuxtla Gutiérrez in Chiapas are also attracting the rural refugees. It will cost billions of dollars to bring air pollution under control and provide water to the multitudes, especially in the arid northern cities.

Nor is there much hope at least in the short term that agroindustry can provide employment to those expelled from the villages. After a brief boom in the late 1980s, commercial agriculture ran up against infrastructure bottlenecks and has largely stagnated. Today Mexico imports a quarter of its food—20 percent of its corn—which puts a strain on the country's hard-currency reserves. Yet the Mexican government marches relentlessly on in its strategy to eliminate "inefficient" producers from the market and encourage the consolidation of agricultural production. In 1992 Salinas reformed Article 27, declaring an end to agrarian reform. For the first time since the revolution, ejidatarios were allowed to legally sell or mortgage their land under certain conditions.

While the shift to commercial, largely export-oriented farming may make sense on paper, the Mexican government has failed to factor in the environmental costs. Most of Mexico's more fertile farmland is in the north, where there is very little water. In order to make it productive, the government has invested billions of dollars in irrigation projects that use both groundwater and surface water. The kind of hybrid crops favored by commercial agriculture demand fertilizers, pesticides, herbicides, and large quantities of water in order to produce. In many areas, water is running out. In the state of Guanajuato, for example, where commercial production of vegetables for the U.S. market has taken off, so much water has been pumped out of the underground aquifer that state authorities estimate it will run dry early in the twenty-first century.

In Sonora the situation is even more precarious. Three times more water is being pumped out of the underground aquifer than naturally flows in. The water level is sinking three to six feet a year, and what remains in the aquifer is coming up salty. In the Guaymas area, 12,300 acres (5,000 hectares) of prime agricultural land have been destroyed by salinization. Nationally, nearly 1 million acres of prime farmland have been damaged by salinization, and nearly half of the country's rivers have been contaminated by sewage and agricultural runoff.

Of course, the intensive and often uncontrolled use of pesticides and herbicides has also had a devastating effect on human health. In Sinaloa most of the largely Mixteco laborers work without respirators or gloves. Without access to showers they are forced to bathe in the contaminated irrigation ditches. Three thousand workers were hospitalized in 1993 in Sinaloa alone; nationwide, acute pesticide poisoning kills five thousand people a year. Although the government has not been forthcoming with statistics, cancer levels appear to be on the rise in Sinaloa, while high levels of residual pesticides have been found in mothers' milk in other parts of the country. Half a dozen pesticides that have been banned in the United States continue to be used in Mexico, including parathion and methamidophos. In 1991, Mexico used 3 million tons of fertilizers and 2 million tons of insecticides.

The contradiction in Mexico's program to strengthen large-scale commercial agriculture at the expense of the small and medium-sized farmers is that to make commercial agriculture successful in the short term Mexico will have to spend billions of dollars that it does not have in developing hydraulic infrastructure. These investments will only pay off if the government can find an effective long-term strategy for mitigating the environmental costs—salinization, depletion of aquifers, and contamination of river basins and ocean fisheries, not to mention the health of the farm workers.

With few opportunities in the Mexican cities or in the countryside, where will the peasants who leave their land go? The United States remains their best hope. Historically, Mexicans, like other immigrants, have been drawn to the United States mostly by a strong demand for labor. Millions stayed and became U.S. citizens, but the vast majority came for a few months or years and then returned to their villages.

Since the 1980s the motivation of the migrants has changed. For many it is no longer the lure of earning a bit of extra cash. It is a question of survival. Increasingly, Mexicans come not because their labor is needed but because they are being pushed out of their country, scraped from the land and expelled from the booming urban slums. By the late 1980s, the U.S. economy was in recession and many could not find work. They could not go home—their villages hardly existed anymore. Instead, they scraped and scrimped and begged and hung on in a saturated labor market, pushing down U.S. wages and fueling a powerful anti-immigrant backlash.

More and more Mexicans who leave the village are finding themselves in Lionel Mendoza's position. I met Mendoza in the Mixteco neighborhood in San Quintín, an agribusiness haven in Baja California three hours south of the U.S. border. Mendoza is from Juxtlahuaca, just down the road from San Juan Mixtepec. His father spent his whole life growing corn. But the younger Mendoza inherited only a small piece of his father's plot and farmed it until "it wouldn't give." He left the village in 1973, went to the United States for a while, then went back to Mexico and settled in the valley of San Quintín. He has had sporadic work in the tomato fields, enough to build a cinderblock home and buy a rusty bicycle.

I spent an hour talking with Mendoza on a foggy morning in June 1994. As I got up to leave he asked me a favor. His son had gone to the United States a year earlier and he had not heard anything from him. He was worried, he told me, that like so many Mixteco boys far from their families he would fall into temptation and became a drunk or a drug addict. He gave me a phone number in Los Angeles and asked if I would try to track him down.

In L.A. I called the number Mendoza had given me. A woman named Juanita who answered the phone said she had not seen the boy in months and had no idea where he was. This is what I put in the postcard I sent to Mendoza. I did not mention the rest of what the woman told me—that the boy had not found work, that he had become listless and depressed, that Juanita had fed him and told him not to worry about the rent until he found a job. But shame had overwhelmed Mendoza's son, and one night he slipped away. Is he living on the street or in a shelter? Is he going to emergency rooms when he gets sick and not paying the bills? I worry that he will get caught one day and become the poster child of some anti-immigrant group—its explanation of what is driving the once great state of California into bankruptcy.

IV

One morning while I was visiting San Juan Mixtepec, I hiked into the hills outside town. After an hour or so I took shelter from the punishing sun under a gnarled pine. From my vantage point about six hundred feet above the valley, I peered down a crumbling canyon. Beyond it, an entire hillside stripped bare of soil gleamed white as marble in the morning sun.

A bit further down the trail I ran into Mario Cruz, who was nattily dressed in purple pants, matching purple boots, and a cowboy hat. Though surprised to see a gringo ambling down the trail, since Cruz was leaving for the United States the next morning he decided to do a little scouting. He asked me about jobs in California, about the best place to cross the border. I offered a bit of advice, but it was clear that he knew more than I did. "It used to be easy to cross the border," he said. "But now that they've installed these new infrared lights in Nogales it could be a bit tricky."

We sat on a bench behind a small store looking out at a recently planted cornfield. Cruz was only twenty-three, but he had already spent eight years working in the United States. His family history was a chronicle of rural downward mobility. His grandfather owned a small orchard, enough land to be able to fallow his cornfield, a hundred goats, a dozen cows. His father had sufficient land but got hooked on fertilizer, caught up in the cycle of debt. He was forced to leave the village to find work. Cruz was practically raised on the road. All that was left of his family patrimony was ten acres (four hectares) of eroded, rocky land, which had to support nine brothers and sisters and their children. "You can't live from the land anymore," Cruz said. "That's why everyone wants to leave."

It was hard to argue with Cruz's analysis. There was little doubt that his future lay outside San Juan Mixtepec. But is it realistic to think that

Mexico City and Los Angeles, Guadalajara and Chicago, can really accommodate the millions who will leave the countryside in the next decade? In other words, do Mexico and the United States have an interest in slowing down the process, in keeping campesinos on their land in conditions of basic dignity?

The answer, both from a social and environmental point of view, is clearly yes. The problem is that tools are limited. For example, the last time the government tried to support campesinos by raising the guaranteed price of corn it ended up subsidizing the large tomato growers in Sinaloa, who stopped growing crops for export and grew corn for the national market instead. Those who were hurt most were peasants themselves, 72 percent of whom are also wage laborers, which means they purchase more of their corn than they grow.

There is simply no easy way to reverse centuries of environmental decay and fifty years of failed rural policies. Nor is there any evidence that the Mexican government has any desire to try. The election day scene in Tototepec made it abundantly clear how the PRI has been able to turn environmental deterioration into a political asset by exploiting the dependence on fertilizers.

The gambit that industrial growth would somehow absorb those displaced from the countryside has not paid off. If the past is any indication, development will continue to be uneven and erratic. Whether Mexico's technocrats like it or not, campesinos will be around in Mexico for the foreseeable future, and ignoring their needs will have social and environmental costs that will reverberate across the continent. In San Juan Mixtepec, the young are leaving while the old are beginning to see the ecological deterioration of their ancient homeland in apocalyptic terms. After leaving Cruz, I walked for several more hours in the hills. Back in town, an old farmer noticed me trudging along looking tired and sunburned and stopped me to apologize for the heat. "There is a veil that covers the sun," he explained. "But it has gotten so hot that it has burned away."

He rubbed his sandal-shod foot in the dirt. "I feel sometimes that the world is coming to an end. The planets are ominous; several of them are unusually close to the sun. That's why the forest is dying. That's why the rain doesn't come. That's why the earth no longer gives." He dismissed me with a wave and turned back to his cornfield.

—three—

The Sinking City

Anyone who has lived through Mexico City's rainy season, when the sky blackens each afternoon and lets loose a thunderous deluge, would never suspect that the city is running out of water. In fact, when Mexico City residents think of environmental threats to their city they look up at the smoggy skies. But that is only because they cannot see what is happening under their feet. The underground aquifer that provides 70 percent of the city's water is being rapidly emptied—its useful life can be measured in decades.

Air pollution receives so much attention because it is so obvious. It is everywhere and its effects are immediate. The water threat is long term—and it takes a trained eye to see the damage. The only visible evidence that the city is running out of water is the fact that it is sinking. So much water has been pumped out of the underground aquifer that the clay soil underlying the city has contracted like a sponge left to dry in the sun. The sinking is not uniform; it varies from street to street, from building to building. After a century of slow subsidence, downtown Mexico City resembles a fun house at an amusement park. Streets are buckled; buildings are pitched forward or balanced at impossible angles.

One quiet Sunday morning, I set out to explore the sinking landscape. I began in the Alameda, a tree-lined park built on the site of an old Aztec market. I crossed Avenida Hidalgo north of the park and descended a flight of stairs to a plaza that was once at street level. On the east side is the Santa Veracruz church, built in 1730. The floor of the church is so slanted that walking on it gave me vertigo. On the other side of the plaza is the Temple of San Juan de Dios. Looking up at the street, all I could make out were shoes and ankles. I was a good ten feet below the level of the sidewalk.

South of the Alameda, Avenida Juárez undulates wildly. From east to west each building leans progressively farther into the street, like spectators along a parade route trying to get a view of the next float.

East of the park, the Secretariat of Education building on Donceles slopes back from the street at a ten-degree angle; the church down the street looks as if it would topple forward if someone pushed it. The building that houses the Mexican Society of Geography and Statistics is buckled; the middle of the building is thrust outward like a protruding stomach. The Santo Domingo plaza is so dramatically tilted that the water in the fountain is six inches deeper on the west side than on the east side.

It is awesome to look across the Zócalo, Mexico City's enormous central plaza, and see the National Palace tilting to the south like the *Titanic* slowly descending into the sea. The Metropolitan Cathedral is sinking in the opposite direction. Inside is a display explaining the multimillion-dollar retrofitting project. The sinking is so extensive and so uneven that engineers have drawn a topographic map of the cathedral floor showing the mini-hillocks and dells.

By far the most dramatic evidence of the sinking is the old Aztec pyramid, the Templo Mayor. The pyramid was torn down soon after the Spanish Conquest and the bricks used to build Spanish palaces and churches. The ruins were uncovered by accident in 1978. The base of the pyramid is twenty feet below the Zócalo and pitched at a thirty-degree angle. Downtown Mexico City is thirty-four feet lower than it was when Cortés arrived.

The problem would be bad enough if only the buildings were affected. But of course, pipes, cables, subway tunnels and the whole underground infrastructure are sinking along with the rest of the city. So many water pipes have burst that 30 percent of the water flowing through the system is lost to leaks. The sinking undermines foundations, making buildings vulnerable to collapse in the earthquakes that periodically strike the city. Sometimes the ground simply collapses and a sinkhole swallows a piece of the city. On July 6, 1996, Pati Ortíz was selling quesadillas on the street corner of a poor neighborhood called Iztapalapa when she heard a loud crack. She grabbed frantically at the skirt of her friend Hortencia Gener, but the ground had fallen away and she was sucked screaming into a twenty-foot sinkhole. The falling earth ruptured an abandoned septic tank, filling the sinkhole with poisonous methane gas. Ortíz and three bystanders who jumped into the sinkhole to save her were all killed.

Because nearly twice as much water is being pumped out of the aquifer as naturally flows in, the water has higher and higher concentrations of salts and other minerals. And because the water level is subsiding at a rate of about three feet a year, it is more and more costly to pump it up from the depths.

Thirty percent of the city's water is piped from distant reservoirs at enormous cost. In fact, 10 percent of Mexico's total energy output is used to meet Mexico City's water needs—pumping drinking water into the city and pumping waste water out.

The situation is clearly untenable. "We've looked at all of the alternatives—every one," said Alfonso Martínez Baca, the head of Mexico City's Water Commission, when I met him in his wood-paneled office. "Not one of them is viable." Martínez Baca has the unenviable task of managing the city's water system. "There is no nearby source that can give us the water we need," he said. "Some people have pointed out to me that we have an inexhaustible source of water, which is the Gulf of Mexico. But you'd have to transport it four hundred kilometers and raise it two and a half kilometers. It's impossible. It would be cheaper to move Mexico City to Veracruz."

Martínez Baca leaned across the conference table and spoke in a conspiratorial whisper. "Water is the most serious threat facing the city," he said. "Tomorrow everyone could ride on bicycles and the air pollution would clear up. But where on earth are we going to get our water from?"

It is a question the city has been asking itself since the days of the Aztecs.

I

Water, or its control, was at the core of Aztec civilization. Tenochtitlan was the amphibious capital of an amphibious people. Water made the

Aztecs feel secure. Their capital was on an island, their enemies were on the distant shores.

Water was also sacred. It descended from Tlalocan, a terrestrial paradise deep in the mountains that was the home of the water god Tlaloc. The gardens, flowers, and trees that filled Tenochtitlan were an attempt to recreate the realm of Tlaloc, a tribute to his power. Since water was believed to come directly from the gods, it represented life itself; rituals attested to its power to purify and cleanse. Bathing, anathema to the Europeans at the time, was a daily activity for the Aztecs. Priests bathed in sacred fountains. Newborns were washed and introduced into the world with a prayer: "Here is the heavenly water, the very pure water, that washes and cleans your heart and takes away all stain."

For two centuries, the Aztecs struggled to bring their watery environment under control. Finding water was the first problem. At first they collected water from springs, which bubbled up around the island. As the population grew, water became scarce. In the mid-fifteenth century the Aztecs began a series of military campaigns to gain control of the valley's water supply. In 1466, after taking over the Chapultepec spring from their old enemies the Tepanecs, Aztec workers completed a stone aqueduct to deliver the water into a fountain in the main square of Tenochtitlan.

At the same time the city was also battling floods. In 1449, with the help of Texcocan King Nezahualcoyótl, the Aztecs built an enormous dike across Lake Texcoco. Over the next several decades, they built dikes and causeways and expanded the canals that crisscrossed the city. The Aztecs realized that Tenochtitlan's spongy soil could not support heavy structures. The temples and a few palaces were the only truly large buildings in the city; only the greatest lord was permitted to add a second story to his home.

These engineering marvels were the pride of the Aztec emperor. Soon after the metal-clad foreigners arrived in his city, Moctezuma II took Hernán Cortés by the hand, led him to the top of the great pyramid, and pointed out the features of his great city. Wrote Spanish soldier Bernal Díaz del Castillo:

> We saw the three causeways that led into Mexico. . . . We saw the fresh water that came from Chapultepec to supply the city, and the bridges

that were constructed at intervals on the causeways so that the water could flow in and out from one part of the lake to another. We saw a great number of canoes, some coming with provisions and others returning with cargo and merchandise. . . . We saw cues and shrines in these cities that looked like gleaming white towers and castles: a marvelous sight.

If Mexicans want to assign blame for their current water woes, they might as well look to Hernán Cortés. Cortés marveled at Tenochtitlan's beauty, but what he inherited at the end of the two-year campaign was a pile of rubble. Tenochtitlan was sacked, burned, annihilated. The Spanish siege specifically targeted the hydraulic infrastructure. The dikes were dismantled to make room for the Spanish brigantines; the aqueducts were destroyed in order to deprive the city of fresh water; the canals were filled in to allow passage for the Spanish cavalry.

Cortés dismissed suggestions that he rebuild on the lakeshore. His capital, like that of the Aztecs, would be on an island. This was a political and perhaps aesthetic decision. In truth, the Spaniards never trusted or understood the lakes. They were land-based people who preferred mules and horses to boats. They grew their wheat in open fields, not in "floating gardens." They found the Indian foods gathered from the lakes repulsive. The fish the Spaniards ate was shipped two hundred and fifty miles from the Gulf of Mexico.

The Spaniards had been in the Valley of Mexico for only two years when they began constructing their new city. They had no empirical understanding of how the lakes worked, and they dismissed the Aztecs' mythological explanations as the ideas of ignorant pagans. Meanwhile, their own ideas about water were based on the theories of the ancient Greeks. The standard authority on lakes and water at the time of the conquest was Hippocrates: he argued that standing bodies of waters were unhealthy because they produced infection.

The great difficulty in controlling the water in the so-called Valley of Mexico is that it is not a valley at all but rather a closed basin. In ancient times the waters drained out of the valley to the south. Then, 2 million years ago, lava sealed off the drainage and rainwater filled five shallow, interconnected lakes—Zumpango, Xaltocon, Texcoco, Xochimilco, and Chalco. Xochimilco and Chalco were freshwater lakes; Lake Texcoco was saltier than the sea. No rivers flowed into the valley and none flowed out.

An underground aquifer regulated the whole complex system. During six months of the year—from May to October—the rain came in torrents. Much of it was absorbed into the aquifer and then disgorged slowly in hundreds of springs along the lakeshore. When the rains were heavy, the aquifer overflowed, the lakes rose, and the valley was flooded. If the rains failed several years in a row, the water table would fall and the freshwater springs would run dry.

Without the infrastructure in place to manage this complex system, Mexico City faced serious environmental problems from the moment it emerged on the ruins of Tenochtitlan. The Aztecs had strictly forbidden that garbage or human waste be dumped in the lakes because it would have affected their food supply. But since the Spaniards did not live from the lakes, they saw no reason to take care of them. The canals that flowed through the city became little more than garbage dumps; human waste fed algal blooms, which covered the canals with a green slime. Since land for burials was at a premium on the small island, the cadavers of dead Indians—along with dogs and horses—were simply hurled into the lakes. The fetid water surrounding the city reinforced the Spanish prejudices.

Forty years after the founding of Mexico City, the Spaniards had so altered the local ecology that the periodic floods became perennial. The construction of Mexico City required enormous amounts of timber. Twenty-five thousand trees were cut down each year for beams. Once the forest was felled, the Spanish opened the land for grazing. Sheep and cows prevented the deforested hillsides from stabilizing, and massive erosion was the result. The soil was washed into the lakes, causing the water levels to rise. Deforestation also changed the climate, making the winter rains more torrential. On October 10, 1555, runoff from heavy rains swept off the mountains. The first of a series of terrible floods struck the Spanish city.

The city flooded again in January 1580. Two decades later, in August 1604, another flood hit: houses collapsed and much of the population fled in panic. Those who stuck around moved through the city in canoes. The city was under water for brief periods in 1605, 1606, and 1607. The Spaniards faced war with their environment. The lakes, fetid and flooding, would have to be destroyed.

Cosmologist Enrico Martínez emerged as the savior of the Spanish city. Born Heinrich Martin in Hamburg, Germany, in the 1550s, he moved to Seville as an adolescent and, after emigrating to New Spain, worked for the Inquisition translating the interrogations of European heretics. In 1607, Martínez's plan to build a series of canals and tunnels to drain the lakes from the northern part of the valley was accepted by the viceroy. It took sixty thousand Indian laborers and ate up a fifth of the entire colonial budget to complete the project in less than a year. On September 17 the viceroy peered down through a skylight and observed water flowing through the tunnel. For the first time since the late tertiary period, when lava had sealed off the valley's natural drainage, water was flowing out of the closed basin into the Río Tula and down to the sea.

The *Desagüe General*—the General Drain—was hailed as the definitive solution to the floods. But in 1629, only two decades after the tunnel was completed, the city was once again flooded. Martínez had refused to open a flood-control gate from Lake Zumpango when the heavy rains hit because he feared that the torrent of floodwater would destroy his new tunnel. He was jailed for his treachery. For five years, until 1634, Mexico City remained under water. Canoes replaced horses, houses collapsed, and all but four hundred of the twenty thousand Spanish residents fled to the nearby city of Puebla. Mass was said in the water-filled Zócalo for parishioners who assembled in canoes. In 1635 the floodwaters retreated. Thirty thousand Indians were dead; a third of the city was destroyed.

Rather than relocating the city or developing more effective techniques to control the lakes, the five-year flood reenforced the Spanish determination to proceed with the *desagüe*. The battle was cultural as well as ecological. Draining the lakes was a way to hispanicize the land itself, a way to show domination over the Indian environment. It was also a pursuit befitting a great civilization. The Spaniards compared the project to the draining of Lake Fucino by Emperor Claudius, an enterprise that opened up new lands for Roman cultivation.

The desiccation of Lake Texcoco, however, exposed not new farmland but dry salt flats. The fierce winds whipped the salty soil into blinding dust storms called *tolvaneras*. The storms remain a feature of Mexico City life to this day and contribute significantly to the air pollution.

In the lake-filled environment the problem was not finding water to drink—it was getting it from the mountain springs to the island city.

The Spaniards invested enormous sums to build beautiful arched aqueducts that spanned the lakes. Special taxes were levied on the Spanish city and thousands of Indians were pressed into service.

By the beginning of the eighteenth century Mexico City had dug itself a hole it would never be able to crawl out of. It had water, but it was paying dearly for it. Meanwhile, the environment surrounding the city was rapidly deteriorating. As the lakes retreated, the water content of the soils decreased and the city began to sink. The Spaniards watched in agony as their palaces and churches sank into the mud. Visitors to the city in the eighteenth century were amazed that every church, mansion, or government building was tilted or sunk down below the street.

Throughout the colonial era, work on the desagüe continued intermittently. In the early eighteenth century, as the waters slowly flowed from the valley and Lake Texcoco retreated, Mexico City finally ceased to be an island. Canoes, at last, vanished from the city.

The city, however, was not rid of the annual floods, because the small tunnel built by Martínez could not fully siphon off the floodwater. City authorities decided to expand the capacity of the tunnel by turning it into an open canal. That was a colossal task. Work responded to periodic panic—it picked up whenever the city flooded and then slowed down again when government coffers ran low. In 1788 the conversion was completed. The canal, called the Tajo de Nochistongo, still functions today. Over the centuries the walls of the hundred-foot-deep ditch have slowly eroded until it now looks like a natural canyon. In 1856, engineer Francisco de Garay began surveying a site for a second tunnel at Tequixquiac near Lake Zumpango, but work was abandoned in the wake of the French invasion.

By that time Mexico City was confronting a second problem that could not so easily be deferred. Centuries of deforestation and erosion were beginning to take their toll, and the flow from the springs providing water to the city began to diminish. In 1847 a deep well dug near the city center drew water up from the aquifer. This was a major breakthrough because the aquifer, filled with the epochal waters of the valley, had never been tapped. It seemed to offer the promise of a definitive solution to the city's water problems. Dozens of new wells were drilled, and by the time Porfirio Díaz came to power in 1876 the capital city was under the mistaken impression that the water problem that had plagued it since Aztec times had been solved. By the turn of the century, there were more than a thousand wells. The aqueducts bringing water from the dying springs were slowly abandoned.

With the water supply seemingly secure, Díaz turned his sights on the lakes. The city was still plagued by flooding, and the remaining lakes, which had been reduced to swamps, were still seen as sources of infection. Since Lake Texcoco received the sewage from Mexico City, that view was not unjustified.

Díaz believed that science was the antidote to Mexico's chronic chaos. Even politics was governed by scientific principles, he believed, and since his administration adhered to them there was no basis or justification for any opposition. During the Díaz administration, engineers were held in especially high esteem. Enrico Martínez, the man who designed the Desagüe General in 1607, was elevated to the status of official hero. His statue was erected in the Zócalo in 1882. He is perched on a marble pedestal and wrapped in a flowing cape. No greater honor could accrue to the Díaz administration than to complete Martínez's great work.

The plan was to build a tunnel near the town of Tequixquiac and then link it to a new sewage canal being dug in Mexico City. Despite the nationalistic implications of the project, the Mexican engineers did not have much luck, and in 1889 a British company was offered the contract. When they too found the work unprofitable, a second British firm was given a crack at it. In 1900 the project was completed. A thirty-six-mile open drainage ditch extended from downtown Mexico City, across the state of Mexico, and then out of the valley through the tunnel at Tequixquiac. Díaz hailed the canal as a symbol of Mexico's entry into the modern world.

In fact, it was, but not quite for the reasons that Díaz envisioned. The draining of Lake Texcoco marked one of the most monumental ecological transformations in human history. After 2 million years, the Valley of Mexico was no longer a basin but once again a valley. The lakes that covered 736 square miles (2,000 square kilometers)—nearly a fifth of the total area—were gone. Their disappearance marked the demise of the valley's ancient lakefront culture. Meanwhile, the enormous salt flats spawned what would become the modern city. Half a century after the lakes were drained, the poor, driven from the countryside, found a new home on Lake Texcoco's dried remains. They would build a whole working-class suburb named Ciudad Nezahualcoyótl after the Aztec king.

Although the Gran Canal finally destroyed the lake system, it did not end the flooding. Severe floods hit in 1900, 1901, and 1910. Even more alarming, engineers observed that the city was sinking rapidly.

II

After three centuries of abuse, the valley's hydrology had been permanently and irreparably damaged. Buildings were cracking, water pipes were snapping, and no one could figure out exactly why. It was not until 1946 that the problem was finally solved. Engineers announced that so much water was being pumped out of the underground aquifer that the ground supporting the city was collapsing.

The Mexican government was not ready to hear the bad news. The economy was poised for takeoff and Mexico City was a big part of the plans. Commercial agriculture had been largely dismantled by President Cárdenas, who had put through the largest land reform in Mexican history. The new landowners were told not to grow crops for the gringos, but for the new factory workers in Mexico City. World War II had spawned the country's great industrialization. Nothing could stand in the way of Mexico's bright future, not even nature itself.

Despite the report on the sinking, the Mexican government went right on pumping water from the aquifer. Between 1948 and 1951 the city sank 4.4 feet; the next decade it sank another 4.75 feet. In one single year—1950—it sank a remarkable 18 inches.

By the mid-1950s, Mexico City was no longer merely the capital of the country. It had became, like Tenochtitlan, an imperial city that demanded tribute from the hinterlands. The tribute was brought in various forms—campesinos provided cheap corn, the rural migrants provided their labor, raw materials from throughout the country were channeled to Mexico City. Like Tenochtitlan, the ever-larger Mexico City embarked on an era of expansion in which it subdued its neighbors and took their water. While the Aztecs could only capture water from within the valley, new technology allowed Mexico City to look farther afield. In the late 1930s, the city's gaze fell on Almoloya del Río, a back-water town of four thousand fishermen on the other side of the 12,620-foot Ajusco volcano.

Eladio Casteñeda was a thirty-one-year-old schoolteacher when President Cárdenas motored into town with a group of engineers. They all took a quiet walk along the lakeshore, staring intermittently down at the water and up at the 14,600-foot Nevado de Toluca, a snow-covered volcano rising above the valley like a jagged crown.

The villagers were honored by the visit but did not think too much about it—not until 1942, anyway, when the engineers returned in droves with slide rules and note pads. They set up camp along the lakeshore in a field where water percolated up through the ground "like it was overflowing from a boiling pot," according to Casteñeda. The water trickled down into Lake Chiconahuapan ("nine waters" in Nahuat) and then formed a series of other, smaller lakes before settling down to become the Lerma River. The Lerma flows through the states of Queretero and Guanajuato before emptying into Lake Chapala, near Guadalajara.

"This was the source of the Lerma River," Casteñeda said with a certain pride as he waved a hand over the landscape visible outside his second-story home. "The whole plain was covered with water—and it was clean, Señor. You could see the fish." Casteñeda had spent his childhood fishing and scavenging in the lake. The Mazahua- and Otomi-speaking Indians who had first settled the valley eight hundred years ago had lived much the same way.

The plan to bring the water to Mexico City got off to a poor start. The engineers dynamited the spring in an attempt to increase the flow of water, but instead the water stopped flowing altogether. Undaunted, the engineers sank pumps into the ground. They sucked up 1,600 gallons of water per second and sent it along a large pipe parallel to the old river channel. In the town of Atrasquillo, the pipe turned east at a ninety-degree angle and climbed the Sierra de las Cruces. Then the water flowed through a three-mile tunnel into the Valley of Mexico. The hundreds of springs in Almoloya quickly ran dry.

The inauguration in September 1951 drew a long line of dignitaries from Mexico City. Once again, the public was assured that the new system would end Mexico City's water problems forever, and that the sinking city would be quickly stabilized.

Meanwhile, Eladio Casteñeda watched as the lake that had sustained him, his village, and his ancestors slowly dried up. "It was like a dream," he said. "One day we woke up and it was gone." More than thirty years later, Casteñeda took me for a walk along what used to be the lakeshore. With the springs gone, what remains of the lake is now filled by sewage and runoff. A small flock of pelicans rested on the water. Casteñeda laughed when I asked if it reminded him of his childhood. "Oh, it was much bigger," he said. "The lakes were not deep, but you could go in a canoe from here all the way to Lerma."

When I asked Casteñeda whether he missed the village life of his childhood, he was less definitive. The engineers who took the water later brought roads, schools, sewage systems, potable water, and a wave of industrial growth. The town's economy shifted from fishing to shoe making and the standard of living rose accordingly. Among Casteñeda's nine children one is a doctor, another a lawyer, and a third an engineer. During a later visit to Almoloya I asked seventy-eight-year-old Taurino Ariscorreta whether he missed the lakes. He sat back in his chair and thought for a few moments. "It was a beautiful life," he said finally. "But we were very, very poor."

Meanwhile, the diversion of the water from Almoloya to Mexico City meant that the Lerma River now began downstream. Unfortunately, it was exactly the same spot were the government of Mexico State had decided to build an enormous industrial park. Today, the Lerma begins its journey carrying 1,000 gallons per second of partially treated sewage and industrial waste. Along its route, it is fed with chemicals from tanning factories, tar from a Pemex plant, and pesticides and fertilizers from the fields that line its banks. It disgorges the muck into Lake Chapala.

The sacrifice of the Lerma River bought Mexico City only partial relief from its water woes, and for only about fifteen years. In 1965, with demand for water continuing to increase and with downtown Mexico City continuing to sink, authorities decided to expand the pumping around the headwaters of the Lerma from 1,500 gallons per second to 4,000 gallons per second. Five hundred new wells were drilled throughout the Ixtlahuaca valley north of the town of Lerma. But the engineers had vastly overestimated the size of the aquifer. By 1970 the land was sinking so rapidly that cracks began to open up in the ground. Still they kept pumping until the aquifer was completely depleted. Today only

1,400 gallons a second can be pumped from the Lerma Valley—a mere drop in the bucket of Mexico City's water needs.

The government had known from the beginning that the Lerma system would buy the city only a few more years. A report released at the time that the Lerma system was inaugurated acknowledged that the next water crisis was only a few years away. In 1951 engineer Adolfo Orive Alba, director of Mexico City's water department, held a press conference to lay out the scope of the problem. Six thousand liters of water per second were coming from the Lerma River valley, he said. But 9,000 liters (2,400 gallons) were still being pumped out of Mexico City's aquifer each second, and the city was still sinking. Water needs, he announced, were destined to increase. Mexico City's population, which stood at 2,942,000 in 1950, had more than doubled since 1930. "If the problem is this severe now, what will it be like in 1960 when it is estimated Mexico City will have a population of 5.6 million people, or 1980 when it will be 9 million?" he asked. Mexico City's population reached 9 million in 1970, a decade earlier than Orive predicted. In 1990 it was 15 million, according to census figures. Unofficial estimates place it as high as 22 million.

III

The year after Orive Alba gave his press conference, Mexico City was hit with a terrible flood. As in colonial times, people moved through downtown streets in canoes. The city flooded because, after decades of pumping water from the aquifer, the city had sunk below the level of the drainage canal and the floodwater could not be evacuated. When the Gran Canal del Desagüe was built in 1900, it was graded to carry the sewage downhill and out of the valley. After the 1952 flood, pumping stations were installed to take the water uphill. Authorities recognized that this was only a temporary solution. As the city grew, more and more water needed to be drained. The pumps consumed large amounts of electricity, and the city remained vulnerable because they could always break down.

Attacking the underlying problem by reducing water consumption and thereby stabilizing the sinking would have been politically unpopular and would have brought the country no glory. Authorities argued that the development process required the consumption of large amounts of resources, and they were convinced that technology and growth would create a solution. Enormous public works were always favored over conservation because they strengthened the power of the central government and became a source of national pride. Mexico would solve the flooding problem with an infrastructure project on the scale of Martínez's desagüe.

Studies for a deep drainage tunnel began in 1959, but ground was not broken until May 1967. The plan was to build a fifty-mile tunnel at a depth of 650 feet, making the system impervious to the sinking. Thirty thousand workers labored on the project, raising 4.57 million cubic yards of dirt from the depths. Workers hoisted from the bowels of the earth had to be put in decompression chambers to avoid getting the bends. The official cost of the project was $43.2 million (540 million pesos), a figure many believe to be far less than the actual investment.

Completing the tunnel took nearly a decade. President José López Portillo personally opened the floodgates in 1975. Supporters were bused in and given T-shirts and banners and instructed to cheer the president and thank him for liberating them from the floods. Officials made a host of self-congratulatory political speeches. "In the years before the nationalist Revolution of 1910 when the Gran Canal was inaugurated you heard names like Reed, Campbell, Harris, Pearson. Today neither these names nor other similar ones appear in the credits," proclaimed Octavio Santies Gómez, Mexico City's mayor. "This work was made by Mexicans."

It was another decade before the deep drainage canal was operating at full capacity, but the Gran Canal continues to handle the bulk of the city's sewage. The pumping stations, viewed as a stopgap measure, still move the water along its uphill journey out of the valley.

There was one last detail to be worked out. What do you do with the 23,200 gallons of raw sewage and industrial waste that Mexico City produces every second? In order to find out, I decided to follow the Gran Canal. It was easy to find—I could smell it from blocks away. The canal begins appropriately enough just behind the Mexican congress. I followed it a few blocks north and stopped at the first bridge to take a look. The "water" was a thick black sludge, the consistency of syrup. It did not seem to flow so much as percolate. I drove through working-class neighborhoods and stopped again at the border of Mexico State, where the canal intersects with the Río de los Remedios; the sludge carried by the river backed up with the canal, forming an enormous swamp of sewage that spread out over acres. I had to hold my breath as I ran across a hanging bridge to a dusty soccer field. Jesús Fuerte García, a sixty-year-old truck driver, covered his mouth with a handkerchief as he crossed behind me and then spat on the ground. "It's a source of infection, of course," said García as we watched the soccer game together. "It hurts your throat. The kids who play soccer here are always getting sick. And when it rains, it overflows the banks."

When I crossed back over the bridge to return to my car I noticed a large object floating under the bridge. It was the carcass of a dog. I recognized it only because of the outline of a jaw poking through the muck.

Despite the stench, houses line the banks of the Gran Canal as it passes through the shantytowns north of the city. Then it flows through open fields until it reaches the town of Zumpango. There, it ducks into a tunnel and then reappears outside the valley in the state of Hidalgo. In 1954 the government created Irrigation District 3 in the Mezquital Valley. This is the same area discussed in Chapter 1, where Spanish sheep turned a highly productive irrigated valley into a mesquite desert. The water that once flowed from springs had returned. Only it had returned black, full of the refuse of millions of *chilangos,* the residents of Mexico City.

I caught up with the black waters in Hermanejildo Estrada's cornfield. Detergents agitated by the passage through the tunnel floated along the irrigation ditch. Foam was everywhere, blowing through the landscape like sagebrush across the prairies. The water is used to grow vegetables. The Mexican government has repeatedly claimed that there are no health risks, but in 1992 a United Nations study found extremely high levels of arsenic, chromium, and selenium and moderately high levels of cadmium, nickel, and zinc in the soil. What effects, if any, these high levels could have on human health is much debated, and from a scientific standpoint the answer is by no means clear. But logic would suggest that there are health risks associated with eating anything grown in raw sewage. Certainly, there are serious risks to the farmers and to the land itself.

When I visited the Mezquital Valley in 1991, cholera was raging through the region. Doctors at local hospitals told me there had been hundreds of cases but added that the government was not releasing the official figures. Farmers, however, defended the waters, saying the organic waste fertilized their fields. Estrada, for example, was undaunted by the recent outbreak. "I've worked with the black waters for twenty years and I've never gotten sick," he told me as we stood beside the toxic canal. "If cholera gets me, so be it."

Cornelio Rosas, meanwhile, was back in his fields only a day after suffering a cholera attack. The doctors told him to wash his hands better. "The black waters don't do anything bad," insisted Gerardo López as he loaded squash into the back of his pickup truck. "We will never let the authorities take them away from us."

As the black waters retreat, they leave the fields coated with a thick crust of salt. The Tula and Salado rivers, which receive the effluence from the Valley of Mexico, empty into the Moctezuma River. The Moctezuma, like every river in the whole watershed, is dead. In most of the world, large cities are in valleys, along river banks, or on the coast, so that if you hike up into the mountains you can find a less-disturbed landscape. But Mexico City's sewage feeds the headwaters of several major rivers. Even if you hike into a remote canyon downstream, you will have to wade through a river full of foam and chemicals.

The black waters have a second destination as well, as I discovered during my travels along the city's sewage canals. On the highway from Mexico City to the city of Texcoco, signs announced a government-funded "ecological rescue" project to restore Lake Texcoco. I pulled off the highway on a dirt road and drove half a mile to a locked gate. A policeman, dressed in black and carrying a machine gun, emerged from a small cubicle. "Entry is prohibited," he told me. "Those are my orders."

The effort to revive the lake began in 1971 as a means of controlling the dust storms caused when dried sediment is whipped up by strong winds. Engineers who began work on the project discovered a major obstacle: the city had sunk so far that Lake Texcoco, once the lowest point in the valley, was now six feet higher than the city center. Allowing the lake to fill with water would have created a serious flood risk. So the engineers did what they knew best—they begun pumping water from the soil around Lake Texcoco until the whole area started to sink. Today Lake Texcoco, which is filled by partially treated sewage water, is two feet below the city. It seems absurd that in an area once covered with water, lake beds have to be created artificially. It is equally absurd that up to 23,200 gallons—both sewage and rainwater—are artificially channeled out of the basin, while approximately 5,300 gallons are pumped in from neighboring valleys. The city is running out of water, and yet it is perennially flooded.

Something in the policeman's tone suggested to me that he thought his orders to keep me out were as stupid as I did. Since he was unmoved by my press pass, I started chatting about the ancient lake. I told him that five centuries ago we would have been under water—or if we were lucky, in a canoe. We could have paddled from where we stood to the town of Texcoco, where the poet-king-engineer Nezahualcoyótl once ruled. We could have paddled or poled across the shallow waters to Tenochtitlan; we would have seen the pyramids rise into the sky as we drew close. If we had some business there, we could have paddled through the streets of the city, directly into Moctezuma's palace. We could have paddled to Lake Chalco, or among the *chinampas* (floating gardens) of Lake Xochimilco. The lakes would have been full of ducks and pelicans; we would have been able to see the fish swim below us.

I do not know if I bored or amused him, but he finally realized that the easiest way to get rid of me would be to let me see the lake. He opened the gate. "Park your car in the bushes," he said. "I could get in trouble."

I walked a few hundred yards over a rise and looked down across a dark lake. Yes, the lake had returned, but the water had not been sent by Tlaloc, the water god. Lake Texcoco was filled with the sewage from Mexico City. The freshwater springs that once filled the lake had been replaced by millions of flushing toilets and the industrial waste from thousands of factories. The tragic cycle had been completed. The pelicans did not seem to notice. They gathered along the lakeshore and flapped lazily into the darkening sky.

As I walked back to my car for the drive back into the smoggy city, I thanked the policeman for breaking the rules. He seemed strangely disappointed that I was leaving. The poor guard was going out of his mind with boredom. "This is my job," he said, as I climbed into my car. "But I hate it. There's nothing here. This spot is so lonely you can't imagine."

IV

Throughout the 1950s and 1960s, as authorities struggled to provide Mexico City with drinking water and to get rid of its sewage, the depth of the environmental crisis remained largely hidden from public view. Mexico City was too busy celebrating its successes to even consider that something might be deeply wrong.

The rapid growth of the city was putting more and more of a strain on the valley's resources. Three million inhabitants in 1950 became 5.5 million in 1960 and nearly 9 million a decade later. In 1954 the banning of residential subdivisions in the Federal District only spawned the urbanization of the neighboring state of Mexico, which welcomed the newcomers. The growth was self-perpetuating. With one-seventh of the nation's population concentrated in Mexico City, no major company would consider locating anywhere else. Besides, everything was subsidized in Mexico City—the cost of gas, transportation, education and, of course, water, were all picked up by the government. Those policies produced enormous growth, but they also fomented a culture of reckless consumption—of water, electricity, and urban space. The size of the city itself, the *mancha urbana* (the urban stain) as it is called in Spanish, grew from 43.3 square miles in 1940 to 281.4 square miles in 1970.

Rather than alarming the authorities, the growth of Mexico City made them proud. Mexico was on its way to becoming one of the world's great metropolises; skyscrapers rose, the subway system was built; monuments, statues, avenues, whole neighborhoods appeared overnight. The colonial prejudice for urban life that had been accentuated during the Porfirian years reached new heights.

What the authorities did not realize was that the so-called golden years were a brief, two-decade transition when the city's size was manageable, when the old dying culture of horse-drawn carriages and market vendors peacefully coexisted with cars and department stores. But the growth that propelled the city into the modern era would soon catapult the city well past its goal. The writing on the wall was a 1958 paper by scientist Humberto Bravo, who made public a new problem— air pollution. A decade later the famously clear air was only a memory. A new generation was raised under smoggy skies.

For the next twenty years the policy of the government was to ignore the air pollution problem. Not until 1979 did President López Portillo present the first comprehensive antipollution program, "The Coordinated Program to Improve the Air in the Valley of Mexico."

The same geographic features that produced the water crisis also explain why Mexico City's air is so polluted. The city is in a closed basin 7,347 feet above sea level and surrounded by mountains. The polluted air has nowhere to go. The Valley of Mexico is—or was—a closed ecosystem. That means that more than any city in the world it is condemned to live in its own waste.

It is difficult to get a clear picture of the early years of the pollution because the government made a concerted effort to withhold information. The initial culprits were probably the largely unregulated factories, which were concentrated in the northern part of the valley, as well as the poor who settled on hillsides and cut down the trees. In 1940 average visibility was more than seven miles. Today it is barely one.

Dirt is also responsible for a good deal of the city's haze. More than eleven hundred tons of dirt blown up from the dried lake beds and off the deforested mountains fills the air each day. At times it can produce a haze so thick that the sky looks like twilight at noon. Airplanes sometimes need to use flight instruments to land during the day. The news gets worse. Each day the haze contains more than a ton of fecal dust—or to put it more crudely, dried shit. Since millions of people on the periphery of the city have no sewage hookups, they use outhouses, and their dried waste eventually ends up windborne. In Mexico City you can get intestinal parasites—as well as typhoid and hepatitis—just by breathing the air.

In the 1970s cars were responsible for less than half the city's air pollution. Today there are between 3 and 4 million cars, and the government claims they are responsible for 75 to 80 percent of the pollution. The average car in Mexico is ten years old and in poor repair. Even the well-tuned ones run poorly in Mexico City's thin air. Because of congestion, poor traffic flow, buses that stop wherever they feel like it, and the ubiquitous speed bumps, traffic pokes through the city at an average of 7.5 miles an hour.

The mass of cars burn 5 million gallons of gas each day, spewing about eight thousand tons of pollution into the air, mostly in the form of carbon monoxide, nitrogen oxides, and hydrocarbons. When carbon monoxide combines with hemoglobin in the blood, the body's ability to transport oxygen is diminished. The heart must race to keep up. Mexican researchers have found that exposure to carbon monoxide over long periods of time can cause heart and brain damage. Nitrogen oxide has a similar effect; combined with hemoglobin, it can provoke throat irritations even at moderate levels.

The real problem, however, is when the sun cooks these chemicals into ozone. Ozone (O_3) is produced in a complex photochemical reaction in which oxygen (O_2) bonds with single oxygen molecules snatched away from other compounds like nitrogen oxides and hydrocarbons. Ozone is a wonderful thing in the atmosphere, where it absorbs the sun's ultraviolet rays, but you do not want it in your lungs. Exposure to relatively low levels will dry out your throat, make your eyes sting, and, if you are sensitive, make you nauseated. Higher levels of ozone will make you tired and dumb. A 1995 study found that high levels of ozone produce cancer in mice. In Los Angeles, ozone forms only at temperatures above eighty-five degrees; in Mexico City's thin air it forms at temperatures as low as seventy degrees. Ozone levels exceed international norms during nine out of every ten days.

If you designed a laboratory to produce ozone artificially you could not come up with anything more efficient than the winter in Mexico City. The dry, cold winter months, which run from November to March, are now known to Mexicans as "pollution season." There is generally little wind, and the wind that does blow enters the valley from the north and blows the polluted air southward until it backs up against the mountains. Because of the variation between nighttime and daytime temperatures, the cooler air that forms along the mountain slopes is sucked down into the valley at night, bringing with it the pollution that was blown against the mountains the day before. The cap of warmer air holds the pollution in the valley like a lid on a boiling pot. This is called a thermal inversion, and it happens almost every day in the winter. The antidote is the sun, which never fails to shine in the cloudless winter sky. But the sun that warms the air all morning also cooks the chemical cocktail trapped below the thermal inversion into ozone. By the time the thermal inversion breaks up by mid-morning, ozone levels are sure to have reached "unhealthy" levels. If it does not break up until noon or so, the result is a smog emergency. On March 16, 1992, Mexico City set its all-time pollution record for ozone—.45 parts per million, more than four times the international safety standard.

The air in Mexico City is the most visible example of the city's ecological demise. Living with headaches, sore throats, tiredness, and irritability is not living. And the government has proved incapable of resolving the problem. The summer rains, which come from July to November, used to clean the air, but for some reason they no longer do so. On July 31, 1995, pollution levels were so high that the government was forced to declare a smog alert at the height of the rainy season—the first time it had ever done so in July. "There is not a single day, a single hour, when we are free from pollution," said Homero Aridjis, Mexico's leading environmentalist, when I talked to him a few days later.

The following winter, during the height of the pollution season, the government announced its latest antipollution plan—"The Program to Improve the Quality of Air in the Valley of Mexico." The authorities pointed to their progress in reducing lead and sulfur dioxide but acknowledged that they had made little headway against ozone and suspended particles (in fact, the Mexico City norm for particles is twice what is considered safe internationally). For the most part, Mexico City authorities have done a remarkable job limiting the political fallout from the air pollution problem by blaming it on the valley's geography and automobile exhaust. In truth, it is much more complicated. Thermal inversions do occur naturally in the valley, but they have been made worse by changes in the local ecology. The sun's heat retained by the growing mass of concrete has caused the daytime temperature on the valley floor to rise over the past few decades. Deforestation and the drying up of the lake beds have also radically increased the diurnal temperature variation.

Nor have enough studies been done to conclusively pinpoint cars as the culprit. In the summer of 1995, U.S. scientist F. Sherwood Rowland and his colleague Donald Blake published a study in the journal *Science* in which they blamed the smog problem not only on cars but on household cooking gas, or LPG (liquefied petroleum gas). The study found high levels of alkane hydrocarbons—butane, butene, and propane—in the air samples analyzed. These gases are not found in car exhaust but rather in the cooking gas distributed in metal canisters to two hundred thousand homes a day. Rowland suspects two problems. First, the gas, which is manufactured by Pemex, is poorly formulated, and the volatile compounds are contributing to the formation of ozone. Second, large amounts of gas are leaking from damaged canisters. Mexico City officials initially rejected his findings. "We continue to believe that automobiles generate 70 percent of the contaminants in the atmosphere," Eduardo Palazuelos Rendón, Mexico City's environmental secretary, told the *New York Times*. "The conclusion that LPG is a major contaminant does not represent a defect in our programs but rather a defect in the study."

By blaming the air pollution on cars, the government shifts responsibility for the problem away from its own policies and onto to individual drivers. When Mexican officials are confronted with the pollution problem they point to the aggressive steps they have taken—closing down the city's oil refinery, replacing diesel-burning buses, ordering all taxis to use unleaded fuel, requiring private cars to stay off the street one day a week. The cause of the air pollution, government officials contend, is that Mexicans love to drive. The implied threat is that, if citizens mobilize against the pollution, the government will have no choice but to take their cars away. Of course the government has not adequately explained why, in 1986, after Pemex reformulated its gas and reduced the lead content, ozone levels soared. Many suspect the new gas is not burning completely. Ozone is also not the only problem. Factories produce 97 percent of the sulfur dioxide and most particles and heavy metals.

Horror stories about the effects of the pollution on human health abound. One 1987 study found that nitrogen dioxide and hydrocarbon levels in Mexico City were comparable to those recorded in New York's Lincoln Tunnel. Babies are born with high levels of lead in their blood (although levels are said to have dropped in recent years); old people and children are routinely hospitalized with labored breathing; lung cancer levels and miscarriages are reported to be on the rise. Doctors blame the pollution for skin disease, heart attacks, and mental retardation. But when the government is confronted with these facts, it points out that no one has been able to establish a correlation between air pollution and long-term health problems. It is a cynical argument—one seemingly borrowed from the U.S. tobacco industry—but the truth is that the government has a point. The smog is so complex, and the normal health risks faced by the population so numerous, that it would take large amounts of money to develop experiments that eliminated all the possible variables. The government has no interest in funding those kinds of studies—it does not want to know the results.

Government propaganda, a culture that for centuries admonished the poor to suffer without complaint, an affluent class that has access to air filters and country homes, and a population that both feels disenfranchised and has other more pressing problems have effectively neutralized air pollution as a political problem for the government. The only real political opposition to the government's program has come from Senator Heberto Castillo of the left-center PRD, who has proposed bizarre quick-fix solutions like blasting away part of the southern mountains to let the polluted air escape, installing enormous fans, and most recently, using electrical charges to disperse the contaminants. But the most common response when you ask *chilangos* about pollution is indifference. "I didn't even notice it," said newspaper vendor Florencio Robles when I asked him how he felt one smoggy afternoon. "I don't think tear gas would affect us at this point. Besides, what can you do?"

But the problem with that kind of nonchalance or bravado is that while you can ultimately make a decision to live with air pollution, you cannot shrug your shoulders when the tap runs dry. The same population explosion that turned the skies black in a few short decades has had an even more dramatic but less visible effect on the city's water supply. But this is a problem that the government has tried to keep secret.

V

In 1972, around the time that air pollution finally became a public concern, the government was working quietly to find a new source of water. The millions of newcomers were a problem, not only because they needed water but also because they often settled on the aquifer's wooded "recharge" areas. As trees were cut down and roads were paved, less and less rainwater was absorbed into the aquifer.

The 1965 strategy to increase pumping in the Lerma Valley was clearly a failure—the friatic level (the depth at which water is found) was dropping rapidly, and water could be guaranteed for only a few more years. The Mexico City aquifer was being exploited at full capacity, and the sinking, though slowed, continued to be a serious problem.

The solution to the water crisis had to be another massive infrastructure project. Los Angeles, it was pointed out, had brought water from the Colorado River two hundred and fifty miles away, and Mexico City could do the same. In fact, it would have to do more. Los Angeles is at sea level, and the water from the Colorado is carried in an aqueduct that flows downhill. At an elevation of 7,347 feet and surrounded by mountains, Mexico City is on one of the highest plateaus in Mexico. Water from surrounding river valleys would have to be pumped at tremendous cost.

On a map, the engineers drew concentric circles around Mexico City. They evaluated various factors—the distance the water would have to be transported, the height of the intervening mountains, the existing infrastructure. The engineers noticed a major dam built in the 1940s at Valle de Bravo in the pine-forested mountains of Mexico State. There was a second dammed reservoir forty miles away at Villa Victoria. The engineers calculated that they could tie the two dams together and then send the water to Mexico City through the tunnel that had originally been built to bring the water from the Toluca Valley. There was only one problem: Valle de Bravo is at 5,700 feet and Mexico City is nearly 1,700 feet higher. Not only that—there is an even higher pass (8,300 feet) between the two. Getting the water to Mexico City would require building dozens of miles of aqueducts, a ten-mile tunnel, a five-mile canal, six power plants to raise the water up the mountains, and an enormous water treatment plant, plus the installation of pipes and tunnels to distribute the water once it reached the city. The system would be a project to rival Hoover Dam. It would fundamentally transform the entire landscape and put it at the service of Mexico City.

When ground was broken on the Cutzamala ("watershed") project in 1974, Mexico was flush with oil money, and future growth seemed ensured. The government did not flinch at the prospect of subsidizing the water delivery system, since its actual cost would be well beyond the means of most Mexicans. But by 1982, when the first part of the system was brought on line, oil prices had collapsed, and Mexico had begun a decade of deprivation and economic stagnation. Still, the work continued apace. In 1985, 1,600 gallons of water per second were being pumped from the Valle de Bravo dam. Over the next few years several other small dams were added to the system, and in 1995 the third phase was completed, bringing the total output of the system to 4,200 gallons per second—about one quarter of the 16,400 gallons per second consumed by the city. It takes 1,650 million kilowatt-hours per year to pump the water to Mexico City—approximately 6 percent of the city's total energy consumption.

The use of surface instead of subterranean water has made the Cutzamala system the most reliable of all of the city's water sources. But it is some of the most expensive water in the world.

One day I tried to follow the aqueduct from the Valle de Bravo back to Mexico City. Valle de Bravo is a quaint cobblestoned village where the Mexican elite have their weekend houses. To get there, I drove through the treeless plains around Toluca and then followed a snaking road that descended from the plateau into a pine-covered valley.

What is ironic about the Cutzamala system is that a city that first trashed its own hydraulic system and then that of its neighbor is now dependent on the conservation and careful management of a third one. All dams have a limited life; over decades they fill with sediment washed down in tributaries, and their capacity diminishes. When the Valle de Bravo dam was built in 1944, the capacity of the reservoir was 108 million gallons; today sedimentation has reduced it to 89 million gallons. Preventing deforestation and erosion in the Valle de Bravo is the responsibility of Santiago Zepeda González, the local delegate from Probosque, the federal forestry agency. With a tiny office and an annual budget of $10,000, Zepeda tries to stop illegal logging, prevent forest fires, and encourage reforestation. In an area in which the Mexican federal government has invested billions of dollars in infrastructure, it has been miserly in funding programs to protect that investment. "Illegal logging is the biggest problem," said Zepeda. "You can get 200–300 pesos for a tree. That's a lot of money for a poor campesino."

The next morning I followed the road to Los Berros, the enormous water treatment plant that purifies the water sent to Mexico City. Five pumping stations raise the water 2,300 feet from Valle de Bravo. What surprised me was that what had appeared as a solid mass of trees was actually forest interspersed with cornfields. Some of the cleared areas were plowed and planted with corn in anticipation of the summer rains; others were eroded and abandoned. At a clearing full of shacks made from freshly cut timber, I talked to Genaro Mari Carranza, who along with about a dozen other men was returning from an afternoon fighting a small forest fire. "It's volunteer work," said Carranza. "We want to save something for our children."

Rangers patrol the woods to ensure that only dead trees are logged, but cutting down a live pine is an incredible temptation for families without enough to eat. Carranza and the 155 Mazahua Indian families who settled in the clearing in 1993 subsist on the corn they produce. But the land they cultivate has been depleted of nutrients; every year they have to add more fertilizers. Carranza leaned against the hoe he was carrying when I asked if logging should be allowed. "For the people who live here, yes, but the government says it's illegal." It must seem nonsensical to be told essentially that a tree is more important than the lives of their hungry children.

Just a few miles up the road was a sad example of why the government is taking a hard line. The forest revealed itself as a veneer, a tree theme park. The trees simply vanished as I drove through them and emerged onto an open plain full of small towns and scraggly cornfields. A few miles farther on I reached the Los Berros water treatment plant, the center of operations for the whole Cutzamala system. In Mexico City I had been told that all visits to the plant had been suspended for "reasons of security," but after a little cajoling Absalón Domínguez, the engineer who runs the facility, consented to give me a tour. We stood in the control room amidst blinking yellow and red lights, as Domínguez used a wall-sized map of the Cutzamala system to make his points. "The Villa Victoria dam was built only fifty years ago and is already full of sediment," he said. "It's only got another fifteen to twenty years of useful life. Valle de Bravo is in much better shape—I give it thirty years, assuming that there is no more deforestation." He pointed to light green spots on the map where the forest had been removed. "This is what worries me," he said. "At some point we'll need to find more water."

The enclosed pipe that carries the water to Mexico City ran across a field and disappeared over an 8,700-foot ridge. From there it is all downhill. The water flows through lonely valleys, across the Toluca plains and through a tunnel in the Sierra de las Cruces before arriving in Mexico City. By the time it comes out of the tap, the cost of a gallon of water is nearly four-tenths of a cent (a liter costs one-tenth of a cent). What you pay, if you pay at all, is less than half that amount. That means that every time you open the tap and take a drink of water in Mexico City (assuming you are brave enough to do so), you strain Mexico's national treasury. The government picks up 60 percent of the tab every time you flush the toilet, take a shower, wash your car, or water your lawn. The total deficit according to Mexico City officials is $125 million a year. An independent study of the water system came up with even more alarming numbers: although the real cost of a cubic meter (1,000 liters) of water is one dollar, the government recovers only ten cents. The annual deficit for water services is $1 billion. Subsidizing the water not only strains the budget; it encourages the illusion that water is plentiful and that there is no reason to conserve it.

The lesson to be drawn from the Cutzamala system is that it is not economically feasible for the government to transport water from other basins. Not only is the infrastructure investment prohibitive, but the government must also make an indefinite commitment to covering the annual budget shortfall. The only way to restore some sort of environmental equilibrium is to treat the valley as much as possible as a closed system. Nearly thirty inches of rain fall in the Valley of Mexico each year, enough to provide a good deal of the city's water needs if it were properly managed. The problem is that the rains in Mexico City are torrential, and the terrain in the surrounding mountains is extremely steep. Left to its own devices, the rainwater would refill the dried lake beds. Unfortunately, they are now occupied by millions of people. The handful of reservoirs within the metropolitan area are used not to store potable water but rather raw sewage, which cannot be accommodated by the city's overloaded drainage system. Because of the danger of flooding, the city must pump rainwater runoff out of the valley as quickly as possible. There are simply no places left in the valley to store large quantities of water for human consumption.

But there is another option: the aquifer itself. The city needs to do a careful study of the exact composition of the aquifer and then inject rainwater collected in smaller reservoirs equal to the amount that is being extracted. One of the greatest untapped sources of water in the city is the water system itself; the sinking has ruptured so many pipes that 30 percent of the water is lost. Alfonso Martínez Baca told me that if he could cut that figure in half, he would suddenly have another 18,000 liters (4,760 gallons) per second of water available for distribution. The city also has a billion-dollar plan to improve drainage and build water treatment plants. If the authorities can find a way to better police industry so that the sewage is less contaminated by chemicals and heavy metals, the water could be treated sufficiently so that it could be reused by industry or perhaps reinjected into the aquifer. There is simply no other solution: Mexico City must find a way to live within its means.

VI

Nearly fifty years after the first scientific report confirmed that extracting water from the aquifer was causing the city to sink, 70 percent of Mexico City's water continues to come from wells in the valley. Once you develop a trained eye you can spot the pumps throughout the southern part of the city—in highway medians, parks, and abandoned fields, and on street corners. There are 4,820 of them, and they pump 11,000 gallons a second out of the aquifer—double the amount that flows in naturally. Because of the "overexploitation" of the aquifer, the friatic level drops more than three feet a year. The danger is not so much that one day the wells will run completely dry, but rather that the quality of the water will continue to deteriorate. More and more of the water pumped up is "fossilized," meaning it has been in the aquifer for an eon. It is so full of minerals and salts that it is not potable. The sinking threatens not only the buildings and the streets but the aquifer itself. In many areas, the direction of the natural drainage has changed; waste water that used to accumulate on the less permeable clay soils of the former lake now flows toward the recharge areas where it filters down into the aquifer. The sinking has opened deep fissures in the surface of the valley. During the 1985 earthquake an enormous crack opened up in Lake Xochimilco, and millions of gallons of untreated sewage poured into the aquifer. Contaminants from the open-air garbage dumps also eventually migrate down to water level. As the friatic level drops, the concentration of both natural and artificial contaminants increases. Since the water has to be pumped from about three feet deeper each year, it is also becoming more expensive.

Beginning in the 1950s, the city began using wells to the south of the valley rather than downtown. This change has reduced the sinking in the city center from a high of eighteen inches a year in 1951 to only four inches a year today—still a very dangerous amount. Meanwhile, the sinking has intensified in the south. Chalco, for example, a squatter settlement built partially on the extinct lake bed, sank about a foot a year between 1985 and 1990. As the south has become increasingly urbanized, it has begun to confront the same problems the city center has; foundations are cracking, roads dip for no apparent reason, overpasses pull away from the main road, and floods are growing worse. A depression formed by the sinking around Chalco becomes a fetid lake during the rainy season. In heavy rains it overflows and floods the town. Xochimilco—once a lake, now a suburb—has had similar problems. On October 4, 1990, fourteen-year-old Sol Aguilar Gallardo, stepped off a city bus and was swept away in the raging river that had replaced the street.

Despite the fact that the city depends on the aquifer for its survival no one I talked to would give me a straight answer when I asked how much longer it would be able to provide water. "I wouldn't dare to guess," said water commissioner Alfonso Martínez Baca.

"But since the city would disappear if the aquifer ran dry," I asked, "why haven't you done a detailed study to find out how much water it contains?"

"There are a lot things that haven't been done," he said.

Even in the unlikely event that the aquifer is able to meet the city's water needs for the next few decades, the cost of the centuries-long battle against the water has already been paid in thousands of lives. At 7:19 in the morning on September 19, 1985, off the coast of Michoacán, the land ruptured along an area 240 miles long and 50 miles wide. The quake, which measured 8.1 on the Richter scale, killed tens of thousands in Mexico City and reduced whole neighborhoods to rubble. Certainly the earthquake was a "natural disaster." The impetus was a cataclysmic event that could not have been controlled or predicted. But a great deal of the tragedy was also manmade, a result of centuries of environmental abuse in the Valley of Mexico.

While the earthquake leveled the small town of Lázaro Cárdenas near the epicenter, forty miles away the damage was relatively minor. That was because much of the energy liberated by the seismic motion was absorbed by the surrounding bedrock. But when the seismic waves passed under the mountains and entered the Valley of Mexico two hundred and fifty miles from the epicenter they were suddenly revitalized. The dried lake bed on which the city is built is made up of volcanic ash and sediments washed down from mountains over millions of years. The soil is highly saturated—in effect, Mexico City is built on mud. The seismic waves were trapped in the spongy soils under the ancient lakes; they bounced around wildly, hurling themselves against the denser basaltic rock that once marked the lakeshores, and then vibrating back through the soft soil until they hit something solid. It was as if four people, each holding onto a different corner, tried to shake out an enormous blanket. Buildings were pulled in two directions at once. In the marshy soil underlying the city center, the destructive force of the earthquake matched that at the epicenter. Meanwhile, in tony neighborhoods like Coyoacán and Lomas de Chapultepec, which were built on firm rock, the intensity was fifty times less.

Above the remains of Lake Texcoco, dust rose into the air. Nowhere was the damage more severe than around the Alameda. Pumping from the aquifer had caused the park to sink more than twenty-five feet since the turn of the century, weakening the foundations of many of the hotels and government office buildings surrounding it. The Hotel Regis, the Hotel del Prado—both spilled their guts into the street, a tangled mass of twisted girders, concrete slabs, electrical cables, splintered furniture. Under tons of rubble were hundreds of bodies. Some were extracted and buried in common graves; others, never found, disappeared into the landfill along with the broken concrete. A block from the Hotel Regis, Lucas Gutiérrez stood outside his restaurant, the Super Leche, "and watched as a hole opened up in the ground into which disappeared his restaurant along with an apartment building in which 300 people had lived." Wrote Mexican journalist Elena Poniatowska: "It was as if a giant vacuum cleaner had sucked it up."

The earthquake represented a terrible payback for the centuries-long battle against the valley's natural environment. Despite clear evidence of its potentially disastrous consequences, city authorities continue to pump water from the aquifer.

The Aztecs believed that the fifth sun, the sun of motion, would be destroyed by earthquakes. Whether or not that prophecy is fulfilled, Mexico City must live under the weight of its history and with the consequences of poor decisions made long ago. The Spanish city has a shallow hold on the land. Despite nearly four and a half centuries of progress, despite an enormous investment in monumental infrastructure projects, the city cannot escape the destiny ascribed to it by the Aztecs. Mexico City is condemned forever to be a city on the brink.

—four—

Jungle Warfare

Standing in the middle of Mexico's Lacandón jungle makes a person feel truly insignificant. It is not so much the jungle's vastness but the amount of life it holds that produces this sensation. If you stand still, you can feel the jungle vibrate. The foliage is so dense that you see neither the ground nor the sun. The air buzzes with insects, birds rustle the treetops. The bone-chilling scream of a howler monkey carries for miles. The jungle is not a hospitable environment for humans—they are prey for insects, snakes, and jaguars. A path cleared through the underbrush will be overgrown in a week; a wooden house can rot in a season; one of stone will be torn down by vines in three.

The first inhabitants of Mexico's Lacandón rain forest acknowledged the jungle's immense power. The Lacandón Indians lived scattered in small huts. They let the jungle take their houses every few years as they moved on and built new ones. Their clans were named for the animals of the forest—the monkey clan, the jaguar clan, the clan of the wild boar.

A century ago loggers began to move into the forest. They responded to what they perceived as a hostile and often cruel environment with cruelty of their own. The loggers felt immune from God's judgment because, as they saw it, to be in the jungle was to be already damned. They kept their Indian workers in chains and whipped them or hung them from trees if they failed to fell the required amount of mahogany.

"Now then, boys, where do you think you are?" asks an old hand named Santiago of a new group of Indian conscripts just brought into a logging camp in B. Traven's novel *The Rebellion of the Hanged.* "On a finca [large estate]? In your village, where only the lice and fleas can eat you? Here you're not just at the entrance to hell; here you're at its very bottom."

The logging camps lasted until the 1950s. At that time the Lacandón was still called the Desert of Solitude, a 3.7 million acre blank spot on the map ("desert" to the Dominican friars who gave the region its name meant "deserted" or "unpopulated," not arid). Today, the jungle is downright crowded.

There is a fundamental difference between the jungle and nature's other extreme environments—the oceans, the mountains, the deserts. The jungle is fragile, and it succumbs to axes, fires, and bulldozers. Humans—even poor, humble ones—can beat it back, transform it. A century ago, the Mexican jungle extended across the lowlands of Tabasco and Chiapas, through Campeche and the Yucatán to the Caribbean coast where it connected with the jungles of Guatemala and Belize. This enormous biomass is often called the *selva maya,* the Mayan jungle.

The ability to cut down the rain forest perhaps explains the utopian vision of many of the Lacandón's settlers. If even peasants could turn the fearsome jungle into cornfields, then they could transform their own lives. This is what the waves of Indian peasants who poured out of the highlands and settled in the Lacandón believed. The priests who came to say mass spoke often of Moses, the River Jordan, and the promised land. The Tzotzil-speaking Protestants also came looking for paradise. Converted to evangelical Christianity by U.S. missionaries and then driven from their homes by corrupt village leaders, they believed that the jungle would deliver salvation.

The dream of a better life took different forms, but it was common to all. The non-Indian or mestizo settlers who poured into a corner of the jungle near the Guatemalan border called Marqués de Comillas cut down the forest and dreamed of becoming prosperous cattle ranchers. Even Pemex, the state oil company, which discovered reserves in the Lacandón in the 1970s, imagined a flood of petrodollars that would save the country.

The Zapatista Army of National Liberation (EZLN), which launched an armed rebellion on January 1, 1994, is only the latest utopian movement to take root in the Lacandón. Although the masked rebels have substantial support in the highlands, they were born in and nurtured by the jungle. For a decade, as the rebels organized clandestinely village to village, house to house, the rain forest kept their secret. Later, when the Mexican army routed them and forced them from the towns they had taken over, the jungle hid and protected them in a way their twenty-year-old rifles never could.

The jungle—from a distance—is also romantic. Part of the rebels' appeal was that in a country in which indigenous people had been deprived of their rights and systematically despoiled of their land, the Indians had risen up to fight back. The rebels were fighting, at least in the popular imagination, against the ranchers, loggers, and oil men who were destroying the jungle.

Although the Zapatistas are Indians, they are not natives of the jungle. They have migrated there within the past thirty years from somewhere else. Unlike the Lacandón Indians who worshipped the forest, their relationship with the jungle is not one of communion. It is utilitarian. They do not despise the jungle as the loggers do, but they do not love it either. They respect it; they know its secrets.

Rather than preserving the jungle, the Zapatistas want to develop it. Even as the nation has become cynical about progress and "development" after decades of disappointment, the Zapatistas thoroughly embrace it. The Mayan soldiers in the Zapatista army are not fighting to preserve a traditional way of life. The list of demands they submitted to the government on the eve of peace talks in February 1995 included land—but it also included "tractors, fertilizers, insecticides, credit, technical advice, improved seeds, cattle, and fair prices for our products." The Zapatistas want telephones, hospitals, and cooperative stores "funded by the federal, state, and municipal government." They want houses with "televisions, stoves, refrigerators, washing machines, etc." The Zapatistas did not rise up because they felt overwhelmed by progress; they rose up because they felt it had passed them by.

This is why the Zapatista conflict represents one of the most complex problems of development versus conservation in the world. Three decades of colonization have brought a hundred thousand people into the Lacandón. They have taken more than 2.5 million acres (1 million hectares) and turned them into cornfields and cow pastures. What is left is the heart of the jungle—815,000 acres (330,000 hectares)—which has been set aside in the Montes Azules Biosphere Reserve. The Zapatista soldiers I talked to told me they had nothing against preserving the trees, but not at their children's expense. They covet the last remaining unoccupied land, and as long as no viable alternative exists they feel justified in taking it.

The Zapatistas base their right to the jungle on the history of the Maya in Chiapas. Their ancestors were run off their land by the Spaniards and enslaved by the plantation owners. These wrongs have never been redressed. Balancing the Zapatistas' desire to develop and exploit the jungle's few remaining resources against Mexico's and the world's right to preserve the last vestige of a dying ecosystem is an exceedingly delicate task. What makes it even more complicated is that no one is advocating for the jungle.

I

In March 1994, two months after the Mexican army advanced along the road from Ocosingo in search of the fleeing rebels, I found myself in a similar position. The vehicle I was traveling in was not an armored personal carrier, however, but a rented Volkswagen bug with "TV" written in white shoe polish across the windshield. My traveling companion was Eduardo Monteverde, a physician turned journalist who specializes in environmental issues (and whose last name conveniently translates as "green mountain"). Monteverde was an ideal companion because he had made the same trip twenty years earlier when the road we were now on was nothing but a trail hacked through the forest.

In 1975 Monteverde had come to Chiapas straight out of medical school. He was a communist and an activist, and during the time he worked with the poor in Chiapas he became friendly with liberation theologian Bishop Samuel Ruiz. The year before Monteverde arrived, Don Samuel, as the bishop is universally known, had hosted the Indigenous Congress to commemorate the 500th birthday of humanitarian bishop Fray Bartolemé de Las Casas. Indians from all over the state bridged language and cultural gaps to confront their common problems.

One of the most pressing concerns to emerge from the 1974 congress was the ongoing transformation of old estates from sugar plantations into cattle ranches as the country's increasingly prosperous urban population demanded more beef. Harvesting sugar requires enormous amounts of seasonal labor. Since colonial times the large estates—called "fincas" in Chiapas but otherwise indistinguishable from the haciendas of the north—had kept the peons around by offering them a small piece of land for growing corn in exchange for work during the sugar harvest. But as the fincas switched from sugar to cattle, the Indians lost their land to cows and were forced into the jungle. "Bit by bit the cornfields are being converted into pastureland," noted the Chol Indian delegation at the 1974 congress.

Tens of thousands of peons were driven from what historian Jan de Vos calls the *franja finquera,* or the plantation strip. Large estates fill the valley of Ocosingo, a swath of fertile land that marks the transition zone between the mountains and the Lacandón jungle. But the fincas were hardly the only source of jungle colonists. Thousands more came from the overcrowded highlands. Monteverde, who was living in a Tzeltal-speaking Indian town called Oxchuc, watched family after family pack their miserable belongings onto their backs and head off down the increasingly well-worn trail from the highland to the jungle.

At the time, Oxchuc was going through some changes that were common throughout the highlands. A population explosion brought about by improved medical care and declining infant mortality was putting a terrible strain on the land. Land-starved campesinos moved onto steep hillsides, causing massive erosion. Others worked tiny plots until the land was exhausted; then they resorted to fertilizers and went into debt. The battle over land exploded into all sorts of conflicts across the highlands as traditional Indian authorities struggled to retain control amidst growing discontent. Because the village leaders in Indian villages were also the religious authorities, they demanded that all members of the community participate in costly religious ceremonies, which often involved purchasing liquor and candles that only the leaders themselves sold.

Protestant missionaries from the United States who invaded Chiapas in the 1960s found fertile ground among the disgruntled Indian villagers looking to escape the yoke of the corrupt village authorities. Slowly, and then more quickly, the word spread: to the east, where the

mountains ended, was a virgin jungle where there was land for the taking. Forced from their communities by a lack of land or by religious
persecution, hundreds, then thousands, then tens of thousands, headed
for the promised land—the Lacandón rain forest.

The government's response was largely passive. It viewed the 3.7 million acre Lacandón rain forest as an enormous green frontier, an area that
could effectively siphon off the unrest growing in the highlands. Throughout the previous century the forest had been divvied up by foreign-
owned logging companies that had set up camps along the Usumacinta
River. Conditions in the camps for the Indian workers were brutal, but
the impact on the jungle itself was slight. The logging companies were interested in only two species—mahogany and cedar. The enormous trees
had to be cut with axes, dragged by oxen to the riverbank, and then
floated to Tabasco. The riverbanks were stripped, but the companies never
penetrated the jungle's interior, which remained virtually unpopulated in
1950. The only inhabitants were a few thousand Lacandón Indians who
lived scattered in small homesteads.

In 1957 the Mexican government declared the jungle "apt for colonization," and peasants streamed in from all directions. Chol Indians from
Salto de Agua and Palenque followed the logging road to Chancalá;
Protestant Tzotziles escaping their eroded highland plots pushed over the
ridges beyond the town of Margaritas; Tojolabales forced off the fincas
and Tzeltales from towns like Oxchuc passed through Ocosingo and
moved along the river channels into a region that came to be known as
Las Cañadas.

Fifteen years after it first opened the jungle for colonization, even the
government realized the process was out of control. What bothered the
officials in Mexico City, however, was not the plight of the jungle colonists suffering as they built a new life in a hostile environment. It was
the fact that peasants were burning down thousands of dollars worth of
tropical hardwood to plant a wretched crop of corn and beans.

In 1972, with environmental protection as the pretext, President Luis
Echeverría granted title to 1.5 million acres of rain forest to sixty-six
Lacandón Indian families. Immediately after the land was given the Lacandones, a government-owned logging company called Cofolasa cut a
deal with the Lacandones to log 10,000 trees a year. Among the reputed

investors in Cofolasa were President Echeverría himself and Chiapas governor Manuel Velasco Suárez.

The Lacandón decree had been drawn up by bureaucrats with no knowledge of the competing local interests. Thousands of colonists who had been granted provisional titles by the government had their rights revoked.

It took years for word of the new decree to reach the isolated jungle settlements. The thousands of Chol, Tzeltal, Tzotzil, and Tojolabal colonists who had spent more than a decade building a life for themselves learned that their land belonged to the Lacandones and they would have to move. They refused to leave. In 1978 President José López Portillo added fuel to the fire by suddenly deciding that a major chunk of the land given to the Lacandón would become part of what was termed "the Integral Montes Azules Biosphere Reserve." López Portillo's motivations remain somewhat obscure, but some have suggested he was gunning for job at the United Nations, which sponsored the international biosphere program.

By 1979 the situation was an absolute mess. Some communities that had been granted a provisional land title in the 1960s found themselves both within the Lacandones' territory and in the biosphere reserve. Pedro Díaz, a Chol Indian who had migrated to the jungle from Tumbala in 1970, was elected to represent his community. He told me he went to see the agrarian reform delegate in the state capital of Tuxtla Gutiérrez.

"It turned out the land belonged to the Lacandones," Díaz recalled. "They said that we were invaders. I told the agrarian reform official, 'If the land belonged to someone else, why did you send us there?' They said they were going to send the Federales to get us out. I told him, 'No sir, alive we will not leave. Only dead.'

"We had no conflict with the Lacandones, it was with the government and the big-time ranchers. I went and talked with the leader of the Lacandones, José Pepe Chambor, and we made an agreement." With the government's backing, the Tzeltales in the region agreed to congregate in a town that came to be known as Nueva Palestina, the Choles were confined to another settlement called Frontera Corozal, and the majority of the Lacandones agreed to congregate in a third town called Lacanjá. The three villages eventually formed what is known today as the Lacandón community in order to administer the 1.5 million acres originally given solely to the Lacandones. Almost immediately the leaders signed an agreement with Cofolasa to log the jungle.

"I never felt good about the arrangement," said Díaz. "So much jungle was being cut down for logging, for growing corn. I told the government that in order not to cut down the forest we needed a technical assistance plan, but they never listened to us."

But the villages west of the reserve in Las Cañadas refused to move from their land, which had also been incorporated into the Montes Azules reserve. The villagers claimed that they were entitled to the land under the agrarian reform laws and banded together to fight the relocation. With the help of the liberation theology–oriented church and the nonviolent Maoist organizers who poured into the jungle over the next decade, they formed an organization called the Union of Ejido Unions and battled the government. Since the government had no economic interest in Las Cañadas, it was not inclined to use force to get the colonists to move. Instead it fought back with bureaucracy, hoping to grind down the independent movement with a phalanx of petty officials who made the campesinos sit for hours or days in the office before listening to their complaints. Not a peso was invested in the region, but the government promised big things if the people would affiliate with the PRI. Instead of breaking the resolve of the settlers, the government created a power vacuum filled by a series of increasingly radical organizations. By 1988— nearly two decades after it was founded in opposition to government decrees supposedly designed to save the forest—most of the members of the Union of Ejido Unions joined the Zapatistas. Environmentalism, not surprisingly, has extremely negative connotations among the rebels' rank and file.

At the same time that the government was trying to coopt the independent organizations in Las Cañadas, it was settling another region of the jungle with government loyalists. As land hunger grew across the highlands, the Echeverría government opened up more jungle areas— not only in Chiapas but in Tabasco, Campeche, and Quintana Roo—to agricultural colonization. Settling the jungle was seen as less politically costly and economically disruptive than redistributing land in the highlands. In the case of the Lacandón jungle there were other motivations as well. In the 1970s, oil deposits were discovered in a fertile, low-lying area near the Guatemalan border called Marqués de Comillas (after the Spanish lumber baron who originally owned the land). Pemex cut roads into the region and began exploration. By the end of the decade the area was being populated with landless peasants from all over the country. They came by the thousands from Guerrero, Michoacán, Veracruz, Tabasco, and even Mexico City. Many found work building roads for Pemex or working on the drill sites. Jesuit priest Mardonio Morales, who worked in the region for thirty years, alleges the government's aim in settling the Marqués de Comillas region was to provide labor for oil development. "Cheap labor was required—meaning people were controlled and controllable. [The government wanted people] who would acquiesce to whatever was coming," Morales told the news magazine *Proceso*.

The government also wanted to settle Marqués de Comillas quickly because it feared that the growing conflict in Central America could cross the border into Mexico. By the mid-1970s, the Guatemalan guerrillas were using Mexican territory as a base to launch attacks in their homeland. In 1982 the government's worst fears came to pass, as tens of thousands of Guatemalan refugees driven across the border by a scorched-earth counterinsurgency campaign flooded the Lacandón. For the Mexican colonists, however, the refugees were a godsend. The Mexicans put the refugees to work clearing the jungle for pasture. Cows poured into the region along Pemex's newly built road. By the end of the decade, Marqués de Comillas was the most deforested region of the whole jungle.

Seeing the destruction wrought by twenty years of chaos and devastation was overwhelming for Monteverde. "The trail to the jungle began here," he said as we drove along the paved highway near Oxchuc. "From here to the horizon there was nothing but forest. One day you'd see a family heading off down the trail and they'd come back months later saying they'd found land."

During my visit in March 1994 we stopped for breakfast in Ocosingo, a sprawling town of twisting streets that advertises itself as the "gateway to the jungle." Ocosingo is not a friendly place. Even at an early hour, the streets were beginning to fill with ranchers in cowboy hats and flared jeans, and off-duty soldiers who listlessly drank cold Cokes in the withering heat. The "coyotes," unscrupulous middlemen who underpay the Indian farmers for their corn and beans, were still asleep but their overloaded pickup trucks were parked outside the cheap dives near the market. The loggers and drug traffickers who also gather there were probably sleeping off their hangovers in the few up-scale hotels.

In the early hours of January 1, 1994, Zapatista rebels using the New Year's revelry as a cover announced their presence by invading five towns in Chiapas. It was the takeover of San Cristóbal de Las Casas, a tourist town in the pine-covered highlands, that garnered the masked rebels headlines, but Ocosingo was their primary target. At a secret training camp in the jungle the Zapatistas built a wooden mock-up of the town's city hall and practiced their assault on the hated building. They knew the town well because it was the center of bureaucratic power for the whole jungle region.

On the night of December 31, 1993, between four hundred and six hundred rebel fighters gathered in the ejido of San Miguel and then rumbled in commandeered buses along the rutted road. At 2 A.M. on January 1 they fanned out through the streets of the sleeping town. The battle with the well-armed police defending the city hall lasted all night. Once city hall was in their hands, the Zapatistas went to work pounding it with sledge hammers and finally setting it on fire.

On January 2 the Mexican army began a counterattack. The fight for Ocosingo was the only sustained battle of the war, and it went badly for the Zapatistas. The well-armed and disciplined soldiers moved relentlessly through the streets, cornering the Zapatistas in the market. Between forty and fifty rebel fighters—as much as 10 percent of the force—died in the battle.

The fight for Ocosingo set the stage for the conflict. The Zapatistas retreated into the jungle. The rebels felt safe there—they knew its muddy trails, its rivers. They were welcomed as heroes in its villages. The Mexican army had already determined that the rebels, armed with an array of old weapons, were not a serious military threat. Even though the soldiers met no resistance as they pursued the rebels into the jungle, the generals realized they would have a long road ahead of them if they tried to pursue them into the bush. The thought of search-and-destroy missions in the dark wilderness struck fear into the hearts of the soldiers in a way that the Zapatistas' arsenal of battered weapons never could. Besides, it would be politically costly. Though Subcommander Marcos, the Zapatistas' charismatic leader, was hardly a military genius, he was master of a much more crucial skill—spin control. Journalists stabbed each other in the back vying for an interview with the irreverent comandante; women sent him love letters; serious writers called his press releases poetry.

On January 12, 1994, Mexican president Carlos Salinas called off the troops and began looking for a negotiated way out. A month later the nation was transfixed as a Zapatista delegation, including the seductive subcommander, met with government negotiator Manuel Camacho Solís in the San Cristóbal cathedral. In a few weeks they had hammered out a peace proposal. As Monteverde and I drove into the jungle in mid-March, the Zapatistas were taking the proposal to their supporters for a vote.

After breakfast we pushed on along the road to San Miguel. The heart of Zapatista territory is not the jungle itself but the transition zone, which ranges between two thousand and three thousand feet above sea level. Here a series of canyons carved by three rivers cuts between oak-covered ridges. Zapatista territory extends beyond the last ridge into the downslope that marks the true jungle—where ceiba and mahogany trees tower above the canopy. As we rolled along, we saw a few crumbling shacks in the middle of broad pasture. For Monteverde, this was especially disturbing because twenty years earlier he had shared the hope that the colonists would improve their lot in the jungle. "That is not a life," he muttered as we drove past a house made of rotting twigs and covered with a cardboard roof.

After a few wrong turns and an unpleasant encounter with some over-zealous Zapatistas guarding a roadblock, we finally arrived at the gateway to Zapatista-controlled territory, a town called La Garrucha. A few days before our visit, PRI presidential candidate Luis Donaldo Colosio had been assassinated during a campaign rally in Tijuana. In the aftermath, Subcommander Marcos reported ominous troop movements throughout Chiapas and released a communiqué saying that only journalists accredited as "war correspondents" would continue to be allowed into the Zapatista-controlled zone. Monteverde and I had brought our credentials and letters of recommendation, along with a formal request for an interview with Marcos. We were told to return a few days later to find out whether our request would be granted. As we climbed back into the car, Monteverde stopped for a minute and looked up at the bit of forest on the ridge and shook his head. There were so few trees remaining, he pointed out, that Zapatista guerrilla fighters would not be able to use the jungle as cover if the army came after them.

"There's nothing left," he said in tone of disgust. "Not even enough to make a war."

II

As it turned out, Monteverde was called back to Mexico City to work on another project. So I hooked up with Susan Ferris and Ricardo Sandoval, a journalist couple with the *San Francisco Examiner,* for my return trip into the jungle. This time I prepared myself for a long wait. I packed cans of food, invested in a hammock, and stuffed blankets in my backpack.

The Zapatista sentries in San Miguel sent us to wait in the town's schoolhouse. There we discovered another waiting reporter, Bill Weinberg, who was sleeping with his feet hanging off the tiny bed. Weinberg is a correspondent for WBAI radio in New York and *High Times* magazine. Among other things, he wanted to ask Marcos whether he favored legalizing drugs.

After two days, we were given permission to drive to the next checkpoint. We piled into the Volkswagen and drove back down the road to La Garrucha. There we waited for a few hours near the basketball court until six chest-high Zapatista soldiers marched rapidly across an open field toward our car. They pulled it apart, tearing through our luggage, patting us down, looking under the seats and inside the spare tire. "Wait here," they ordered and then marched off into the gloom.

Three hours later we were still waiting. Susan and Rick finally went to sleep in the Volkswagen while Bill and I hauled out our blankets and passed out in the schoolhouse. Sometime after midnight I was awakened by a flashlight shining in my face. The first thing I noticed was the sweet smell of pipe tobacco. "Get up," I heard a voice say in Spanish. Then in accented English. "Let me see your credentials." The man in the ski mask peered intently at my press pass. He was wearing a ragged brown uniform and a weather-beaten gray cap adorned with three plastic stars. He had a bandolier of red shotgun shells strung across his chest and carried a sawed-off shotgun over his shoulder as if it were an umbrella. "O.K. Get your things together and get in the truck," said Marcos.

The four of us climbed into the back of Marcos's bright red pickup truck while Marcos got in the passenger seat. We were driven past the roadblock at La Garrucha and down the rutted road for forty-five minutes to the town of Patihuitz. Marcos promised to return the following day for an interview, but he never did. We shouldered our backpacks and followed our Zapatista guides down a dark trail. Around midnight, we were shown to our bunks. I wiggled into a foot-high crawl space, the second tier of a triple-decker bunk. The two sleeping Zapatistas were already cramped, but they made a little more space for me, and the three of us squeezed into the same small bed. I wrapped myself in my blanket, and immediately fell asleep.

When I opened my eyes the morning sun had crested over the forested ridge, bathing the valley in a diffused, liquid light. I scrambled out of bed to explore the camp. It consisted of two buildings made from soft jungle wood lashed together with vines. Our unit consisted of eighteen rebels—ten men and eight women. The Zapatistas' uniforms were hand-stitched; their backpacks, holsters, and the various pouches hanging off their belts were made of cheap nylon. Their weapons ranged from a few old .22s to the AR-15 semi-automatic rifle that belonged to the unit's nineteen-year-old captain. The unit had participated in the assault on Ocosingo on January 1. They had seen death, but they were also excited, enthralled really, by their warrior status. The government's peace proposal was inadequate, they said in unison. (It would be rejected by over 95 percent of the rebel rank and file two months later.) "We didn't train to negotiate," said Captain Ignacio, who went by the nickname Nacho. "We trained to fight."

The rebels would not tell us the names of their hometowns, but they all had similar stories. Nacho's family had been expelled from a finca and had migrated to the jungle twenty years earlier. "In my town there is no school, no teacher, there is nothing," he said. Lieutenant Lucio said he had a small piece of land, "but nothing grows, it's pure rocks." "Where I'm from," said a recent recruit who had chosen "Paul" as his nom de guerre, "there is no place to plant a milpa [cornfield] and the corn hardly grows."

Héctor, another insurgent, said that in his town "the children don't know how to read or even speak Spanish." His primary complaint against the government was the reform of Article 27 and the end of land reform. Under the Mexican constitution, poor peasants were at least theoretically guaranteed a right to land.

The spark that ignited the Zapatista revolt was the reform of Article 27, which held out the promise of land and also affirmed Mexico's historical obligation to the campesinos. Arguing that there was no more land to be distributed and that the campesinos had "grown up," President Salinas pushed through the reform in 1992. Ejidatarios would be allowed to form partnerships with private investors, sell their land, and generally treat it as private property.

"Before, the land was for the campesinos," Héctor told me. "Now it's for the *finqueros* and their cows."

Despite Marcos's tirades against Salinas, most of the Zapatistas' grievances were much older than the president's six-year term. The Zapatista rank and file were interested in national politics to the extent that it affected their central grievance—land. All of the Zapatistas I talked to mentioned poor land as their reason for joining the rebels. Everyone was fighting for a new, better plot.

The Zapatistas were hemmed in between a nature reserve on their eastern flank and the fincas to the west. Where were they going to find land? Their first choice was to take land from the finqueros, and in the aftermath of the January 1994 uprising they did so. The Indians who had been living on the rocky hillsides moved into the valleys, invaded the ranchland, and planted corn. In the Zapatista heartland, Las Cañadas, the rebels exacted revenge on a general who was also the region's largest landowner. General Absalón Castellanos, the former governor of Chiapas, owned approximately 37,000 acres (15,000 hectares) in the region. He had spent his six years in office defending the interests of his landowning cronies against any Indian who dared invade their property. On January 2, 1994, a group of Zapatista soldiers took the general hostage at his 500-acre San Joaquín finca, releasing him six weeks later after condemning him "to live to the end of his days with the pain and shame of having received the pardon and the good will of those he had killed, robbed, kidnapped, and plundered."

But while 37,000 acres may sound like a lot, it suddenly seems small when divided up among thousands of land-hungry peasants. The majority of the fincas in the region are only a couple of hundred acres. Just outside the Zapatista stronghold of Guadalupe Tepayac, I visited a finca that had been invaded by local peasants soon after the Zapatistas rose up. Peasants from the Buena Vista Pacheco ejido had taken over a 500-acre plot that was previously home to forty-two head of cattle. Now it would be divided up among 113 families.

"There's just a little piece for each one," said Gustavo Morales López, the leader of the invasion. Not only would each family receive only six acres—about the size of several football fields—but turning degraded pastureland into cornfields is no small feat. The best-known method is to allow the forest to regrow and then burn it to return nutrients to the soil—a process that can take twenty years.

Around Ocosingo, on the fringes of the Zapatista zone, peasants seized another 37,000 acres belonging to owners of large and medium-sized ranches. The ranchers were furious—so furious that the Salinas government had to buy them off with millions of dollars in rent to prevent them from embarking on a murderous rampage. Yet even by the time of my visit in March 1994 it had became clear that the Zapatistas lacked the military strength to hold on to the plantations. And even if they could, they would have the inevitable problem of turning ranchland back into cornfields.

The Zapatistas often point out that Chiapas has the most skewed land distribution in all of Mexico. Eighty-five years ago when the original Zapatistas rose up in Morelos, a counterrevolutionary force organized by the landowners and nicknamed Los Mapaches (the raccoons) came to dominate Chiapas. Los Mapaches held off land reform for twenty years, until the Cárdenas era. But even then, the land reform consisted mostly of redistributing moderate-sized plots within Indian communities or of giving land title to a piece of rocky hillside. Many truly large plantations—some of which reached tens of thousands of acres—survived the land reform through legal maneuvering or political influence.

The large plantations, however, are not distributed evenly throughout the state. Most are concentrated in the Grijalva Valley near the state capital of Tuxtla Gutiérrez and in the Soconusco region on the Pacific coast, where the Zapatistas have little influence. The Zapatistas lack the military capability or political force to impose a statewide land reform.

Meanwhile, there is not enough land in the area under Zapatista control to meet their long-term needs. A regional land reform would put enough land in the hands of Zapatista villages to relieve the land hunger for perhaps a decade. And even if the Zapatistas are able to hold on to the invaded land, they would soon be back where they started because the problem is not just the lack of land but also its quality and how it is used. Most of the original land grants in Las Cañadas were for plots of fifty acres, nearly ten times larger than the average holding in the highlands. But fifty acres deteriorate fast when you slash and burn and then put cattle on the cleared land. The process is especially devastating in Las Cañadas, where the rocky hillsides rapidly erode. When families have an average of six or seven children, there is never enough land for the next generation. The jungle region, with its fragile soils, simply cannot sustain intensive agriculture. By 1990, only two decades after the first wave of settlers arrived, the population of Las Cañadas had grown to more than twenty-three thousand.

The town next to the Zapatista encampment where I was staying is a good example of the problems the settlers faced. Patihuitz—the name means "beyond the mountain" in Tzeltal—was settled in two waves as peons expelled from the fincas left for the jungle. The land was rocky and the soil shallow; it produced corn for two years, and then a new area had to be cleared. The settlers planted grass on the cleared land and bought cows. Although they had learned ranching on the fincas, they did not have access to the same specialized grasses and technical training in the jungle. In many cases the cattle grazed for five years until the land was destroyed.

By the 1960s, land in Patihuitz was becoming scarce. The children of the original settlers were forced to leave Patihuitz and hike into the jungle to found new settlements. They were joined by wave after wave of expelled peons until they were pressing up against the land claimed by the Lacandón Indians and later incorporated into the Montes Azules Biosphere Reserve. Today, half of the cleared land in Las Cañadas is in pasture, and most of it belongs not to the large fincas but to the Zapatista villages themselves.

Another way out for the Zapatistas is to make do with the land they have and somehow make it produce. This is why they are asking for roads, schools, fertilizers, and credit. But the Mexican agricultural economy is in deep crisis; the market for traditional peasant products like corn, beans, beef, and coffee has virtually collapsed, and unless the Zapatistas can singlehandedly transform both Mexico's economic policy and international economic trends, there is little hope that whatever they can produce on their rocky land—even with the tractors they want— will find much of a market.

So the Zapatistas have few options, but there is one. There are several hundred thousand acres of good land only twenty miles from the Zapatista front lines. They are part of the Montes Azules Biosphere Reserve, and the land is empty, claimed only by a few Lacandón Indians, the contemptible government, and environmentalists in Mexico City and the United States. The rebels have adopted the battle cry of the earlier revolution—"Land to those who work it!"—and they see no reason why that logic should apply any less to environmentalists than to finqueros.

III

After three days in the Zapatista camp, Subcommander Marcos's driver (nom de guerre: Monarca) came to take us back to La Garrucha. Marcos, he said, may or may not be available for an interview.

La Garrucha was not as we had left it. The following day, April 10, 1994, was the seventy-fifth anniversary of the death of Emiliano Zapata. The Zapatistas were planning a military parade in his honor and had invited the press to attend. All afternoon, carload after carload of journalists and Zapatista fellow travelers were let through the roadblock at San Miguel. They pulled up at the basketball court and disgorged their occupants. Slowly, it filled with gringos and *chilangos* who stood around and talked as if they were at a cocktail party. Marcos was nearby—we could feel his presence. Everyone was in a state of high anxiety, hoping he or she would be selected for an interview. Monarca delivered the subcommander's love letters to two pretty young women who had come from Mexico City with some vague purpose. Later we saw an armed phalanx form around a tree and supposed Marcos was holding a meeting with a gringo we had seen plucked from our midst.

By evening it was a circus. Marcos parked his red pickup truck fifty yards from the basketball court, while Monarca made his way through the press corps calling out the names of a few selected journalists who were granted an audience, one at a time, in the truck. Rick, Susan, Bill, and I felt like wallflowers at a high school dance; we realized that we were not among Marcos's crop of current favorites. Around 10 P.M., we could still see the glow of Marcos's pipe through the windshield of the truck. We decided to call it a night. We retreated to the school, where three Mexico City college students had already staked out the floor space. After a week in the Zapatista camps we had no desire to stay for a media event the next day. We decided to leave in the morning.

I woke up around 1 A.M. because Rick and Susan were having a loud discussion about the San Francisco 49ers. It was not until I saw the tell-tale pipe light up a ski mask that I realized they were talking with Marcos. He was reclining comfortably on one of the two beds, his head propped up against the headboard.

"WBAI—99.5 in New York!" Marcos yelled to Bill. Remarkably, he knew the station's FM frequency. "Very good," said Bill. We were surprised when we didn't hear another peep out of Bill all night.

Marcos was both media savvy and remarkably knowledgeable about U.S. and Mexian popular culture. He asked Susan and Ricardo, from the Hearst-owned *Examiner,* what had ever happened to Patty Hearst. When Susan asked the subcommander if Chiapas could turn into another Vietnam he said, "Why? Are you guys planning to come down here as well?"

Sensing that Marcos might get up and leave at any moment, we kept trying to get him to answer a few serious questions. But when asked how he had learned English, he launched into a fanciful tale about working as a waiter in a San Francisco restaurant. "I was fired for being gay," he quipped. He said that he worked next doing demonstrations on blow-up dolls in a sex shop before getting a film part in Los Angeles ("I played the kid in *Kramer versus Kramer,*" he said). He worked as a cab driver on Bourbon Street in New Orleans, a security guard for the Dallas Cowboys cheerleaders, and a ski instructor in Aspen. "That's were I got the ski masks," he said.

After about two hours of this banter, we realized that Marcos, an insomniac, was settling in for the night. Two of the Mexican activists, whom we had seen receiving the love letters from Marcos earlier in the day, climbed into bed with the subcommander. He snuggled up to them, one woman on each side. I was never able to figure out exactly what had brought them to the rebel camp, but one had brought a bag full of medicine to donate to the Zapatistas. By three in the morning our proposed interview had devolved into a slumber party. The Mexican activists launched into Cuban protest songs. The subcommander refused to join in but pointedly corrected them when they mangled the words.

Clearly, Marcos, whoever he was behind the mask, was starved for company. The all-night interview had already become a Zapatista tradition (in fact Marcos would give another one to Alma Guillermoprieto of the *New Yorker* the following night). But the clowning around with journalists was not mere frivolity. Every positive story written about the Zapatistas raised the political cost of a military assault of the ragtag rebels. Marcos had succeeded in capturing Mexico's—and the world's—imagination.

But good public relations would not help the Zapatistas solve their most serious problem—the absence of adequate farmland. Toward dawn I asked Marcos where the Zapatistas would find new land to farm. Suddenly he got serious.

"This land originally belonged to the Indians," Marcos said. During the colonial period the Indians in Chiapas lived in scattered settlements. The Spaniards gathered them into villages and put them to work on fincas owned by the Dominican friars and the descendants of the conquistadors.

"The white people, the big farmers and ranchers, forced the Indians into the mountains," Marcos continued. "The good land belongs to the fincas. The Indians have the rocky land in the mountains. But Indians see the good land below and say, 'Originally that was my land so I have a right to recover it.' We need to redistribute the land. But we also need roads, water, schools, hospitals, technology—like tractors, like planes. The next question is the price. You can grow a good crop of coffee but when you take it to the city, the *coyote,* the intermediary, thinks 'you don't speak Spanish, so I can lie to you and cheat you.' You can bring in one hundred pounds and he will say it is only fifty."

If the Zapatistas did not get what they wanted, Marcos implied, they would be forced to cut down the rest of the jungle. "There's a certain kind of environmentalist who loves trees more than people," he said. "We want trees, we want the mountains. But we also want a dignified life for our people. If the government makes a good plan and we have what we need, then we will not have to attack the trees. The government cannot just declare that there will be no more cutting of trees. Here we have no option but to cut the trees, burn them, and put the seeds in the land. It doesn't matter how the land is taken when you are hungry."

The morning sun finally began to pour in through the cracks in the hut, and as the light came up we looked around to see that Bill was still asleep. None of us had the heart to wake him. He had not realized that the man teasing him the night before was the subcommander himself. "I thought it was some obnoxious *chilango* who wouldn't go to sleep," he told me later.

Later that morning, Bill caught up with Marcos, who good-naturedly gave him a long interview. Did Marcos think that the war on drugs was being used as a pretext to militarize Chiapas? He did. Would he support legalizing drugs as a means to undercut that kind of militarization? "Well," said Marcos, "we must think about this, reflect on it. But our problems are very urgent. I mean our problem is dire survival. Our principal work is in that direction."

IV

For the first year of the Zapatista revolt Marcos did an amazing job of keeping the rebels in the spotlight. But he should have taken a lesson from Madonna. In today's MTV world, you need to change your image every fifteen minutes to sustain interest. A year after the Zapatista uprising began, the media and the public seemed to lose interest in the Zapatista story. That was the moment that newly inaugurated Mexican president Ernesto Zedillo chose to counterattack.

On February 9, 1995, Zedillo told the nation that Subcommander Marcos was actually Rafael Guillén Sebastián, the son of a furniture salesman from Tampico, a former university professor, and a tired old socialist from a two-decades-old underground organization called the National Liberation Front (FLN). The Zapatista leaders, the government claimed, had exploited the ignorance of the Indians and turned their legitimate grievances into an armed movement whose true goals were those of the leadership alone.

The propaganda offensive coincided with a military one. With the Zapatista leadership unmasked, President Zedillo sent the army to arrest Marcos and his gang. The Zapatistas turned on their heels and fled without firing a shot. Once again, the jungle was their only weapon.

In the year before the government military offensive, and with fewer than five hundred deaths, the Zapatistas had accomplished what had taken the Salvadoran guerrillas a decade of brutal fighting. If Chiapas were an independent country instead of a state in Mexico, the Zapatista revolution might have triumphed. Across the country, the rebels had raised fundamental questions about the direction of the economy and had rattled the cages of the political elite. In Chiapas, they had weakened the political machine, they had taken over thousand of acres of land, and they had put the issue of indigenous rights on the table.

But by the time of the military offensive in February 1995, the Zapatistas' appeal was already waning and their options were running out. They had tried and failed to build nationwide support for their movement and to defeat the PRI. They had sponsored an anti-PRI political gathering in August 1994 called the National Democratic Convention, bringing a caravan of 234 buses with six thousand delegates to a specially constructed amphitheater near Gaudalupe Tepayac. The journey, which normally takes six hours, took thirty. The convention was excellent political theater, but it did not spark a significant political movement.

When Zedillo and the PRI won easily in the presidential elections, the Zapatistas tried to apply a bit of military pressure. Claiming that the state elections in Chiapas were fraudulent, the Zapatistas "mobilized" throughout the highlands on December 19, 1994. A few hundred armed rebels took over towns that their supporters already controlled. They were easily chased out by the army, which used the offensive as an excuse to further militarize the region.

Meanwhile, life in the jungle was taking its toll. The Zapatista propaganda war was falling apart amidst the government's barrage. The sycophantic attention that had been lavished on the rebels in the months after the uprising convinced Marcos and the Zapatistas that there was an enormous groundswell of support which they could tap into if they could only find the right formula. Marcos continued to write long missives, mostly about the adventures of a beetle named Durito. They were sent out on the Internet. No one in Mexico read them.

By the time the Zapatistas arrived at the table for the second round of negotiations in the highland town of San Andrés Larrainzar in February 1995, both their political and their military gambits had failed. The government had successfully marginalized the rebels from national politics, while the finca owners in the Ocosingo valley were counterattacking against the land invaders. Armed militia called *guardias blancas* pushed the peasants off the invaded land. Whatever shape peace took—and no one expected it to happen quickly—it was clear it would ultimately depend on finding some formula that would allow the Zapatista supporters to survive on their degraded land.

Against this backdrop, I set out in September 1995 to do a circuit of the Lacandón jungle. I wanted to visit different communities in different regions. I wanted to see how the people lived, what their relationship was with the land. My trip would take me around the Montes Azules Biosphere Reserve.

I began in the town of Palenque. In 1841, John Lloyd Stephens, the American explorer, visited the nearby Mayan ruins and found the muddy trail so steep he had to be carried through the jungle by a Mayan porter. Today, the ruins can be reached in twenty minutes on a microbus. The jungle begins thirty miles south of Palenque. To get there you must pass through a devastated landscape, an enormous treeless valley in which a few dozen humped Zebu cattle graze listlessly. In the past three decades, the area has been logged, burned, planted, and ravaged by cattle.

Past the town of Chancalá, the jungle closes in. The area along the road has been cleared, but trees cover the nearby ridges. Road crews were everywhere, and the Zapatistas deserved the credit. In an effort both to create employment and to improve access for the military, the government was spending millions of dollars grading and paving the rutted old jungle trail.

In the town of San Javier I met a Lacandón Indian teenager named Rodolfo who lent me his bicycle so I would not have to walk the five miles to Lacanjá in the hot sun. "Did you see what the Tzeltales and the Choles have done to the jungle?" asked Rodolfo. "The Lacandones take care of the *selva*, we take care of the trees. Before, all of this was jungle, but then the Choles came and they cut it all down."

I rode Rodolfo's bike through town right up to the front door of a small ecolodge run by a Lacandón named Kinbor. Soon after I arrived, Kinbor himself pulled up in a blue pickup truck. He wore brown pants and no shirt. His enormous pectoral muscles looked as if they had been developed hauling mahogany trees down from the mountains. His hair was cut in the Lacandón style—it hung down below his shoulders in the back but the bangs were cut straight across his forehead. It made him look a bit like an aging rock star. Kinbor is one of a half-dozen Lacandones in Lacanjá who have built lodges for the tourists. He offers guests a creek for bathing and two sheds for sleeping (he is building another), a large, heavy mahogany table with a barbecue pit, and a cabana with a thatched roof where you can string your hammock. Guests usually spend a night or two. Kinbor takes them to see the Mayan ruins at Bonampak or the Lacanjá lagoon or the nearby waterfalls. "How's business?" I asked when Kinbor sat down at the mahogany table.

"It's picked up a bit," he said. "After the Zapatistas started up no one was coming. They heard 'Lacandón jungle,' they thought 'Lacandón Indian.' So they were completely afraid.

"But the Zapatistas have never come here because we don't support them," Kinbor continued. A Zapatista delegation had visited the Lacandón village at Lake Nahá, where Kinbor was born and where he still has relatives. "The Zapatistas told the people there that they had nothing against the Lacandón Indians, that their only enemy was the government, which never keeps its word."

In Kinbor's view—and in the view of many of the other Lacandones I talked to over the next few days—the Zapatistas represent the interests of the Chol and Tzeltal corn farmers who are cutting down the jungle. Tzeltales from Nueva Palestina, where the rebels are rumored to have significant support, have also been advancing into the jungle, knowing that the government will not risk a confrontation.

"They want more and more land," said Kinbor. "Because they want cattle. They have twenty hectares and they say they don't have enough to eat. Me, with two hectares, I never lack corn."

The difference between the farming techniques practiced by the Lacandones and those practiced by the Choles and Tzeltales can be traced back to the late 1950s and early '60s, when the Lacandón was first opened for colonization. At the time, little was known about the complex ecology of jungle soils. The officials who promoted the colonization scheme figured that if the soil was rich enough to support the exuberant jungle foliage it was certainly suited for growing corn. But jungle soil is quite thin. Most of the nutrients are not in the soil itself but in the successive canopies of growth. When the peasants burned the jungle to clear the land for their corn crop, they deposited this enormous mass of organic material into the soil. Corn, watered by the abundant rain, virtually sprang from the earth. But the torrential rains also leached the soil, quickly carrying away the nutrients. Within two to four years the corn would not grow. The old plot was abandoned and a new one cleared. Then the real damage was done: the peasants planted grass before moving on. They put a few cows to graze on the land. As the rains further leached the soil, the pasture gave way to weeds that even the cattle would not eat. The final result is land that is so degraded that it takes several acres of grazing land to feed one mangy cow. That is what has happened along the road to Chancalá.

The Lacandones, meanwhile, have in some instances been cultivating the same plots for centuries with no discernible damage. The difference is the use of what is called an *acahual,* or fallow plot. Kinbor still grows his corn on a milpa, as his ancestors have for centuries. He clears two and a half to five acres of low-lying land but leaves the big trees standing. He burns the undergrowth and then plants a complex garden plot that imitates the jungle's natural canopy—he grows corn and beans but also sweet potatoes, yucca, squash, sugar cane, tomatoes, cilantro, onions, pineapple, and plantains (some of these crops are nontraditional, introduced in the past few decades). After three years—four if the particular farmer has exceptional skill—yields fall off and the forest is allowed to regenerate. The dormant plot is called an acahual. Another five-acre plot is cleared and the process is repeated. After seven years the jungle on the original acahual will be "twice as tall as a man's head." It is once again cleared, burned, and planted. A Lacandón can grow corn in perpetuity without damaging the jungle by rotating his milpa on a fifteen-acre plot.

What fouls up the process completely is planting grass and raising cattle—then the acahual never regenerates and the farmer must chop down virgin jungle every two or three years to plant his milpa. Cattle are banned in Lacanjá; I did not see a single hoofed animal during my visit there. "We're not fucking ranchers like the Choles," muttered a teenage Lacandón. "Fucking cows destroy the jungle. Here you will not see a single cow—nothing but the corn flower."

If cattle are so destructive, then why are the Chol and Tzeltal farmers so reluctant to give them up? The answer must again be traced back to the 1960s. When the Choles and Tzeltales began to invade the jungle, the finqueros followed right behind them. Often the colonists earned money by leasing their cleared land to the large cattle ranchers. Since the land seemed abundant, they pushed deeper into the wilderness.

By the 1970s, when the government resettled the Tzeltal colonists in Nueva Palestina and the Choles in Frontera Corozal, both groups saw cattle as an important part of their personal economies. Peasants must do two things to survive: they must grow enough corn to feed their families, and they must earn enough cash to buy other essentials like clothing and medicine. Small-scale cattle ranching has become an important part of the cash economy. A few head of cattle function exactly like money in the bank. If a peasant can manage to clear twelve acres of pasture and graze five cows, then he can raise cash if the crop fails or a child gets sick. (Many Zapatistas sold their cows to buy guns.) In the meantime he is earning interest—every year, if he is lucky, he gets one or two calves, which he sells at market.

Cattle ranching has been a prestige occupation in Mexico since colonial times. It is also a way of asserting ownership of the land in a region where land titles are uncertain. Frontera Corozal has three thousand inhabitants and Nueva Palestina has five thousand. A new generation is coming of age, and it is hungry for land. Land that is privately owned but uncleared could be invaded—remember, "Land to those who work it!" Even an acahual is potentially fair game. No one is going to invade pastureland because it is being "worked." Finally, peasants worry that their uncleared land will be expropriated by the environmentalists and declared a reserve. The peasants have learned that once you clear a piece of land and remove all the trees the environmentalists lose interest. That's why you see acre after acre of cleared land in Frontera Corozal without a cow in sight.

Anthropologists who have studied the Lacandones for several decades are saddened by the changes. In the past three decades, the only Mayan group to escape the Spanish missionaries and to preserve its ancient culture in almost complete isolation has been Christianized, abandoned its rituals, lost its ancient knowledge, and seen enormous portions of its jungle home destroyed. But for me, contrasting Lacanjá with the devastated landscape along the road from Chancalá, it was striking to see how the Lacandones had reached an accommodation with these inevitable changes. Kinbor drives a pickup truck, he often wears jeans instead of his traditional white tunic, and the satellite dish he bought recently has turned him and his family into television addicts. But Kinbor and all the Lacandones I met maintain a fierce love for the jungle and a powerful desire to protect it.

I saw that best when I walked with Kinbor's cousin, Pancho López, from Lacanjá to the Mayan ruins at Bonampak. Pancho stopped every few minutes to tell me the name of some plant or point to animal tracks. "A jaguar passed this way," he said pointing to paw prints in the mud. He showed me cedar and mahogany trees whose enormous branches waved with surprising grace above the jungle canopy. Butterflies flitted everywhere—yellow and blue, swirling and dancing around our heads. A small deer crossed the path, stared at us for a second, and wandered off into the bush. Pancho was able to detect a resting troop of spider monkeys hidden high above the jungle floor. He scooped up a turtle along the bank of a river and handed it to me. "You can eat this," he said. "But it's still too small." When I put it back on the trail, Pancho picked it up and deposited it along the riverbank. "Otherwise it can't get back into the water," he said.

Arriving at the ruins in Bonampak, my jaw went slack when I saw the enormous pyramid rise on a hillside. Pancho, who as a young man came here to make offerings to the gods, was not impressed. He wanted me to notice something else. "Nothing but jungle," sweeping his hand across an unbroken horizon of green. "Not like the Choles—they cut everything down."

There are only about two thousand Lacandón Indians left, and their needs cannot take precedence over the tens of thousands of Choles,

Tzeltales, and Totziles who now call the jungle their home. Still, one day I asked Kinbor if the Lacandones had talked with their neighbors about the way they cultivate their milpas, about the destruction caused by cattle, and about their love for their forest. He said, "We talked to them and they just laughed."

V

After a week of hard rain, the bridge along the road to Benemérito de las Américas was washed out. I got off the bus and walked across a twisted girder to the other side. There I met Niseto Contreras, who was going in the same direction. Benemérito is the largest town in the Marqués de Comillas region of the Lacandón. After two decades of cattle ranching, logging, animal trafficking, oil exploration, and drug smuggling, hardly a tree has been left standing. Marqués de Comillas is also the most prosperous area of the jungle.

Contreras himself was quite a success story. Twenty years earlier, his father had heard that the government was giving away land in the Chiapas jungle. He packed his family up and left his home on the coast of Oaxaca. Today he owns 250 acres of land and 500 head of cattle. "Producing good pasture takes skill," said Contreras. "You have to plant high-quality grass and then you have to burn it every few years. Otherwise the cows will destroy the land in a few years and it will be good for nothing. See that land over there?" he asked, pointing to an empty field. "The people who planted it didn't know how to take care of it. Now it's useless."

As we pulled into town, I stared out the window at a man in a white T-shirt who staggered along muttering to himself. Contreras noticed my gaze. "He's crazy," he said. "He saw the devil and it frightened him. Since that he's never been the same."

"No kidding," I said.

Contreras waved out to the window to a friend. "Have you seen the devil?" he asked me.

I admitted that I had not.

"He's about your height," Contreras continued. "But he's got goat hooves instead of feet. I saw him last year when I was out herding cattle. He didn't frighten me, but he scared my horse. A lot of people around here have seen the devil."

That revelation did not surprise me. Benemérito has a reputation for lawlessness. Small planes carrying cocaine from neighboring Guatemala routinely airdrop their cargo into the Usumacinta River, where it is picked up by waiting boatmen. The night before I arrived, two soldiers had been killed in a firefight with drug traffickers along the riverbank.

A decade ago Benemérito was a center for animal smuggling. Macaws, parrots, toucans, spider monkeys, jaguars, and rare reptiles and insects were captured as their habitats were destroyed. The animals were sold to government officials in the region, who often moonlighted as smugglers. Eventually many of the animals found their way into the hands of an international animal smuggling company called José Vera, S.A. de C.V., which illegally shipped them to buyers around the world. The company was able to get the animals through Mexican customs because its owners were well connected: David Ibarra, whose father of the same name was a former treasury minister, and Jorge Hank Rhon, a Tijuana businessman and son of the former agriculture minister Carlos Hank González, were the reputed partners. The elder Hank is a stalwart in the PRI and a billionaire businessman.

In 1989, Graciela de la Garza, the director of ecological conservation in Mexico's environmental ministry, began investigating the two men. She was beaten up twice, the tires of her car were shot out, someone tried to force her off the road, and one of her investigators was murdered. As the result of her investigation, David Ibarra was fined $15,000 and Jorge Hank had to cough up $30,000.

Over the years, the Marqués de Comillas region has also lived from logging. In 1989 logging was banned in Chiapas, but there was always a thriving market if one could float the lumber across the border into Guatemala. In 1994, with the state economy reeling as a result of the Zapatista uprising, the authorities lifted the logging ban. The people of Benemérito managed to remove their allotted 1.5 million cubic meters of tropical hardwood in less than a month. During my visit I saw dozens of piles of cut mahogany stacked along the roadside.

All that remains of the jungle in Benemérito is the heat. Without a tree to provide shade, the sun burns down with unbelievable intensity. The energy I expended to stand up caused rivulets of sweat to roll down my chest and my face to turn bright red. The rain forest had become a distant memory. On the wall of the boarding house where I stayed, someone had painted a colorful mural showing a macaw perched on the branch of a tree while a jaguar prowled in the background. Something about the jaguar caught my eye. Looking closely, I saw that it had stripes, not spots. It was a tiger. Whoever had drawn this picture had relied on some sort of picture book, not on personal experience. The jungle had been so thoroughly annihilated that it had already been reduced to an idyll.

What is perhaps most unsettling from a conservationist standpoint about Benemérito and the other towns I visited in the Marqués region is that this unmitigated destruction of natural resources has translated into a higher standard of living. Benemérito is full of pickup trucks, sturdy houses, restaurants, schools, pharmacies, doctors, and hotels. Many people who came with nothing twenty years ago could now be considered prosperous. One young woman named Mirena, whose parents ran a restaurant in town, was taking the unprecedented step of studying journalism at the state university in the capital of Tuxtla Gutiérrez.

José Olan Martínez, the mayor of another town called Pico de Oro, arrived with nothing and now owns a dozen cattle, 125 acres of good land, a solid house, and, of course, a pickup truck. "It was a good decision to come here," he told me. He was planning to cut the last twenty mahogany trees on his land, which would bring in about three thousand dollars. Olan Martínez acknowledged that he will not be able to leave any mahogany trees or much jungle to his children, but so what? His children will have something more important—capital.

The economic success in the Marqués de Comillas area sends a clear message to other, less-developed areas of the jungle: destructive practices like logging, ranching, and animal trafficking can create wealth. Of course, the correlation is not automatic. Cattle have wrecked whole regions without contributing to the welfare of the inhabitants. In other regions, the money from the logging operations has gone into the pockets of functionaries and investors who live in other parts of the country. But with its large, fertile plots of land, abundant cattle, roads, schools, and even hospitals, Marqués de Comillas had achieved the kind of development that Captain Nacho, Lieutenant Lucio, and Subcommander Marcos were talking about during my visit to Las Cañadas the year before.

The Zapatistas do not want the same kind of devastation. Could Las Cañadas be developed without destroying the land?

It would be difficult. Making the land produce is enough of a challenge. The land in Las Cañadas is less fertile; it is rocky and already eroded by grazing and slash-and-burn farming. There is not as much of it either. The largest plots in the region are 50 acres. Families in Marqués de Comillas received 125 acres, which have allowed them to diversify their personal economies; they can graze thirty cows and still have enough land left over to raise corn and leave something to their children. The people who settled the area came from more developed areas of the country and were therefore more educated. They also benefited from government credit, roads, schools, and the jobs provided by Pemex.

What would happen if the same kind of development strategy were applied in Las Cañadas? In other words, what would happen if the government built roads and schools, granted credit for cattle ranching, and allowed logging? How about if the government looked the other way as parts of the biosphere reserve were logged and cleared? My view is that it would cause widespread environmental destruction without raising the standard of living, because many of the resources in the region have already been depleted. The difference between a 125-acre plot and a 50-acre plot in a region that cannot withstand intensive farming is enormous. Exploiting the natural resources on the larger-sized plot allowed the settlers in Marqués de Comillas to create capital while they destroyed the jungle. Applying a similar strategy in Las Cañadas would probably not create capital; it would do little more than buy the Zapatistas a few more years. Of course, that is what the government is looking for. If the government believed it could squelch an armed rebellion by sacrificing a bit of the rain forest, the trade-off might prove irresistible. From the vantage point of officials in Mexico City, what value does the jungle really have?

VI

That seemed like a good question to put to Ricardo Frías, a Mexican research biologist I met in the furthest corner of the Lacandón. Frías is the scientific coordinator of the biological research station at Boca de Chajul inside the Montes Azules Biosphere Reserve. His research is on the interaction between plants and animals in the jungle, specifically the ants that live in the cecropia tree. "In a single cecropia tree there are more species of ants than you will find in all of North America," said Ricardo.

The 815,000 acres of the Lacandón that remain constitute less than one-fifth of 1 percent of Mexico's territory, yet contain 20 percent of the country's biological wealth. There are more than four thousand different species of plants alone in the Lacandón. In 1994 a whole new plant species was discovered near the ruins at Bonampak. It is called *Lacandonia schismatica* and is, according to Ricardo, "the current star of the plant kingdom." There are healthy populations of all animals native to the region in the reserve, but large expanses are necessary to ensure the survival of a breeding population. A single jaguar, for example, needs twenty square kilometers to hunt.

Aside from the enormously diverse flora and fauna, much of which has not even been recorded, the swath of remaining jungle anchors the regional ecosystem. Destroying the jungle changes rain patterns (perhaps even globally) and increases the intensity of flooding, since heavy rains tend to run off more quickly. A part of Mexico's fishing industry also depends on the Lacandón, since fish that breed in the Gulf of Mexico thrive on the nutrients carried there by the Usumacinta River.

The rain forest's role in converting carbon dioxide to oxygen has been well documented. It is also highly possible that valuable drugs for treating everything from cancer to AIDS could someday be manufactured from the plants found in the jungle. "Just imagine what one of the Lacandón elders could tell you about the medicinal uses of the native plants," said Ricardo.

The problem is that none of these arguments—however utilitarian—is going to carry much weight with a Tzeltal corn farmer.

"If you try and present this kind of argument in an impoverished community it's not going to work," argued Ricardo. "Their moral imperative is to feed their children. You have to give them an alternative."

Many have been suggested. Ronald Nigh, an anthropologist and expert on jungle agriculture, has developed a strategy called "productive reforestation." Nigh points out that reforestation of degraded jungle regions has not been successful because the poor inhabitants cannot afford to wait twenty to thirty years until replanted mahogany trees can be harvested.

He has developed a system in which each phase of the natural process of regeneration can be exploited, either for subsistence or for the cash economy. Each region, Nigh argues, must be evaluated to determine which products can be produced and what roads, schools, marketing techniques, and credit are needed to develop these resources. If infrastructure development is not combined with a search for new forest products, then roads just accelerate the destruction of the region.

One controversial strategy for creating a nontraditional source of income is being carried out by Roberto Ruiz, a Spanish primatologist studying spider monkeys at the Chajul research center. Once a week, Ruiz takes a boat across the river to the town of Chajul. Residents there line up to sell him their week's catch—of rare butterflies. The insects are shipped to Mexico City, where they are carefully catalogued, warehoused, and eventually sold to museums and international collectors.

The income generated from capturing butterflies has helped change the perception of the jungle in the town. Many families take in between $25 and $200 a month. Leonardo Cabrera caught five agrias, an extremely rare butterfly of luminescent fuscia and deep blue. He used the $500 he earned to buy a gas-powered generator. Meanwhile, Ricardo Estrada's teenage son convinced his father that he could make more money collecting butterflies on their land than they could from cattle ranching. Estrada decided not to cut down the jungle. In order to participate in the butterfly project, the town of Chajul agreed to set 300 acres of jungle aside as a community reserve.

The butterfly project is not without its critics. Collecting and marketing rare insects makes a lot of conservationists uneasy. The project designers say that a more critical threat to the butterflies is habitat destruction. Others I talked to in the region describe the Chajul biological research station as a jungle playground for Mexico City's environmental set. They feel it is inappropriate for a research station to have solar panels, flush toilets, and a fleet of motorboats in a region where most of the population lives without plumbing or electricity. Porfirio Camacho, a former agrarian reform official who is now an adviser to an indigenous group called the Comunidad Lacandona, argues that all scientific investigations should be approved by Indian representatives, that investigators should live in the same conditions as the local population, and that all research should have applications that directly benefit the local community—research on malaria, for example.

That kind of thinking makes primatologist Ruiz furious. "On what basis are they going to evaluate my project?" he asks. "The Indians need to understand something. Yes, the jungle belongs to them. But it also belongs to the whole world."

But does it? Or is it more accurate to say it belongs to the Mexican nation? Or to poor farmers everywhere who need a bit of land? Or to all the indigenous people of Chiapas who were robbed of their land centuries ago? Or to the indigenous farmers who migrated to the region? Or to the Zapatistas who have begun to invade the reserve? Or maybe to the few remaining Lacandones whose ancestors have lived in the Lacandón for centuries? How can all these interests share a resource that is rapidly vanishing?

What argument could anyone make to a Tzeltal corn farmer if he perceived that his family's welfare depended on chopping down the forest? Given the history and the militancy of the region, the only one that would work is an economic one. Somehow, the real economic value of the forest has to be increased. Many extremely creative, resourceful, and dedicated people have tried to come up with ways to do this—from ecotourism, to sustainable logging, to butterfly collecting. The projects sometimes work in a few communities. But if the Lacandón is to survive, there must be a regionwide shift from extensive and destructive corn farming and ranching to intensive exploitation and management of the jungle resources. Making the regional economy sustainable will require not only a sizable investment to identify new products and bring them to market, but also an adjustment on the part of the jungle's impoverished inhabitants, who will have to invest time and energy in projects that could fail. Peasants are not averse to innovation, but they do try to avoid risk because they have such a tiny margin for failure. From their vantage point, slash-and-burn corn farming, small-scale cattle ranching, and logging the region's mahogany still offer the most security. None of the proposed alternatives can match it.

In fact, in the months after my visit the circumstances continued to deteriorate in the Lacandón. Zapatista communities, driven from their homes by the army, moved into the reserve around San Quintín and

Ocotal and began clearing land to plant corn. The government, meanwhile, granted a legal land title to a squatter community called Indio Pedro in the reserve's supposedly untouchable core zone. There were also land invasions from Marqués de Comillas and from a Tzeltal village called Palestina; the government did nothing.

By March 1996, the Comunidad Lacandona was beginning to split along ethnic lines. A group of Lacandones, including Kinbor, ousted community leader Carmelo Paniagua because he was making too many concessions to the Choles and Tzeltales who wanted to cut down more of the forest. Chol and Tzeltal leaders responded by threatening to split up the Montes Azules Biosphere Reserve and begin clearing the jungle.

The government seemed to be accelerating the destruction by signing a limited agrarian reform agreement with peasant organizations in March 1996 and then sending the police to dislodge peasants who had invaded privately held lands that were not included in the accord. Eight people were killed and dozens were wounded in clashes between police and peasants.

With the government taking a hard line against those who invaded privately held land and turning a blind eye toward those who moved into the reserve, the strategy seemed to be to buy peace for a few more years by sacrificing the remaining jungle. The future looked bleak. One must have a heart of stone not to sympathize with a peasant's basic struggle for a bit of productive land. Still, as I rode home in a motorboat down the swollen Lacuntún River, I found myself trying to comprehend the staggering loss if what remained of the rain forest were turned into cornfields.

After two weeks of heavy rain, the river itself was as muddy as the Mississippi. Enormous tree trunks turned cartwheels through the water. On the right bank the jungle rose as an impenetrable wall. From a boat it looked still and beautiful. I watched two macaws fly awkwardly above the trees, their black silhouettes turning to red and blue when they passed between the sun and forest. The clouds spread across the enormous sky, turning ominously dark as they stacked up against a distant ridge. A feisty chicken belonging to one of the passengers threw itself overboard. We circled back and rescued the bird.

I was let off in a small town called Nuevo Tenejapa. From there it was a three-hour walk to Flor de Café, where the road from the city of Comitán ends. I struggled to keep up with a young couple who were traveling from Chajul to Comitán for a doctor's appointment. The trail was a maze of rocks and mud. If I took a wrong step I sank in up to my knees. After two hours, I stepped onto a bluff and saw an enormous pasture-covered valley. Below me was a dirt road weaving through valleys off into the distance. This was the border of the Zapatista zone, and somewhere to the north, perhaps along the same ridge, the rebels were hiding. I could not help but be reminded of Eduardo Monteverde's comment of more than a year before—that there was not enough jungle left to make war. After a long, hard trip I had come to a different conclusion: there is not enough jungle left to make peace.

—five—
The New Treasure
of the Sierra Madre

The ritual drinking party had been going all night and a new round of guests had arrived with the morning sun. Some of the most revered men of the community lay face down in the dust, too drunk to stand. The newcomers crowded around an enormous earthen pot full of a frothy, fermented corn beer that was being doled out by a smiling, red-faced host. He passed two tiny crosses over the drinking gourd, blessing the beverage in his native Tarahumara.

As far as the Tarahumara Indians are concerned, it is never too early for a swig of *tesguino*. Tesguino—the name of both the fermented corn beer and the get-together at which it is drunk—is a sort of cultural glue that binds the Tarahumara together. Business is transacted, community issues are discussed, ailments are analyzed, appointments are made. Men, women, children, visiting journalists, all are invited, indeed expected, to share in this small bounty.

I took the gourd of tesguino offered to me and looked around at a dozen smiling faces eager to see how I would respond. I drank it in a single swig, as I had seen them do. It was highly carbonated, sweet and bitter at the same time. I poured the remaining sediment on the ground and handed the gourd back to my host. He filled it, blessed it again, and handed it this time another member of the drinking party—a young girl who was not more than ten years old. Even though the sun had crested over the forested hillsides I had the sensation that I had just walked into a dark room and my eyes had not yet adjusted.

Fights and misunderstandings, I soon learned, are common at tesguinos. The night before, Gumercindo Torres had suddenly stood up, punched two people in the face, and then wandered off into the darkness. He staggered across a plowed cornfield, crossed a dry arroyo, and stumbled up the embankment to his small house. A red and white Jeep Wagoneer was parked out front. Gumercindo, even in his drunken state, recognized the vehicle—it belonged to his boss, Edwin Bustillos. Bustillos is the director of Casmac, a regional environmental organization fighting the drug traffickers and loggers who are terrorizing the Tarahumara and destroying Chihuahua's ancient forest.

Gumercindo had heard that a gringo was visiting and set out to find him. I was sleeping in the schoolhouse. Sometime after midnight, I awoke to a loud banging on the door. Gumercindo swaggered into the room. "Who gave you permission to sleep here?" he demanded. I could tell he was looking for a fight but I did not know he was armed. Luckily, I greeted him enthusiastically, shaking his hand and introducing myself. The next morning, despite mumbling about his raging hangover, Gumercindo was back at the tesguino lolling in the sun. The previous night's events were forgotten.

One of the most liberating aspects of a tesguino is that in Tarahumara culture one is not responsible for one's own behavior when drunk. Public drunkenness is an exalted state in which every action is forgiven. Murder, as the Tarahumara understand it, is when a sober person kills someone to steal his property—that is a heinous crime and is duly punished. If someone attacks another with a knife or a gun or a rock at a tesguino, that is closer to an accident. If someone dies, the killer will be made to work for the family of the victim for a week or so and pay a small fine. If it happens twice, the punishment will not be much more severe. If it happens three times, only then will the offender be asked to leave the community. In the previous two years, there had been five tesguino-related murders in the isolated Tarahumara town of Pino Gordo.

At that moment, however, I felt safe because everyone seemed too drunk to cause any trouble. And besides, Lupe Rivas Vega was looking out for me. In two days we were leaving to hike through the three-thousand-foot deep canyon to Lupe's hometown of Baborigame. Lupe was to be my guide and armed escort, since we would be passing through an area full of drug plantations—places where the old-growth forest has been cleared to plant marijuana and poppies.

Like Gumercindo, Lupe works with Casmac. He is tall and light skinned, with shaggy sideburns and a thick mustache. His grandfather was an Arab who came to work in the mines of the Sierra Madre, but Lupe is culturally a Tepehuan Indian, a cousin of the Tarahumara. In his own community he had stood up to the loggers and drug traffickers, and they had tried to kill him. "I'll tell you about it later, this not the place," he said. "They learned that I don't die so easily."

Lupe handed me a gourd full of tesguino. "I killed a man," he said. "And I feel *muy macho.*"

I

The Sierra Madre Occidental, the chain of rugged mountains that extends from the U.S. border south of El Paso through the states of Chihuahua and Durango, is one of the most ecologically diverse areas in all of North America. There are as many as one hundred species of oak and twenty species of pine. In all, seven thousand different plant species have been catalogued, more than are found in a tropical rain forest.

This explosion of species is fueled by a series of deep canyons called *barrancas,* which extend into the mountains like the fingers of a giant hand. Over tens of millions of years, the rivers that drain the Sierra to the Pacific have gouged out the soft volcanic rock to a depth of between three thousand and five thousand feet. The Barranca del Cobre (Copper Canyon), along which a famous rail line runs, is deeper and wider than Arizona's Grand Canyon. As species spread across the fractured landscape, they evolved and adapted to microclimates and tiny ecological niches. There are thousands of endemic plants—found nowhere else in the world. In the barrancas, mesquite trees, fresnos, copal trees, and cactus dominate; oaks take over at higher elevations but make room for pines on the plateaus, which reach eight thousand feet. The pine forest is positively riotous—it is full of so many colors that it looks like the sort of picture drawn by a nine-year-old with a box of 128-color Crayolas. Ponderosa pines, with their orange-hued scaly bark, alternate with more exotic bushlike species with clusters of needles sprouting from the branches like water pouring from a fountain. *Tascaté,* a kind of juniper, is common in the mesas. There are so many different oaks in so many different sizes and colors that I could not believe they were all the same species. The trees were sometimes stunted and gnarled, sometimes expansive and soaring. Their bark ranged from black to beige; their leaves from dark green to red. The most psychedelic tree in the forest is the madrone, whose peeling bark is sometimes as red as a bad sunburn.

What is really mind blowing, however, is the wildlife—a bizarre mixture of species common to the northern pine forests and those more commonly associated with the jungle. In the forest, the familiar squawk of the Steller's jay can drown out the more subtle "koa, koa, koa" of the trogon, a colorful relative of the Guatemalan quetzal. Flocks of thick-billed parrots occasionally come screeching through the pines, while military macaws share the barrancas with eagles and hawks. The barrancas represent the northern limit of many tropical species; leaf-cutter ants meander across the trails; there are palm trees and figs; spiny-tailed iguanas and boa constrictors.

Sadly, many species have been wiped out or are severely threatened by logging and hunting. In the 1930s and '40s, sport hunters eliminated the grizzly bear from the region. The current practice in the Sierra regarding wildlife among both Indians and mestizos is to shoot first and ask questions later. Nearly every species big enough to eat is threatened. Deer, once abundant, are rarely spotted; the black bear, ocelot, and jaguar, and the very rare Mexican gray wolf, are generally shot on sight. Even squirrels are not terribly common.

For centuries the landscape itself was a kind of natural fortress for the Tarahumara. The Jesuits who came in the seventeenth century hiked through the Sierra until they found a few houses. They settled there and tried to convince the Tarahumara to live in towns and worship Christ. The Tarahumara liked some of the missionaries' ideas—the powerful symbol of the cross, which they incorporated into their ceremonies, and the reasonable-enough idea that there was a devil who was the source of all evil (although in Tarahumara mythology the devil is God's older brother).

They liked the goats and chickens the missionaries brought. But they did not want to live in towns.

Today, they still do not. In Pino Gordo, what passes for the town center is a single building—the school. The more than one hundred families who are part of the community live spread out in the woods, sometimes several hours' walk from their nearest neighbor. In their forested isolation, Tarahumara families have learned to produce or collect just about everything they need for survival. They clear a bit of forest by burning to plant corn and beans; they raise goats and chickens; they hunt occasionally; and they collect hundreds of plants from the ancient forest for food and medicine. Traditional Tarahumara lifestyle requires large expanses of relatively undisturbed woodland, something that has grown increasingly rare. In fact, less than 2 percent—420,000 acres (170,000 hectares)—of old-growth forest remains. Pino Gordo is one of the few Tarahumara communities in all the Sierra that has never been logged. That is why Edwin Bustillos is here.

"When I was a kid, Cabórachi was like Pino Gordo is today," Edwin told me. Cabórachi, where Edwin had grown up the son of prosperous farmers, is on the other side of the four-thousand-foot-deep *barranca sinforosa,* a two-day walk from Pino Gordo. As the only mestizo in the tiny schoolhouse in Cabórachi, Edwin had been teased mercilessly by his Tarahumara classmates. The forest was his refuge. When the teasing became unbearable, he would take sanctuary among the pines. Atanasio Cruz, a Tarahumara healer whose small house was near Edwin's favorite creek, had observed the lonely Edwin as he sat crying. He knew the boy had a good heart because he had had a dream about him.

After several months the old man invited Edwin to walk with him in the woods. "See that cactus," he said one day, pointing to a fuzzy green plant sprouting a red flower. "I want you to cut the flower." A few weeks later Atanasio took Edwin to a secret place where rare crystal-filled rocks called geodes could be found.

"After that I never had a problem with the kids," said Edwin. "Every time they wanted to hit me I showed them the rock and the flower and they left me alone."

At sixteen, Edwin left the forest for the jungle—the concrete jungle, that is. For the next decade, he was something of a professional student. He studied agricultural engineering at the University of Chapingo outside

Mexico City and then, in 1988, spent a year at Crown Business Institute in Manhattan. In 1990 he came home to the Sierra Madre and took a government job with the National Indigenous Institute (INI).

In 1989 the World Bank approved a $45.5 million loan to develop the forestry industry in Chihuahua and Durango. Most of the money was to go to road building. Project guidelines required that the Mexican government produce environmental and social studies of the region. Edwin was hired as a consultant.

With both technical training and nostalgia for a childhood spent walking in the woods, Edwin was in a unique position to evaluate the impact of the World Bank project. As he traveled through the Sierra, he was not encouraged by what he saw. Logging in the Sierra Madre began around the turn of the century but did not really take off until the 1940s and '50s. During those fifty years or so, much of the forest was divided into ejidos—holdings owned and managed collectively by the entire community. That was a good idea on paper, but in many communities a few mestizo residents began to dominate village affairs. They used their language skills and their ties to government officials to bully the Tarahumara into accepting them as leaders. Once they gained control of the ejido, they cut deals with the logging companies in Chihuahua or Parral. The companies built roads into the region to haul the timber out. They paid the ejidos on a per-foot basis for the trees they logged. It was not a lot of money. Loggers in the Sierra Madre used to walk into bars and order "a couple of pines." The bartender would plunk two beers down in front of them. One pine tree sold to the logging company earned enough to buy a single beer.

The most common method of logging practiced in the Sierra Madre is called "highgrading." Forestry officials survey the area to be logged and then mark the trees that can be legally cut. The trees selected are normally the largest and most mature. The result is a reverse natural selection and a genetic impoverishment of the forest. All the best trees are gone; those that reproduce are the runts. The problem is compounded by the fact that in many cases the forestry officials, the logging companies, and the ejido officials conspire to overcut the forest. Today, many Tarahumara ejidos are logging trees so small that they can serve as nothing but fence posts. Meanwhile, springs are drying up, medicinal plants are disappearing, and rains—so the old-timers say—are becoming more erratic.

The influx of mestizos who came along the logging roads also changed the Sierra culture forever. With logging work readily available, many Tarahumara entered the cash economy, quickly acquiring a taste for manufactured goods. New land pressures and government credits caused many Tarahumara farmers to switch from fallowing to using chemical fertilizers. When the bottom dropped out of the logging industry in the 1980s, many Tarahumara found that both the destruction of the land and their new taste for Western products made a return to a subsistence economy impossible. Many left the Sierra for the tomato fields in Sinaloa. Others entered the drug economy.

Logging and drug production, in fact, go hand in hand. The isolated, rugged terrain of the Sierra made it ideal for drug cultivation—and the new logging roads and landing strips provided an easy way to get the drugs out. A logging operation is also the perfect way to launder money because it allows the narcos to hide profits earned from the drug trade.

In the 1960s, drug producers began colonizing the Sierra—clearing small plantations on which they grew marijuana and poppies themselves or making agreements with Tarahumara who produced the drugs and then sold them to the traffickers in exchange for corn or liquor.

By the middle 1980s the Sierra Madre had became the second largest drug- producing region in the world, shipping billions of dollars worth of opium and marijuana to the United States. The traffickers grew increasingly violent and sophisticated, buying off or attacking police or soldiers who stood in their way. In the mid-1980s, the traffickers made alliances with the larger cartels, which had expanded into transshipment of cocaine from Colombia. Alexandro Fontes, a mestizo cacique from the Tarahumara ejido of Coloradas de la Virgen, became the leading drug trafficker in the region and eventually became the chief of the State Judicial Police. After his plane was shot down by the military in March 1986, Alexandro's brother Artemio stepped into his shoes.

By the early 1990s, Artemio Fontes had instituted a reign of terror in Coloradas de la Virgen. He forced families to grow marijuana and opium instead of corn. Thirty-seven people were killed between 1988 and 1993, and dozens of other families fled. In 1993 Fontes began to illegally log Coloradas's old-growth forests. According to Edwin, Fontes is also the secret owner of a logging company, which he uses as a money laundering operation.

All of this was not exactly what the World Bank wanted to hear. When the Mexican government tried to suppress the information Edwin was digging up, he resigned in protest in July 1992. A few months later, Edwin founded Casmac—the Consejo Asesor de Sierra Madre A.C. (Advisory Committee of the Sierra Madre). Randy Gingrich, who was working with the U.S. environmental group Forest Guardians, hooked up with Edwin and quickly nailed down $25,000 in seed money from the Biodiversity Support Program of the U.S. Agency for International Development. "Edwin had just quit a good job in Mexico on ethical grounds," recalled Randy. "I knew that he was the person I wanted to work with."

Casmac's goal is to work with Tarahumara communities that want to protect their forest. The program provides legal advice, training in sustainable agriculture, and small-scale development projects. It was never Edwin's intention to take on the drug traffickers. "Some of Edwin's best friends are narcos," joked Randy. The problem is that once the narcos move in, the Tarahumara lose control. Increased drug enforcement has forced the narcos deeper and deeper into the forest. They clear the woods through uncontrolled burning, destroying on the average sixteen hectares of forest to sow a one-hectare plantation. They often lose control of the fires as well, creating huge blazes, which, in the remote mountains, are left to burn themselves out. On the drive up from Chihuahua to Pino Gordo I had seen dozens of smoky fires rising above distant canyons. "Every one is going to be a drug plantation," said Edwin.

In the 1990s, Pino Gordo has been fending off the narco-loggers who have been moving into their community. The neighboring ejido, called Coloradas de los Chávez, is controlled by a mestizo named Gonzalo Loera who, in alliance with a Chihuahua-based logging company called Impulsora, had plundered the forest. According to Casmac, Loera is also involved in drug production.

Prudencio Ramos Ramos, the mayor of Pino Gordo, told me that Pino Gordo has been able to fend off the Loeras for now. But only a few hours after I talked with him, four armed men from Coloradas de los Chávez showed up in Pino Gordo and went trudging across a field in the direction of the tesguino. Half an hour later they returned with Lupe and Gumercindo—Casmac's promoters. At first, I was afraid that this was some sort of shakedown, but it was soon clear that it was just a social visit. The narcos hauled a case of beer out of the cooler in the back of their pickup truck and began blasting ranchero music on the car stereo. Gumercindo went into to his house to get his gun, and soon the gang was whooping it up, shooting at trees and rocks and generally having a good time. The narcos were friendly enough. One of them, a young mestizo with a 9-mm handgun tucked into his belt, came over to say hello and talk about the time he spent working on a ranch in Oklahoma. Still, I found the fact that Casmac's promoters would shoot around with these guys vaguely unsettling. One of the narcos, a Tarahumara carrying an automatic rifle, had a long chat with Pino Gordo's sheriff, which looked from my vantage point to be rather intimidating. Two days later, when Edwin showed up in Pino Gordo, I asked him what was going on.

"I am not against the drug traffickers," explained Edwin. "That would be futile and self-destructive. There are many drug traffickers who work with the communities—they ask the people to plant poppies or marijuana and they pay them a fair price for it. What I am fighting for is human rights—against the violence and destruction. If the community doesn't complain to me about the traffickers, then I don't get involved."

II

The next morning we were all a bit hung over. We had spent the night before standing around a campfire drinking some strange concoction that Gumercindo had brewed up and finishing off the last of Edwin's tequila.

That morning Gumercindo showed me his scar. The entrance wound was on his right hip, the exit wound on his left. In November 1992, Artemio Fontes's gunman had burst into the church in Coloradas de la Virgen, where Gumercindo and his brother Luis were praying. The two brothers had become Edwin's most important allies in his effort to wrest control of the town from Fontes. Luis Torres was killed in the attack; Gumercindo survived only because the women in the church threw themselves on top of him. He was carried to the airstrip at Baborigame and put on a plane to Parral. There, he spent three months in the hospital. After he recovered, Edwin brought him to Pino Gordo to recuperate and hide out from his enemies. Gumercindo spent months in bed. Medical doctors predicted that he would never walk again.

But Agustín Ramos, an old healer in Pino Gordo, was not ready to give up. He scouted the forest for medicinal plants; Gumercindo drank herbal infusions and applied compresses while Agustín chanted in Tarahumara. Today, Gumercindo walks without a limp.

After breakfast, we packed our knapsacks for the hike to the town of Baborigame on the other side of the barranca. Lupe kept reminding me that he could do the hike in one day but that it would take me three. I was excited to be venturing into the forest. To me, the woods had always been a sanctuary, a place I went to escape the city, to think, to be transported from my daily life. But in the Sierra Madre I needed to make a mental adjustment because the forest here also served another function—it was a refuge from the law, a place where the narcos ruled and the good guys fought back with guns. Lupe picked up an M-14 (a Korean war–era automatic rifle), while Edwin, who was to accompany us as far as the next town, shoved his 9-mm handgun down his pants. You never know who you might meet on the trail.

Then, just as we were leaving, Diana Venegas made us all listen. She and Ramiro Uranga had arrived with Edwin the night before. The two biologists were planning to spend the next few weeks scouring the remaining old-growth forest for signs of the imperial woodpecker. There had been no sighting of the bird—the largest woodpecker in the world—for a decade. Many ornithologists now classify it as extinct. We looked up in the tree where Diana pointed. It was not the imperial woodpecker but another rare bird—the eared trogon. It flew from its perch, its long green tail feathers flowing behind it. We picked up our bags and began our walk. This sighting seemed like a good omen.

As soon as we were in the forest, Lupe, as I had asked him to do, began pointing out the different medicinal plants. The small yellow flower of the lechugilla plant is made into an alcohol rub and applied to bruises; an infusion made from the green-striped leaves of the small encenilla plant is used to relieve kidney pain; the oval-shaped leaf of one variety of madrone can be brewed into a powerful tea that lowers a fever.

At the top of a ridge we stopped to gaze down over the endless forest spreading out across a series of smaller ridges. Lupe offered to let me fire his M-14. I do not like guns, but I wanted to give it a try because they seemed so much a part of the Sierra culture. Every fourteen-year-old boy learns how to handle a rifle. I rested the heavy wooden stock against my shoulder, lined up a large rock in the sights, and gently squeezed the trigger. I have no idea where the bullet hit. All I know is that the explosion made my ears ring for half an hour. That was enough of gun culture for me. I handed the gun back to Lupe, who thoroughly chastised me because I forgot to put the safety back on.

We scrambled down the ridge into a small valley of juniper and pine. Half an hour later we came across a devastated landscape where trees had been felled and acre after acre of forest had been ravaged by fire. Narcos, Edwin pronounced. They would probably be back to plant before the rains came. After several more hours hiking through the shady forest, Edwin veered off the trail and hopped a split-rail fence. A small field of poppies grew next to a cornfield. The poppies had probably been planted by a Tarahumara who sold the opium gum he collected to a middleman; the fleshy bulbs that support the fluttering orange and red flowers bore the spiral scar from the shallow incision made to collect the gum. Edwin picked a flower, turned it upside down, and shook it. Black seeds rained into my hand. Where had I seen these seeds before? I know—on a bagel!

We stopped in a small Tarahumara settlement called Mesa de los Pinos, where Lupe had been living and hiding out since fleeing his hometown of Baborigame. Edwin wanted to talk to the community about building a school, and so, partially to provide food for the meeting and partially to fortify us for the long walk ahead, we decided that we should slaughter a goat. I am not sure whether Lupe asked me to hold it down while he slit its throat just because I was standing next to him or because he thought it would be amusing to give the gringo a nasty job. (The day before, I had been handed a live chicken and knife and given one word of instruction: lunch.) Lupe expertly skinned and butchered the goat until all that was left was the bloody head dangling from a rope looped around its horns. We built a fire and then threw the meat on the burning coals to cook it.

A mangy dog straggled up and began sniffing around. I picked up a small rock and threw it at the dog to scare him off. What had happened to me? After less than a week in the Sierra I found myself throwing a rock at a dog to keep him from eating the goat I had just helped slaughter. At first I did not like that image of myself, but then it occurred to me that this was a less romantic function of the wilderness—not solace, but freedom to break the rules. Besides, the people I was with saw my behavior as entirely normal. If I had let on that I normally did not approve of pelting dogs with rocks, my companions would have been either baffled or amused.

After lunch we sat in a dusty clearing, staring into the barranca. "That's what you're going to have to cross," said Edwin as a fierce wind rocked the trees. Actually we had to cross two canyons; the first one was formed by the river that ran from Coloradas de los Chávez. We would have to climb down two thousand feet to get to the streambed, and then we would walk along it until we got to the Túpure River. There we would make a U-turn and head up to the Mesa de los Martínez. The two rivers had left an enormous peninsula of rock in the middle, which reached into the canyon like a giant tongue. Fires rose from the depths of the canyon— again future plantations. On the other side, we could see a large clearing where the forest had been scraped away. A small house was perched on the ledge. This was the home of Trinidad Urtusuastegui—known simply as Doña Trini—who controlled drug production in the region. Already she had killed seven Tarahumara, according to Edwin, either because they stood up to her or because she coveted their land. I had always imagined that drug production was controlled by organized gangs that fed the cartels, but in this remote region it was simply the person with the most firepower who ran the show. Edwin estimated that Trini made about $50,000 a year, enough to pay the salaries of seven well-armed gunmen.

Artemio Fontes, on the other hand, had moved out of mere production and into smuggling, where the real money was made. He was worth millions. "The first time I went to Coloradas de la Virgen when I was working for the government, I had a meeting with the people there and Fontes showed up," recalled Edwin. "He said, 'I need to speak with you in private.' He had gold chains around his neck, gold in his belt, a gold hat band, gold in his cowboy boots—gold everywhere. I estimate he was wearing about $100,000 in gold. Fontes took me aside and said, 'Mr. Bustillos, let me explain how things work. I control things here. So I give you money and you do what I want.'"

Obviously, Edwin did not take Fontes up on his offer. Just the opposite, against all the odds, and at grave danger to his own life, he decided to take Fontes on. He has already paid the price. In October 1993, soon after

Casmac stopped Fontes's illegal logging operation in Coloradas de la Virgen, municipal police from the town of Guachochi, who Edwin thinks were linked to Fontes, dragged Edwin from his car and beat him nearly to death. Edwin had lost his left eye in a childhood accident, and the police beat him repeatedly around his one good eye. Edwin was blind for four days. No sooner had he recovered than a truck came up behind him and forced him over a three-hundred-foot embankment. His left arm was crushed, his ribs were broken, and his spine was severely damaged.

Edwin survived, but his left arm and his back will probably never recover. He walks stiffly, like a boxer the day after a fight. Gumercindo had barely survived and his brother Luis was dead. Lupe was an outlaw—and other volunteers had been beaten and threatened. The Fontes cartel had been weakened, but Fontes himself, despite an order for his arrest, was living comfortably in his mansion in Chihuahua. Could Casmac really have an impact? What would prevent new narcos from moving in, even if the old ones were taken down? Army patrols and helicopter raids had barely put a dent in production—what good were a few hundred soldiers and a bunch of corrupt cops against one of the most powerful markets in the world? As Edwin saw it, they were helpless. But if he could knock out the biggest and most violent drug lords, then the Tarahumara ejidos could regain control of their forests. They would certainly continue to grow drugs on a small scale, but the Tarahumara, unlike the drug lords, would have little interest in opening up the forest to logging. This was Edwin's vision.

He was going back to Pino Gordo, and I was heading down into the canyon. Edwin and I shook hands. Lupe, carrying his M–14 as always, and Manuel, who had tied a bloody goat leg onto the back of his pack, and I went down the narrow trail. That night we roasted the leg on an open fire.

III

In 1519, before the arrival of Cortés, Mexico was a country of trees. Pine-oak forests extended across the central plateau—from Veracruz to Michoacán and Guerrero and south to Oaxaca. They reached northward across the deserts in two enormous mountain chains—the Sierra Madre Occidental and Oriental. In the heavily populated valleys, the trees provided firewood and lumber for construction, and burning was common to clear

areas for farming. But without metal tools, grazing animals, or any industry that consumed large amounts of timber, the forests were exploited in
moderation. Three-quarters of the national territory was covered by forest.

That changed dramatically after the conquest; by 1550 the Indians
around Taxco in modern-day Guerrero were complaining to the authorities that trees had been stripped to use in the mines. By the end of the
century, Indian communities around all the logging centers had lodged
similar complaints. The mines consumed enormous amounts of timber,
used for bracing the shafts and burning in the smelters. By 1600 not a tree
was left standing in the previously wooded hills around Zacatecas, and
firewood had to be brought from distant regions by mule. The building
of Mexico City and other colonial cities also put a terrible strain on the
forests. In fact a lawsuit was filed against Cortés for cutting too many trees
to build his palace in Mexico City. Forests were also cleared to make way
for the cattle herds. The result was widespread desertification. Forested
areas in Tlaxcala, Guanajuato, Oaxaca, Zacatecas, Guerrero, Hidalgo, and
the Valley of Mexico were permanently destroyed.

But accounts of the journeys by the friars into the wilderness suggested
that away from the area of Spanish settlement, large areas of woodland
were undisturbed. The friars described valleys full of oaks, pines and ce-
dars; they commented on the rabbits and deer and on the clear streams full
of fish. Baron Alexander von Humboldt, the German naturalist who visited Mexico at the beginning of the nineteenth century, marveled at Mexico's enormous resources and estimated that half of the country's territory
was covered with woodland (still, a dramatic decline from the time of the
conquest). But Humboldt also noted the terrible damage where the forests
had been clear-cut. "The crumbling hills have increased . . . the violence
of the floods," he wrote. French naturalist Jean Louis Berlandier, who traveled from Veracruz to Mexico City in 1823, described enormous stretches
of wooded wilderness where "everything is fertile." He saw monkeys,
jaguars, raccoons, wolves, coyotes, rabbits, and birds everywhere, and was
amazed that the deer approached him without fear.

Not until the 1860s did Mexico begin to take action against the destruction of its forests. But the first forestry law passed under President
Benito Juárez was limited in scope (it applied only to public lands) and was
never enforced. A government circular published in 1880 by the Secretariat

of Development noted that uncontrolled destruction of the forests had caused climatic change, air pollution, the drying up of springs, erosion, and the loss of agricultural land as well as increased flooding. The construction of the railroads during the Porfirian era greatly increased the demand for lumber, used both for railroad ties and as fuel for the locomotives. The railroads also opened up new areas of the country to development and logging. In 1895 the first logging company was founded in Mexico.

In the aftermath of the revolution, one of Mexico's greatest environmentalists, Miguel Angel de Quevedo, began to have increasing influence on the nation's forest policy, and for a brief time destruction was curtailed. Quevedo, who had been trained in France, founded a forestry school in the Mexico City suburb of Coyoacán in 1914. He was concerned that the destruction of forests was damaging the nation's watersheds and aquifers. He was instrumental in getting a comprehensive forestry law passed in 1926, which used Article 27 of the 1917 constitution as the basis for the state's asserting broad control over forest use. Quevedo was appointed head of the autonomous forestry department under President Lázaro Cárdenas, and he convinced the president to ban logging in many parts of the country. The bans were expanded throughout the 1940s and '50s.

This conservationist policy was well intentioned, but it was not appropriate for Mexico at the time. During the 1930s, Cárdenas had distributed millions of hectares of forests to the ejidos. Then he told them they were responsible for their care and maintenance, and that logging was strictly banned. That did not go over well with the campesinos; they had fought and died to get control of the resources of their community—not so they could preserve them for the good of the nation, but so they could use them to feed their children. Zapata repeatedly mentioned access to the woodlands as the one of the principal goals of his insurrection.

Since legal logging was banned, many of the new ejidos cut deals with clandestine logging companies. These were not small-scale operations. The advent of the logging truck in the 1940s had opened previously inaccessible areas of the country. Logging roads were put in, sawmills were constructed, and the local authorities were bought off. Because the logging was illegal, it was geared toward short-term profit. There was no reforestation or management. Usually only the tree trunk was used, while the limbs were left on the ground to provide fuel for forest fires. And once the forests were gone, they were gone forever. Campesinos moved in with their corn crops and their animals, preventing the forests from regenerating. Much of Mexico State, Michoacán, and Guerrero were converted from forests to pasture in this way.

Legal, managed logging might have created an economic dependence on logging that would have given the campesinos an incentive to preserve the woods. Instead they saw the forest merely as potential farmland. When they could not find a logging company to help them out, they sometimes just burned the forest in order to clear it.

Beginning in the 1950s, the Mexican government tried to remedy the problem by lifting the logging bans and licensing both private and state-owned companies to log legally. In some instances, the government was able to control the worst abuses, but the logging industry had gained too much momentum to be stopped. Logging laws were widely ignored, and the logging companies continued to cut deals with ejidos or private property owners for the right to log a stand of forest. Because they did not own the land, they considered only short-term yields. And since government officials were getting a cut, they were not interested in enforcing the law.

Today, Mexico continues to clear as much as 2.5 million acres (1 million hectares) a year of forest—the highest rate of deforestation in the world. Most of the formerly forested highlands have been logged out. Once a sea of trees, the forest is now a series of scattered islands in the most remote and least accessible areas in Chiapas, Guerrero, and the Sierra Madre Occidental of Durango and Chihuahua, all of which are being logged. In fact, the Sierra Madre comprises two-thirds of Mexico's forested reserve.

Throughout the Mexican highlands, the forests anchor the whole ecosystem. Once the trees are gone and the corn farmers move in, erosion, floods, and a permanent loss of natural resources are the result. An equally important but less visible loss that comes with the destruction of the forest is the centuries of knowledge about medicinal and edible plants, which is stored in the historical memory of the native inhabitants. What has already been lost is incalculable, but Lupe's impressive knowledge of medicinal flora in the Sierra Madre gave me some sense of its dimensions.

As we descended into the barranca—scrambling down steep hillsides along a narrow, treacherous trail—the climate grew warmer until the cool pine forest was only a distant memory. We passed through an enormous number of vegetative zones and microclimates; every few minutes Lupe stopped to break off a twig or point to some flower. Hierba la juanita, a twiggy plant with red bark and small green flowers, is used to treat diarrhea. It is especially effective when mixed with lemon. An infusion made from guareche is used to treat bruises and broken bones. Tepeguaje is used for headaches. The thorny venorama is used for back or chest pain. The thick-barked copalquin tree will lower your fever; the red bark of the copal tree is used to treat coughs; a tea made from the bark of the fresno tree alleviates nausea. The barranca is full of more gynecological remedies than most ob-gyn wards: the flowering pasote can be made into a tea that relieves menstrual cramps; the red-flowered tabamin regulates menstruation; the brazilito de la sierra, when mixed with other herbs, is a potent fertility drug; pelo de la piedra is taken during labor to expedite childbirth. When I asked Lupe if there were any plants that could be used for birth control, he said that the woman should drink a glass of ice water immediately after sex. "It's a natural spermicide," he said. Lupe has five children.

Lupe's remedies were slightly different from those given me by a Tarahumara healer in Pino Gordo. They sometimes coincided and sometimes differed from those listed in Francisco Cardenal's authoritative book, *Remedies and Curative Practices in the Sierra Tarahumara*. That is not surprising, since knowledge about medicinal plants is transmitted orally—from parent to child, or from healer to pupil. Part of the explanation for the curative properties of plants involves magic, ritual, and folklore. Lupe is a Tepehuan Indian who learned about medical plants from his father (according to Edwin, Lupe is studying to be a healer). His tradition is different from that of his Tarahumara neighbors. Still, both cultures exploit the ecological diversity of their shared homeland. Over generations, the indigenous people have acquired knowledge about the medicinal qualities of more than three hundred and fifty plants, and new ones are discovered all the time. "If I see a plant I don't know, I taste it and see what it does," said Lupe. He recently discovered a plant that numbed his mouth—good for treating canker sores. Until recently, native knowledge about medicinal plants was of little interest to Western scientists. But in the 1980s and '90s biomedical companies have turned many indigenous treatments into Western medicine. Nearly a quarter of all medicines are derived from plants. South San Francisco–based Shaman Pharmaceuticals is devoted exclusively to developing medicine from medicinal plants used by indigenous cultures around the world.

Lupe's enthusiasm was contagious. I walked with notebook in hand, writing down a few brief lines about each plant Lupe showed me (I have included only a few here). As night fell, we were swallowed up by the canyon, two sheer cliffs of red rock rising on either side of us. The full moon rose, but we continued walking to take advantage of the cool night air. Springs soon filled the dry creek bed we were following, and we hopped from boulder to boulder to keep dry. The moonlight made it seem as if we were moving in slow motion, walking under water. Even though I could barely see, Lupe continued to collect plants from among the rushes that grew near the shore. I dutifully put them in my pack to catalogue in the morning.

We stopped at an abandoned farm and made camp under an orange tree. During our hike we had passed about half a dozen plantations where marijuana and poppies grew side by side in small plots. These belonged to poor Tarahumara families; Lupe said it was too dangerous to take me to the larger plantations planted by the narcos. As night was falling, we passed a large clearing where an army patrol had recently destroyed one of Doña Trini's poppy fields. The small stone house was abandoned, its Tarahumara owner a refugee in La Mesa de los Pinos. It was the same story at our campsite; we were sleeping in a destroyed drug plantation. The owner of the abandoned farmhouse was either dead or too terrified to came back; several dozen cows wandered about in the darkness and smashed through the underbrush.

While I rolled out my sleeping bag in the soft sand, Lupe went fishing in the creek. He returned an hour later with a handful of small trout. "There's no way to starve to death in this forest," he said. He did not seem so much to build a fire as to conjure one from the earth. One second there was nothing; the next a bonfire lit up the night. Lupe cooked the fish and then curled up around the embers to sleep as the night grew chilly. He was traveling without a blanket.

Every time we stopped to rest, Manuel pulled out a small tape recorder and began playing ranchera music, Mexican ballads of betrayal and life on the run from the law. As I drifted off to sleep, I listened to El Vampiro y Sus Fantasmas (the vampire and his ghosts) sing about El Bandido Generoso, the generous bandit, a heroic outlaw and his epic fight with the law. That was followed by a *corrido,* or Mexican ballad, from Chalino Sánchez, a narco who gained fame as a singer before he died in a shootout with police. I woke again in the middle of the night and stared up at a sky full of stars. Strangely, I had been dreaming about e-mail.

IV

Just up the canyon is the town of Tuáripa, a mixed Tarahumara, Tepehuan, and mestizo settlement renowned for having the most dangerous landing strip in the Sierra. We arrived in the late morning just as a small plane took off. It banked sharply and flew along the canyon wall before it pulled up and barely climbed over the rim. It had left behind supplies—bags of cornmeal were neatly stacked at the end of the airstrip. Nearby, I noticed a prosperous-looking mestizo in a cowboy hat and gold chains sitting in the bushes drinking, with a certain degree of determination, an entire case of warm beer. Already, half a dozen empties were strewn around his hiding place. He nodded at me as I walked by.

Lupe's cousin lived a mile up the creek in a one-room adobe house. Lupe had left two of his children here in the care of his cousin, but after a week apart they greeted their father with such restraint (as is the Tepehuan custom) that it took me a few hours to realize that these were his children. Ten-year-old Juan looked like a Mexican version of Huck Finn; he was light skinned and freckled, wearing a palm hat and, like Lupe, a large knife tucked into his belt. His younger brother, Alvino, was armed with only a slingshot, from which no creature winged or furry was safe. The two of them came and went without warning. One moment they were playing in front of the house, the next they were scrambling along the creek.

Manuel, as usual, pulled out his tape recorder and began playing rancheras. We rested in the shade, watching two eagles circle above the cactus- and scrub-covered hillsides. "Probably looking for a goat," said Manuel. The trail we would climb the next day went straight up the canyon wall. "There's hardly any water," said Manuel. "I don't know if you're going to make it."

The Tarahumara's isolated existence has made them incredible runners and walkers. They can hike thirty miles up and down a barranca with a forty-pound sack of corn on their backs. Running is their official sport;

children will run for miles through the woods kicking a wooden ball in front of them. By the time they get to be adults, such endurance becomes a more serious business. A Tarahumara routinely bets his most essential possession (such as the ox he uses to plow his field) on running a race between villages.

One Tarahumara creation myth tells how God made the Tarahumara from clay while the devil created whites from clay and white ash. God and the devil then organized a foot race between the two, which was won by the whites. God was angry that the Tarahumara had lost. From that moment on, He vowed, the whites would be rich and the Tarahumara would be poor. Perhaps God will be happy that a delegation of Tarahumara recently won a rematch. In 1993, led by fifty-five-year-old Victoriano Churro, Tarahumara runners wearing huaraches made from old car tires finished first, second, and third in the Leadville, Colorado, 100-mile ultra-marathon. Over the years, the Tarahumara have learned that the longer the race the better when it comes to competing against the *chabochi,* as they call white people. Tarahumara runners who raced in the 1928 Olympics had to be stopped by race officials when they continued running after they crossed the finish line. "Too short, too short," they complained.

Perhaps it is this history, or perhaps it was just a friendly ribbing, but Manuel was constantly on my case about my deficiencies as a hiker. Although I may not rank high in the other realms of Tarahumara masculine virtue—drinking, fighting, and siring children—hiking is something I can do. "I don't walk like a Tarahumara," I told Manuel defensively. "But I'm pretty good for a gringo."

In the afternoon, we all went down to the river to bathe and wash our clothes. Lupe changed out of the sweatshirt he was wearing, which had probably been donated to some Christian charity in Iowa and, through a series of middlemen, ended up for sale in a used clothing shop in remotest Mexico. On the front it read "Jesus Is Better Than Santa Claus." On the back it said "Time to Sing Joysongs for the Lord." Lupe does not read English. The sweatshirt was replaced by what amounted to a military uniform except for the huaraches—dark green pants, a military jacket, a camouflage baseball cap. "If we run into a military patrol they're going to kick the shit out of me," said Lupe. "I'm dressed exactly like them and I don't have a permit for my gun."

That night, as the sun disappeared behind the canyon wall, Lupe decided it was time to tell me about the night of October 24, 1994, when he killed one man and wounded another. It all started in June 1992 when a three-person commission from the ejido of Baborigame traveled to Mexico City to investigate what appeared to be a fraud perpetrated against the ejido. According to Lupe, a corrupt ejido administration had conspired with a logging company in Parral to illegally log the ejido and pocket the proceeds. The three-person delegation, of which Lupe was a member, also discovered the administration had taken out a 464,000 peso loan from the government-run rural development bank, and the money had disappeared. The leader of the alleged scam was Cirilo Ríos, a part-time narco who grew poppies up on the mesa. Backing the narcos was the town priest, Francisco Chávez Acosta. Lupe charged that the priest used his plane to fly the narcos around. In a letter to Father Luis Verplancken, the respected priest who directs the Tarahumara mission, Randy Gingrich wrote that the townspeople in Baborigame allege "that Padre Francisco Chávez is corrupt and is damaging their culture, dividing their communities. They further allege that he is a cacique and that his conduct is immoral—accusations abound of sexual misconduct, alcohol abuse, interference in land issues, drug trafficking, embezzlement of church funds, and arms trading. The accusations against him are very strong, there are many witnesses."

In the fall, as the investigation into the embezzlement scheme began to make headway, Cirilo Ríos started getting nervous. So he hired Lupe's old enemy, Isidro Ramos, to do him in. "Isidro was bragging all over town that he was going to kill me," said Lupe.

The showdown took place at a tesguino when everyone was a little drunk. Isidro Ramos had come armed with a knife—he stood up and suddenly lunged at Lupe without warning. Ramos slashed at Lupe seven times, but aside from the wound to his armpit the attack did little damage. Lupe pulled out a .38 special he was carrying and got off two shots, wounding Ramos before a crowd threw itself on top of him and wrestled the gun away. Ramos's wife got hold of the gun and took one shot at Lupe before he managed to escape. But no sooner had Lupe gotten away from Ramos than he was caught in an ambush. Cirilo Ríos and his brother Alberto were waiting for him outside the tesguino, armed with a rifle. Lupe scrambled through the darkness and then jumped the Ríos brothers, again wrestling the gun away. He turned the rifle on Alberto and killed him with a shot to the chest as Cirilo looked on. Then he high-tailed it into the woods. Although no official charges have been filed, Lupe is an outlaw in Baborigame. If he shows his face there, he will be shot or arrested.

Ever since that night, Lupe has lived as a fugitive. He spends most of his time in the Mesa de los Pinos, doing work for Casmac, but you never know where you might find him. If he goes home to see his family, he goes at night and leaves before dawn. He never goes anywhere without his gun. "If I see one of my enemies on the trail, I keep him in my sights, and then I walk away backwards," said Lupe. "If he raises his gun, I'll shoot him. If they arrest me, I know someday I'll get out of jail. Once I'm dead, I'll never get out from under ground."

That night we slept like children at a slumber party, spread out across the floor of the small adobe hut. Manuel, Lupe, his two children, several other Tarahumara and I shared the same blankets. At four in the morning, the fire in the corner of the house began to glow when Lupe's cousin's wife stoked it to begin making tortillas. By five thirty, we were on the trail, scrambling through the deciduous forest, full of what Lupe called jarrilla trees, cactus, and nopales. Lupe's children led the way, laughing and clowning around as I trudged, step after careful step, along the narrow trail that clung to the canyon wall. Alvino, Lupe's youngest, carried a sprig of palm. "What's that for?" I asked Lupe. "We bless it and then we use it in ceremonies," he said vaguely.

Lupe continued pointing out medicinal plants: tea made from the green bark of the torote reduces inflammation; the mesquitelike cacachil tree will bring down a fever; the scrubby hierba de tigre is used for earaches. Lupe eyed me with amusement when I put purification tablets in water we scooped from a spring. "I never worry about getting sick," he told me. "If I get diarrhea, I cure it with plants."

Within hours, the scrub had given way to an oak forest; by noon we spotted our first pine. The air cooled as we approached the rim of the barranca; by early afternoon we were resting on some rocks, back in the shady and familiar pine forest. From here to Baborigame, Lupe pronounced, it was all downhill.

Lupe mentioned that his enemies, the narcos from Baborigame, had a plantation just a few hundred yards away. I decided to take a look. The other members of the party pushed ahead, while Lupe pulled a black Zapatista-style ski mask out of his pack. He clicked off the safety of his gun and climbed up onto a small embankment to cover me as I snuck down a dry arroyo. I heard voices as I approached the poppy field hidden from sight beyond another small rise. Then I heard something move in the bush. I looked up and saw Lupe emerge from behind a tree. He had thrown a rock to get my attention and was now waving frantically for me to retreat. I ran as best I could with my blistered feet, scrambling up the hill where Lupe had kept lookout. "The compañeros are there, working," said Lupe. "You catch up with the others on the trail. I'm going to check things out."

He bounded off into the woods like a deer, a terrifying sight, surely, dressed in military fatigues, carrying his M-14, his face covered in a ski mask. We moved quickly along the trail for the next hour, with Lupe covering our back just in case the narcos decided to come after us. We sped through some of the most beautiful forest of the whole trip; the trail wound about enormous pines and along ridges that offered a spectacular view of the barranca. After an hour, we decided we were in the clear and stopped in a dell next to a small creek to eat a lunch of pinole—a drink made from water and cornmeal—and tortillas and beans we had hauled form Tuáripa. At the top of the next ridge, we hit a logging road that would take us to Baborigame. Here Lupe said good-bye. It was too dangerous for him to walk out in the open this close to town—this was the same road the narcos used to get out to their plantations. Lupe had become a forest creature, half hunted, half hunter. He avoided clearings where his enemies could take him by surprise. The forest was his refuge, his sanctuary; to those who knew its secrets it was full of edible plants, clear streams, and a veritable pharmacy of natural remedies. There, Lupe could hide out forever. He called to Juan and Alvino and they disappeared down a trail, back into the woods, like rocks vanishing into a pond.

V

Baborigame is a town of silent, brooding men. They gather in the afternoons, and early on Sunday, in front of the stores, on dusty street corners, around pickup trucks blaring ranchera music. All the men dress the same, in sombreros, western shirts, flared jeans, and cowboy boots. To be clean shaven is considered effete; a mustache is as much a part of a man's face as his nose. The street is a man's realm; women are scarce. You find women in church, in the market, and standing in the doorways of their homes.

Baborigame is also a town of bloody feuds—you can sense it. All heads turn and stare silently when a new person walks into a room. Conversation with strangers is limited to *buenos días.* What most would call chit-chat is considered unduly invasive. It is no one's business what your name is, where you come from, what you do for a living. The surest way to make enemies in Baborigame is to ask too many questions.

Baborigame is one of the main areas of drug production and is therefore a center of the drug-fighting effort. There is a large army base in the middle of town, and the Judicial Police have an office. In a town full of *cabrones* (tough guys), the *Judiciales* are *más cabrones.* They cruise around in a white pickup truck carrying machine guns, their side arms hitched in their belts. On Saturday afternoons and all day on Sunday they are likely to be drunk. That was why Loreto Rivas Vega was lying low. Loreto, the Casmac promoter in Baborigame since Lupe went on the run, had been called in for a meeting with the Judiciales the day before I arrived. They told him they had received three reports that he owned an AR-15, a knock-off of the M-16 automatic rifle, and that he had two days to turn it in or they would *"partirle la madre"*—fuck him up good. Loreto insisted he did not own the rifle, and that his enemies—the same folks who had tried to kill Lupe—were out to get him. Loreto borrowed 100 pesos (fifteen dollars) from me an hour after I arrived because the Judiciales wanted to talk to him again and he wanted to have money in case he needed to pay a bribe. It turned out they just wanted to remind him that time was running out. When I asked for the money back the next morning, Loreto said he had spent it on beer.

On Sunday, I decided to check in on Father Francisco Chávez Acosta, known in the town as "Pancho Cura," Frankie the Priest. He was in the church saying mass. A crowd of women (the men were off drinking) overflowed the church into the plaza.

After mass, I introduced myself to Chávez. He is tall, handsome, with dark curly hair and, of course, a thick mustache. "I've been in this parish since 1972," he told me. "I'm a native of this area—the only priest who speaks both Tepehuan and Tarahumara."

I waited in the pews of the one-room church as Father Chávez baptized half a dozen babies, speaking to the parents in Tepehuan. One woman had asked Chávez to be the godfather of her child. Chávez placed a cloth on the floor of the church and knelt down across from the mother. They passed the infant back and forth, making the sign of the cross and patting each other on the shoulder.

"We're having a picnic today in the countryside to celebrate the first communion," said Chávez to me after the service. "Maybe you'd like to come with us."

I hopped in the back of his new pickup truck with a group of excited teenagers—mostly girls in short dresses and cowboy hats. "You drink beer?" asked the padre, handing me a cold can of Modelo Especial and cracking one for himself. We drove through the town and into the treeless countryside where the wind blew the earth into dust devils that spun back and forth on the dry cornfields. Past the sawmill and gas station, the forest began. It had been highgraded; all the big trees had been removed and many areas were cleared. Still, the grove where we stopped under an enormous gray cliff was a pleasant enough place for a picnic.

Father Chávez and I sat under some pines; a nun delivered two overflowing plates of picnic fare. The padre had had some seminary training in the United States and spoke passable English. I asked him what he thought was the greatest problem his parishioners faced. "Survival," he said. "Lack of employment. Every year the earth produces less—people die here if they don't have fertilizers. And of course the deforestation here is monstrous."

And drug-related violence?

The priest stopped eating for a moment and stared at me. "Who do you work for?" he asked. "The DEA?"

After I assured him that my interest was entirely journalistic, he began to talk. "Edwin Bustillos has exaggerated the drug problem here for his personal reasons. He's looking for publicity to help his program. There are some drugs grown around here, but the Indians rent the land and then they help grow the drugs. The drug traffickers get together with the Indians—they work together."

What about Artemio Fontes? What about Doña Trini who had driven the Tarahumara off their lands?

"I've never heard of this Trini, and the problem in Coloradas de La Virgen is much reduced," said the priest. "I was threatened with death in 1984 for helping the Tarahumara there.

"Historically, the problem in this region has been the army," Chávez went on. "Up until five years ago, I got complaints all the time that the army would come and break into people's houses and beat them to find out where the drugs were being grown. I had to found a human rights office here. I remember this general, General Fonseca, accused me of helping the traffickers. He called me into the base and he said to me, 'How come you're always defending the narcos? By the way, where did you get the fancy new pickup truck?' Well, I belong to an organization called the Catholic Church. The bishop gave me the money to buy that truck." The same was true of the small plane Chávez piloted around the Sierra. I later confirmed that it was indeed loaned to him by the bishop's office.

The army, Chávez said, was behaving itself, and the violence was greatly reduced. As for Lupe, Chávez said, he had nothing against him and no particular interest in the murder case. But it was not, as Casmac claimed, a question of self-defense. He took my notebook from me and began drawing a diagram. "The tesguino took place at the house of Vicente Carrillo," he began. "The first fight was Lupe versus Isidro." He underlined both names. "Lupe's brother Macario had killed Isidro's brother—I can't remember his name—three years ago. So there was bad blood between them. Isidro couldn't have come to kill Lupe because he didn't have a gun—all he had was a knife. So Lupe shot Isidro, and then after they got the gun away from him he ran back to his house to get his rifle to finish Isidro off. On the way back, he ran into Alberto Ríos, who was carrying a gun. Lupe, in his drunken state, thought Alberto was coming to get him. He ordered Alberto to drop his gun, and when he didn't do it, Lupe shot him. It was murder, plain and simple."

Chávez's explanation made a bit too much sense for me to feel comfortable. If Isidro had been sent to kill Lupe, why had he come armed with a knife instead of a gun? Why hadn't Lupe mentioned to me that his brother had killed Isidro's brother? If Alberto Ríos was really waiting outside with a rifle to finish Lupe off if Isidro couldn't do the job, why didn't he just pull the trigger before Lupe got close enough to take the gun away? As I was ruminating over this, Chávez leaned toward me and asked how I had arrived in Baborigame. He had not seen me fly in at the airstrip, nor he had seen a vehicle parked in front of my hotel.

"I walked here," I stammered. I was thinking of Lupe. "From Pino Gordo." I described how I struggled to keep up with my Indian guides, how they kept ribbing me that a walk that was taking me three days they normally did in one.

Luckily, Chávez didn't ask me who my guides were. "They're like animals," was all he said, referring to the Indians' walking prowess. "Rational animals."

VI

I caught up with Edwin a week later, back in Chihuahua. The biologists had spotted a number of rare birds but found no sign of the imperial woodpecker. Agustín Ramos, the healer in Pino Gordo who had cured Gumercindo, told them he had seen the bird when he was a child, but "whenever the sawmills come the animals go."

"Where do they go?" Edwin asked.

"I don't know," said Ramos. "But they go. The plants go to the same place. Many things have gone."

"When I was child in Cabórachi," continued Edwin, his memories stirred by the old healer's discourse, "the Tarahumara depended on nature for everything, they were entirely self-sufficient. Then they started logging the forest and today it is completely logged out. In the interim, they have created a culture of dependency. They have to continue to cut down the pines in order to buy the beans that they can no longer grow. If they get sick, there are no medicinal plants or they have lost the knowledge of how to use them. They have to go to the doctor. They have no choice. I need to give them an alternative."

Edwin took on a different persona when we were not in the woods. We sat at his kitchen table drinking coffee. He was dressed in a plaid western shirt, revealing only a triangle of his white T-shirt at the neck. He looked officious, ready to take on whatever bureaucrat stood in the way of his project. Edwin smiles constantly—to make a point, to disarm his opponent. In the Sierra I had seen him get angry once. He had sat for a moment and stared at the ground. Finally, he looked up and a smile spread across his face. "I am angry," he announced.

The alternative that Edwin wants to offer the Tarahumara is a program of community reserves, economic diversification, biodynamic agriculture, and support in taking on the violent narcos who try to take over the communities. The trail I had walked from Pino Gordo to Tuáripa and on to Baborigame was the heart of what Edwin hopes will be a series of linked community reserves. Already, many of the ejidos were on board. In Pino Gordo, all but 6 of the 183 ejido members had voted in favor of the proposal. Within the reserves, logging would be prohibited or severely restricted. Traditional Tarahumara practices such as allowing animals to graze on the undergrowth and clearing the forest for agriculture had been developed when resources were more abundant. With the forest disappearing, Edwin hoped he could convince the villages to build pens for the animals and switch to more intensive cultivation. At his family ranch near Cabórachi, Edwin has installed a pilot agroecology training center where workshops are held with delegations from various communities. The idea is to teach people how to reduce the use of chemical fertilizers, restore degraded soils, and diversify production into fruits and vegetables. In areas where medicinal plants have been wiped out, Edwin is trying to convince communities to cultivate them themselves. "At first they find that idea amusing, but in the end they accept it," he said.

In order to make up for the loss of logging revenues, Edwin has proposed that Sierra communities develop more sustainable industries. One plan is to manufacture tool handles out of oak, which has been successful in the Zapotec community of Ixtlán, Oaxaca. Another is to promote ecotourism in the region. Casmac has already constructed a small hostel in Pino Gordo. Visitors, led by Tarahumara guides, would hike from one community to the other. Few tourists would probably want to venture into a region infested with drug traffickers, but if the situation improves, perhaps one day the hike I did will make it into the guidebooks.

A second alternative that is picking up steam is to create a biosphere reserve in the Sierra. The U.N.–funded biosphere program calls for the creation of a "core area" that would be maintained in a pristine state. In other areas, low-impact, sustainable development would be the goal. This is not much different from the community reserve program that Casmac already promotes, but the biosphere reserve would receive international recognition and funding. Edwin is lobbying government officials to get behind the project. In the summer of 1996 he was granted preliminary approval.

It is an ambitious program, especially when one considers that Chihuahua has almost no environmental culture (Casmac is virtually the only environmental group in the state), and powerful interests from narcos to the logging companies would be adversely affected by it. But my hike through the canyon had convinced me that it could work.

I had started the walk with a conception of wilderness developed during visits to U.S. national parks; a postindustrial wilderness preserved as a monument to a mythical past and a refuge from urban alienation. Mexico, however, is still using its wilderness. It is a resource it cannot afford to preserve for preservation's sake. A significant but rapidly shrinking number of Tarahumara and Tepehuans continue to rely on the forest for food and medicine; logging interests must be accommodated; the narco-economy has gained far too much momentum to be eliminated. The challenge is to convince all these interests that in the long run they depend on the survival of the forest. That will be no small feat. Logging as an industry generally recognizes the concept of sustainability, but unless it is effectively regulated, short-term profits usually win out. The outlaw drug economy is even harder to reach. It is, by its nature, geared toward short-term profit, and the concept of sustainability is anathema. The only solution is to target the violence or the environmental destruction rather than the drug production itself. Narcos who kill Tarahumara or burn the forest will run into problems with the authorities. Those who grow their crops peacefully without causing destruction should expect more benign treatment. It is a sort of de facto decriminalization. Active prosecution has no impact on production; all it does it foment a culture of violence and corruption and drive the narcos deeper and deeper into the forest.

Even getting the Tarahumara and Tepehuan communities to go along with the plan is not exactly easy. In Cabórachi, Gregorio Moreno, who runs the community-owned sawmill, is fighting with government authorities who have ordered the town to reduce logging. "The authorities are blocking us," he said. In the town of Aboreachi, which has already signed on to the community reserve program, Mayor Petronilo Bustillos complained that logging had stripped the forest of all the big trees and caused the streams to dry up, the animals to disappear, and the rains to become less frequent. But the town has become dependent on manufactured goods, and logging continues apace. When I asked whether Pino Gordo should consider logging, he said, "If they have big trees, I think so. There have been problems, but there have been many benefits."

The other serious obstacle for Casmac and its plan to protect the Sierra is the physical survival of Edwin and his personnel. Edwin has survived two assassination attempts. His house in Chihuahua has been shot up. Gumercindo was nearly killed; his brother Luis is dead. Lupe, meanwhile, is a wanted man. "After the fight, when Lupe was wounded, I went to see him in the mountains," said Edwin. "Immediately, he offered to resign. He didn't want his problem to affect the program. But you have to defend yourself. Some more of us might die, but some of them might die also."

Edwin insists that although Chihuahua State authorities have decided not to prosecute Lupe, Father Chávez, despite his denials, is leading the crusade against Lupe in Baborigame in order to discredit the Casmac program and protect his narco-buddies. My impression of Father Chávez was not wholly positive, but I did not find any evidence that he was involved in the drug trade, as Edwin alleged. Nor was I completely convinced that Lupe had told me the whole story.

Lupe, I realized, is a Mexican archetype as threatened as the imperial woodpecker. Like the men in the corridos that Manuel kept playing on his tape recorder during our walk, Lupe is a righteous outlaw. The cult of the outlaw thrives in a culture that values fierce independence, regional loyalty, and machismo and shares an overwhelming contempt for a meddling and corrupt central authority. During his early career as a horse thief, Chihuahua native Pancho Villa would hide out in the mountains where the Judiciales seldom ventured. There, far from any town, a gun was the law. Since the government has no moral authority, the ethos of the Sierra is that feuds are settled honorably by fighting it out. To kill someone in self-defense or in a fair fight carries little stigma. It is also why narco-culture has taken root so easily in the Sierra; it a place where guns, death, and life on the run were already deeply embedded.

In Baborigame I had talked to Felipe Molina, a mestizo who had served on the commission with Lupe to investigate the alleged fraud by former ejido officials. "We were getting so close, we were about to break the case open, and then this happened," he told me. "When Lupe ran away to the mountains, we sent a message that we wanted to meet with him in secret. We wanted to know if this really was an assassination attempt, because then our lives would be in danger. He also had some documents we needed for our investigation. But he never showed up."

I could tell that Molina missed Lupe, missed the work they had done together. In this hard culture, where death is met with a shrug, Molina's voice grew dim and I thought I saw a lump rise in his throat. "I don't know what happened on that night," he said. "But I do know this. What happened is between him and Isidro and Alberto Ríos. It's got nothing to do with me and Lupe; it's got nothing to do with our friendship."

Here, at last, was an explanation I could accept.

Postscript: In 1996 Edwin Bustillos was awarded the Goldman Prize, the world's top environmental award, for his work in the Sierra Madre.

—six—

Pemex: A State within a State

A few minutes before six in the morning on November 19, 1984, a massive explosion shook the 45,000 residents of Mexico City's San Juanico neighborhood. Hundreds never woke up. They were killed even before they realized what had happened. Enormous flames leapt from the nearby gas storage plant and shot a mile into the air. Bodies simply disappeared in the fireball, snatched from the earth without a trace. People ran through the street, some with their clothes and hair on fire, all screaming in fear. The sun had not yet come up, but the light from the flames lit up the scene as if it were noon. Whole families, in their pajamas and their underwear and even naked, dropped to their knees in the middle of the street and prayed. Some prayed for God to end the nightmare; others assumed that the end of the world had come and asked God only to take pity on their souls. The air smelled of gas and burned flesh.

Between six and nine in the morning, there were five explosions as the Pemex plant at San Juanico was blown to pieces. Enormous hunks of twisted metal landed more than a mile from the blast.

For Pemex, and for all of Mexico, the explosion marked the end of an era. For forty-six years, since Petróleos Mexicanos was created through the nationalization of foreign oil companies in Mexico, Pemex had been a source of national pride and a symbol of Mexican independence and know-how. The San Juanico explosion, coming on the heels of the collapse of international oil prices, and coupled with alarming reports of environmental destruction and massive corruption, changed the public perception of Pemex forever. Pemex was publicly excoriated, a symbol of everything that was wrong with both Mexico's political culture and the country's take-no-prisoners drive toward development. Environmental destruction became the battleground.

The roots of the crisis lay in the expectations created initially by the 1938 nationalization and then by the discovery of enormous oil deposits in the mid-1970s. Pemex had never been run as a business; its function as conceived by President Lázaro Cárdenas at the time of the nationalization was to foment the country's industrialization by producing oil and gas for national consumption. In the 1950s and '60s, the government promoted vertical integration of the oil industry. Pemex produced, refined, and distributed oil, gas, and petroleum products often at highly subsidized prices. This strategy provided employment and helped foster technological development. Cheap oil and gas were also an enormous boon to industry and the development of a consumer economy.

In the midst of the boom, however, Pemex was digging itself into an enormous hole. Since its mandate was to sell oil and gas cheaply for the domestic market, the company was not profitable and had no money to invest in exploration or even day-to-day maintenance. By the early 1970s, growing demand had forced Mexico to import oil from Venezuela. When oil prices skyrocketed in 1973 with the Arab oil embargo, Mexico found itself in deep trouble.

The trouble was soon washed away in a river of oil. In 1972 Mexico discovered a massive oil deposit in Tabasco on the Gulf Coast, and by the mid-1970s it began to exploit it. Over the next decade Pemex's role expanded from serving the national market to exporting oil to the world. Bankers flooded the country, lining up to lend Mexico money; governments from around the world sent delegations to discuss contracts. Mexico became a powerhouse in the developing world, and the billions of dollars in loans pegged to future oil earnings financed a decade of massive infrastructure investment. Mexico, its leaders firmly believed, would follow the rising price of oil into the first world.

Pemex's motto is "at the service of the nation," but with so much riding on the company's performance, the nation was put at the service of Pemex. As Mexico's economy began to depend more and more on oil exports, Pemex grew in power until it became an almost autonomous arm of the state, operating with few legal restraints and no public oversight. Corruption on the part of both the oil workers' union and Pemex officials was massive and allegedly reached directly into the presidential palace. Little effort was made to control the cost of production, limit waste, or invest in industrial safety or environmental controls. Enormous demands were made on campesinos and fishermen in Tabasco, Veracruz, Chiapas, and Campeche, where Pemex was drilling. If Pemex needed your land, it took it. If you complained that an oil spill wiped out the oyster harvest or your corn crop you were being selfish and unpatriotic, putting your personal needs above those of the nation. "Our only responsibility was to obtain the maximum production regardless of the cost," recalled a Pemex engineer who told me he would be fired if I printed his name. "No one gave a moment's thought to the environment."

But the environmental damage was piling up, especially around Villahermosa, Tabasco, where drilling operations were concentrated, and Coatzacoalcos, Veracruz, where refining and petrochemical production were rapidly expanding. Millions of gallons of industrial waste were discharged into the region's rivers and oceans; obsolete refineries sent enormous quantities of contaminants which damaged crops into the sky; oil spills and leaky pipelines fouled the oceans, coasts, jungles, and swamps; and industrial accidents cost dozens of lives.

Not only peasants found Pemex unresponsive when they complained about environmental damage. The U.S. government fared no better.

In 1979 an offshore well called Ixtoc I blew out in the Bay of Campeche. It spewed 30,000 barrels of crude oil a day into the ocean. By the time the spill was capped, 3.1 million barrels of oil and 3 billion cubic feet of gas had fouled the entire gulf—more than ten times the amount that was spilled by the *Exxon Valdez* in 1989. When part of the spill began washing up on the shores of Texas, U.S. authorities demanded that Pemex pay damages to property owners in the state. Pemex balked. "There is no international regulation for this type of accident," said Pemex director Jorge Díaz Serrano. "Therefore, we must abide by Mexican laws and principles."

That, of course, was a political slap in the face, since Pemex never abided by any Mexican law it did not like, and its principle regarding environmental damage was to ignore it. Mexico was not in the mood to be contrite. The reason the well blew out was because the oil had erupted

from the earth with explosive force. That fact suggested the size of the
new strike. By the following year the new offshore reserve was estimated
at 24 billion barrels. Resisting U.S. calls for indemnification was a way for
Mexico to assert its new economic and political clout.

There is another reason why Pemex dismissed charges of environmental damage, whether they came from peasants or foreign governments. To
Pemex officials, the damage was not real. Environmentalism, as they saw
it, was a first-world luxury, an idea that did not apply in a developing
country. How can one compare the cost of a corn crop, or the catch of
river trout, or even a tar-free beach, to the benefits that accrued to the
nation from developing its oil industry? From a financial standpoint, Pemex was completely insulated from the cost of the environmental damage because it was untouchable legally. Under Mexico's constitution, the
state owns all subsoil rights, and so Pemex is entitled to expropriate privately held land for oil production with a minimum of compensation. As
a state entity, Pemex has not made any attempt to internalize environmental destruction into the cost of production. Either the state itself
picked up the tab for environmental damage or the problem was ignored.
The company was so insulated from any sort of legal action that it rarely
even considered the cost of industrial accidents in which people were
killed, except to address the damage to its own facilities.

But not every Mexican was willing to sacrifice his or her well-being for
the sake of the nation. By the late 1970s, peasants and fishermen in Tabasco
and Veracruz began blocking wells and demanding compensation for the
harm caused to their crops and their rivers by Pemex's negligence. Dredging, dikes, road building, and hundreds of miles of leaking pipelines that
carried the crude from the wells to the petrochemical plants caused immense damage. One frequent problem was the insufficient capacity of the
batteries that separated the oil and water drawn up by the pumps. Oily
water, which overflowed from the batteries, damaged cornfields and lagoons and spread through the regions' extensive river system into the fragile wetlands. A 1979 report on the Laguna Limón near Ciudad Pemex in
Tabasco noted that "the results indicate that the water in the lagoon is in
a state of putrefaction, completely full of grease and oil. It is a threat to public health and it is not in conditions to be used even for irrigation." Fishing and agriculture were severely affected; oyster collecting was wiped out.

Isolated complaints about pollution soon coalesced into a social movement that brought together seven thousand fishermen and farmers in a coalition called the Pacto Ribereño. The group demanded millions of dollars in compensation for lost crops, damaged land, and fouled waterways. Pemex director Jorge Díaz Serrano dismissed the damage and smugly declared that the people of Tabasco would have to learn to live with the "abundance" of the oil economy. In response, members of the Pacto Ribereño blocked fourteen wells and had to be dislodged by the army.

At the same time that the people of Tabasco began to examine the social and environmental costs of runaway development, the bottom fell out of the oil boom. A worldwide recession in 1981 caused a sharp drop in oil prices while Mexico, in a fit of nationalist pique, raised prices for its crude. Billions of dollars in orders were canceled at a time when the international market was shrinking. The Mexican oil industry, and the whole petrolized Mexican economy, has never recovered. The promised prosperity had been short lived; Mexico had gone on a spending binge and incurred huge and rapidly mounting international debt. With its massive corruption, its arrogance, its false promises, Pemex became the scapegoat for the entire economic downturn. President Miguel de la Madrid, who took office in 1982, promised a "moral renovation" and made some efforts to rein in the company. Pemex mounted an advertising campaign to improve its environmental image and promised to channel more funds into social development in the oil zone. Díaz Serrano was arrested in 1983 and charged with masterminding a $34 million corruption scheme. He was released in 1988, after serving five years of a ten-year sentence.

But with creditors clamoring for dollars, Mexico had to continue to rely on petroleum exports to generate hard currency. Instead of reinvesting revenues in further development, or throwing money around to buy off opponents, Pemex's profits were used to pay off creditors and run the government.

Also in the 1980s, Pemex began to pay the environmental costs it had dismissed the decade before. In 1983 the state governor in Tabasco got behind the Pacto Ribereño movement, and Pemex was forced to cough up tens of millions of dollars in compensation. Throughout the oil zone, campesino groups grew increasingly strident and blocked hundreds of wells. In Chiapas and Tabasco, production dropped off in overexploited wells. Maintenance was curtailed, leading to a series of industrial accidents like the one at San Juanico; poorly formulated gas produced a dark cloud over Mexico City; high-grade light crude was shipped out of the country, and power plants were forced to burn heavier crude, increasing air pollution throughout the country. In fact, many of the nation's power plants burn an extremely dirty fuel called *combustol,* which has as much as 6 percent sulfur. Sulfur dioxide, a byproduct of sulfur emissions, is extremely noxious and can cause serious lung damage in high concentrations.

Pemex, however, did not appreciate the depth of the anger and disappointment directed against it. Officials continued to act as if they were the nation's heroes. When newly appointed Pemex director Mario Rámon Beteta was asked if the company planned to pay damages to the victims of the San Juanico explosion, he answered, "But it was Pemex that suffered the damage."

Indeed it had, but the damage was also to its image. Even though evidence linking Pemex to the blast was overwhelming, the company tried desperately to worm its way out of taking responsibility. It blamed the explosion on a nearby private gas facility, which the San Juanico plant supplied. "The accident did not begin in the Pemex plant because the installations are subject to rigorous safety checks and constant maintenance," said Beteta. Local residents reported otherwise. They claimed that the whole neighborhood had reeked of gas for years and that in the days preceding the blast the smell was even more intense. There had been a small explosion at the plant several months earlier, and neighbors had noticed large flames periodically shooting into the sky. In fact, the whole plant was in violation of the law: Pemex was prohibited from locating gas plants in residential neighborhoods.

It was a month later that President Miguel de la Madrid finally accepted Pemex's responsibility for the explosion, and the company, despite Beteta's outrageous statements, was made to cough up several million dollars in damages (a pittance when one considers the extent of the losses). Still the company resisted environmental controls. Wrote Mexican social critic Carlos Monsiváis in an essay on the San Juanico explosion:

> Oceans and lakes had been contaminated, marine and jungle species had disappeared, campesinos' rights had been violated and the atmosphere had been poisoned. The implicit response pays homage to the Cult of Progress: "If you want to live in a modern nation, stop crying about the

environment. Just look at Tokyo and Los Angeles. Oil is what puts food
on our plate, not environmental dreams."

In the wake of the San Juanico blast, protests about environmental destruction reflected Mexicans' larger concerns about development in general. Massive demonstrations were organized to protest the construction
of a nuclear plant at Laguna Verde on the coast of Veracruz; air pollution
and urban growth emerged as political issues in Mexico City; and intellectuals like Carlos Fuentes began to describe Mexico City as an urban
monster, a third world dystopia, progress gone to hell. Pemex found fewer
and fewer defenders. Campesinos in Tabasco continued to take over wells;
taxi drivers in Mexico City bitterly cursed the company that had led the
country down the wrong path. The hostility Mexicans felt toward Pemex
was not entirely rational. It was in part the bitterness that comes from
betrayal. Mexico was seduced by oil. It believed the promises, the lies, the
sweet talk. Oil persuaded Mexico to leave home, to run off, to elope. Its
reputation now sullied, Mexico could not go home.

Pemex, however, could not adapt to this new reality. It was used to
adulation, not criticism. It continued to operate above the law, further
fueling public anger. After taking power at the end of 1988, President Salinas made the now perennial promise to attack corruption and force Pemex to operate more like a business. A month later, Salinas sent the army
to arrest Joaquín Hernández Galicia (known as La Quina), Pemex's notoriously corrupt union chief, who had made a fortune through kickbacks,
subcontracting, embezzlement, and selling jobs. Mexicans initially cheered
the arrest but soon realized it hardly represented the triumph of the rule
of law. Salinas went after La Quina not because the union boss was corrupt but because he refused to support Salinas's presidential campaign.
Salinas used the army to arrest La Quina in clear violation of the constitution; the primary charge against him was the murder of a federal agent;
but witnesses placed the agent hundreds of miles away at the time that he
was said to have been killed at La Quina's house in Tampico. There was
also widespread suspicion that the enormous quantity of high-powered
weapons found in his home were planted.

In any case, whatever public good will was generated toward Pemex by
the arrest of La Quina was squandered three years later when an enormous
explosion ripped apart the Guadalajara sewage system. At 10 A.M. on

April 22, 1992, the streets in a twenty-six-block radius near downtown burst open, tossing cars onto nearby rooftops, flipping tractor trailers as if they were toy trucks, killing more than two hundred people, injuring fourteen hundred, and destroying thousands of homes. Pemex once again tried to cover up its responsibility. The day before the blast residents had complained of a powerful gasoline odor coming from the sewers. Inspectors who responded had warned that an explosion was imminent but did not order evacuations because they lacked the authority to do so. Initially, Pemex blamed the explosion on a small cooking oil factory. That explanation quickly became untenable; the leading theory today is that workers at the Pemex storage facility who were illegally selling gas on the black market dumped the gas down the drain to avoid detection during an audit. In any case, Pemex has still not been found legally responsible for the blast. Partial payments have been made to the victims, but the money has come out of the coffers of the federal government's social ministry, not Pemex itself.

When President Salinas asked Pemex to develop a plan to address industrial safety in the wake of the Guadalajara sewer explosion, the company proposed splitting itself into four divisions—exploration and production, refineries, gas and basic petrochemicals, and secondary petrochemicals. This was an opportunistic response to a terrible human tragedy because it did not address issues of industrial safety or environmental protection. Instead, Salinas saw the explosion as the political opening to push through a financial reorganization that would make the company more efficient and open the door for privatization.

The Guadalajara blast showed Mexicans that nothing had changed. Pemex, as it had for decades, continued to operate outside the law. The only way to get the company's attention was to take over a well and demand payment. In such cases, Pemex found it easier to pay off the campesinos than to dispute their claims. This response only encouraged takeovers. In 1993 and 1994, 123,000 fishermen and farmers lodged complaints against Pemex, and the company agreed to shell out $130 million. In 1995, Pemex received more than 60,000 complaints, recognized 14,000 of them, and paid $46 million in damages. Pemex complained that many of the claims were bogus and that it was forced to pay them because public opinion had turned against the company. "We will not pay one centavo more to the claims industry," vowed Pemex head Adrián Lajous.

But the real problem was that no adequate legal framework had been developed to regulate the relationship between Pemex and Mexican society. When the relationship turned hostile Pemex was at the mercy of the social forces it once dismissed out of hand.

I

If anyplace in Mexico has suffered from the excesses of oil development, it is the twin cities of Coatzacoalcos and Minatitlán on the coast of Veracruz. Along the banks of the Coatzacoalcos River are a major refinery and four enormous petrochemical plants, which supply dozens of other smaller industries. At times, the air is as polluted as Mexico City's, and the river receives more than 35 million cubic feet (1 million cubic meters) of waste water a day. Thirteen hundred years ago the rich ecosystem of estuaries, lakes, lagoons, wetlands, and rivers spawned Mexico's first great civilization—the Olmecs. Today, the industrial corridor is Mexico's New Jersey.

From the window of my plane, the chemical plants loomed like miniature cities, outposts on an alien planet. On the ground the scene was even more dramatic. I could smell what the nearest factory was producing; the sharp, bitter odor of ammonia gave way to a sweeter, more diffuse smell of a strong solvent as I drove through town.

Biologist Lorenzo Bozada Robles, a small man with thick glasses and a warm smile, met me at my hotel soon after I arrived in August 1995. "Have you ever seen it rain oil from the sky?" he asked. "One day in 1978 or 1979, it started to rain like any other day. Then I realized that it was not water, it was oil. Everything was covered in a fine film. People were sliding around, falling down in the street. My clothes were soaked, I had to throw them away. I couldn't get the oil off my skin. I had to bathe with solvents."

Coatzacoalcos has been a company town for most of the twentieth century, ever since British engineer Weetman Pearson constructed a rail line from the Pacific port of Salina Cruz across the Isthmus of Tehuantepec to the delta of the Coatzacoalcos River. The rail line, which was designed to move freight between the Atlantic and the Pacific, was quickly made obsolete by the completion of the Panama Canal in 1914. But by then Pearson had already found an alternative business. He struck oil in 1906; in 1909 he built a refinery a dozen miles inland from the mouth of the Coatzacoalcos River in Minatitlán.

Over the next several decades the Minatitlán refinery became the center of Mexico's booming oil industry. Up the coast near Tampico, American prospector Edward Doheny had struck oil a few years before Pearson on May 1, 1901. The strike erupted with such force that it blew the drill out of the ground. Mexico had its first gusher—and also its first oil spill. Later, the oil was shipped down the coast to the refinery at Minatitlán before being sent to the United States and Europe.

What allowed Doheny, Pearson, and a slew of other foreign companies to develop the oil fields was a very important legal development. In 1884, Porfirio Díaz had changed Mexican law, relinquishing the state's historical ownership of the subsoil. Production in the oil fields continued to expand even during the revolution because the oil fields were isolated from the fighting. By the time the war was over, Mexico was producing a quarter of the world's oil—almost 80 percent of it was shipped out of the country, along with the profits. While the foreign companies grew wealthy and powerful, Mexicans received almost no benefit. Positions that required skill or technical training went to the foreigners.

The country made some effort to remedy the situation with the passage of Article 27 of the 1917 constitution, which returned subsoil rights to the state. But the oil companies used their clout in Washington and the threat of a U.S. invasion to extract open-ended concessions.

The oil companies met their match, however, in Lázaro Cárdenas, who took office in 1934. In the wake of the world economic crisis, Cárdenas had shifted Mexico's economic strategy away from the development of commercial agriculture and natural resources for export and toward industrialization and the development of an internal market. Meanwhile, the oil companies were losing interest in Mexico. The discovery of new oil deposits in Venezuela and the Middle East in the 1920s had made Mexican oil uncompetitive on the global market. From Cárdenas's point of view, retooling production for the domestic market would not only stimulate his industrial development scheme but would also provide employment for Mexicans at a time when the international market had collapsed. In 1937 oil workers went on strike and the government ordered the oil companies to submit to binding arbitration. Based on its conclusion that the Mexican oil industry was enjoying unusually high profits, the arbitration board ordered the oil companies to grant a 27 percent pay hike. The companies appealed to the Supreme Court, which upheld the board's ruling. When the companies balked at the decision and suggested that they would not comply, Cárdenas, as was his right under the Mexican constitution, nationalized the oil industry.

The nationalization is sometimes referred to as the last act of the revolution and Mexico's greatest moment. In Mexico City, crowds surged into the street to celebrate and everyone from peasants to socialites contributed to the national fund that was to be used to indemnify the expropriated companies. In Coatzacoalcos and Minatitlán, according to stories Bozada heard from his father (who was an oil worker at the time of the expropriation), soldiers diligently recorded the donations, which ranged from live chickens to gold jewelry. A captain who was caught pocketing a pair of gold earrings was summarily executed by his superior officer with a bullet to the head; the officer then explained to the aghast bystanders that this was the punishment for stealing from the nation.

"That was the first and last time there was an honest accounting of anything relating to the oil industry," said Bozada. "Every peso made it to Mexico City." It was also the last time the law was brought to bear in a meaningful way against the oil industry. The justification for the nationalization was the fact that the foreign-owned oil industry had failed to comply with Mexican law when the companies were ordered to increase wages. In its own way, and with an entirely different justification, Pemex would be just as contemptuous of the law as the foreign companies. The emotional significance of the nationalization also insulated Pemex from the kind of political pressure that could be applied to the foreign companies. Yes, the oil industry had started working for Mexico instead of for shareholders in New York or London. But the country's needs were determined by ministers and bureaucrats in Mexico City who wanted to make Mexico a first-rate industrial power at all costs. In Coatzacoalcos—again, according to Bozada's childhood memories—the love fest with the newly formed state oil company quickly faded when the new Mexican managerial class took over the houses of the British engineers who had lived in a walled compound near the refinery. Each morning Bozada heard the plink of tennis balls from behind the wall as he walked to school.

What had originally brought the British engineer Pearson to the Coatzacoalcos area was its potential as a continentwide transportation hub. In the 1950s, when new oil fields were discovered in the region, Coatzacoalcos emerged as a likely spot to develop the nation's petrochemical industry. The first step was to increase capacity at the Minatitlán refinery. New equipment was installed throughout the 1950s. The first petrochemical plant, Cosoleacaque, was opened in 1960. It produced ammonia, much of it sold to the state-owned Fertimex plant, which used it to manufacture fertilizers. Over the next two decades, three other plants came on line: Minatitlán began processing benzene in 1964; Pajaritos began producing ethylene and other products in 1967; and La Cangrejera, which produces everything from naphthas to nitrogen, began functioning in 1981. Morelos, opened in 1991, was the last plant to be built. It produces ethylene and propylene derivatives, largely for the national market.

These plants are linked by hundreds of miles of leaky ducts, which tie into the marine terminal at Pajaritos. Only the Morelos plant has installed a full water treatment facility—the rest dump untreated industrial waste in the Coatzacoalcos River. Sixty-five other plants and related industries, many of them privately owned, also contribute to the contamination, as do the more than half a million residents of the region whose untreated sewage is dumped into the river. Within living memory, pods of dolphins ventured up the Coatzacoalcos River. Today, the river is so polluted that it has been known to catch fire, and the accumulated oil that has settled on the bottom of the lagoon is six feet deep. The beaches near town, littered with tar and contaminated by industrial and human waste, are closed to swimming.

Soon after the Pajaritos plant went in, local fishermen began noticing a drop in their catch. "Before, we caught trout, bass, and river shrimp," remembered sixty-six-year-old fisherman Eusebio González. "The net was so heavy we couldn't haul it in."

González is the president of the 516-member Miguel Alemán fishing cooperative founded in 1948, "before the industry arrived," he reminded me. "Every year there were less and less fish, so we went to Pemex and complained," continued González. "We saw the chemicals being dumped into the river; we saw clouds of vapor rising above the water at night. We saw that when we scooped up the mud from the bottom of the river it was yellow, the consistency of Jell-o. We saw that the tankers rinsing out their hulls dumped oil into the river. After a spill we saw all the fish wash up on the shore, and we said to Pemex 'fish don't commit suicide.' But they never listened to what we had to say."

The catch that the fishermen took in often reeked of chemicals. "You'd cut the fish open and a smell would come out like ammonia," said González. "I'd yell, 'throw that out, it smells terrible.' If you eat it, your stomach swells up like a balloon. Still we have to sell it. What else are we going to live from?"

The blame, insists González, belongs to Pemex. "They should declare this a dead river, but they know that if they did they would have to pay off all the fishermen," he said. Fishermen have presented dozens of legal complaints and taken over Pemex facilities. Pemex has responded not by cleaning up the mess or even by acknowledging the damage. Instead it has treated the demise of the local fishing industry as a development issue. Since 1982, Pemex has channeled money into a regional development program and paid off individual fishermen. In 1994 the Miguel Alemán cooperative received $2 million in cash and equipment, and some of its members shifted from fishing in the river to venturing out into the open ocean.

Pemex has also shelled out millions to local peasants who claim that their wells have been contaminated and their crops lost because of toxic spills. But it has done so grudgingly.

"A lot of people around here are making a living out of charging Pemex for nonexistent damage," said one Pemex engineer in Coatzacoalcos. "A lot of fishermen who are upriver from the plants are blaming us for a poor catch."

"If it rains, if it's hot out, it's our fault," added Pemex spokesperson Rodolfo Vizcaino. "All this stuff we get blamed for is not our responsibility. We couldn't get away with it because we're under constant scrutiny. I'm telling you we live in a glass house."

While I saw plenty of real damage during my visit to Coatzacoalcos, it did seem everyone was taking potshots at Pemex. When I gave a local journalist who was showing me around a recording of an interview I had done with a Pemex official on the condition that he use it only for background, it appeared on the front page of the local newspaper the next day, naming me as a source. Pemex was not happy. A day later, I talked to local photographer Guillermo Estudillo about the 1991 explosion at the Pajaritos plant, which many suspect left more than the officially claimed eight people dead. Estudillo, who has made his career photographing the victims of Pemex explosions for the local press, had been first on the scene at Pajaritos. He invited me to look over his photographs of the explosion, which were published in the local scandal sheet called *Gráfico.*

When I went by the office, editor Javier Salas had already put aside the March 14, 1991, issue with a banner headline reading "¡Explosión!" There was Estudillo's handiwork—a headless corpse, another body protruding from a pile of rubble. As I looked over the photos, Salas began to ask me questions. "Would you say that Coatzacoalcos is the most polluted city in the world?" he said. Then a flash fired in my face and I realized I had been caught in a journalistic ambush. I did not stick around to buy the paper the next day, but I am sure there was a story about an American journalist who visited the *Gráfico* offices to warn the people of Coatzacoalcos that their city was about to explode.

Despite Pemex's self-righteous indignation, the attacks by the local press and a few fishermen and farmers have done little more than bruise a few delicate egos. The millions of dollars the state government and Pemex have shelled out in damages is pocket change. If Pemex is ever made to pay the real damage for its misdeeds, it will reach into the billions of dollars. In the early 1980s, with support from the Centro de Ecodesarrollo in Mexico City, the Mexican National Autonomous University (UNAM), the University of Veracruz, and the municipality of Coatzacoalcos, investigators began studying the ecological transformation of the river region. Biologist Bozada, an expert on aquatic life, was one of the key researchers. The reports found alarming levels of hydrocarbons and lead in the atmosphere, as well as regionwide acid rain. The results from studies of the river were mixed. There was widespread damage, especially on the river bottom where contaminants were concentrated, but the tropical system showed a remarkable ability to withstand abuse. The problem was grave, Bozada noted, but it had not passed the point of no return.

Pemex responded to the publication of the reports in 1987 with an immediate denial. But President Miguel de la Madrid, who was in the last year of his six-year term, realized that the reports were politically sensitive and tried to prevent the opposition from using them to its advantage by promising immediate action. Opposition to the Laguna Verde nuclear power plant up the coast from Coatzacoalcos had already become an explosive issue in the presidential elections, which were planned for the following year. The nuclear plant was originally conceived in 1972 as part of an ambitious plan to build between twelve and fifteen nuclear power plants throughout the country. The strategy was to develop Mexico's technical capacity and at the same time provide energy for domestic consumption, freeing up oil for exports. From the beginning the plants ran into political and technical problems. A report by the U.S. Atomic Energy Commission, which was leaked in 1978, expressed concerns about flaws in the boiling water reactor, which had been designed by General Electric. By 1987 the nuclear power program had been trimmed to a single plant—Laguna Verde. Construction was ten years behind schedule, and cost overruns had raised the estimated cost from $128 million to $3.5 billion—an increase of 2,600 percent. In addition, the reactor vessel at Laguna Verde was dropped from a crane during construction and sea water entered the reactor during operating tests, contributing to corrosion. The San Juanico accident in 1984 led Mexicans to question the industrial safety standards, and the Chernobyl accident in the summer of 1986 revealed the potential consequences of an accident. Opposition to the plant included national and international environmental groups as well as the growing leftist opposition. With the 1988 elections on the horizon, de la Madrid sought to demonstrate his commitment to industrial safety and environmental protection by recognizing the depth of the problem in Coatzacoalcos. He visited the region four days after the environmental reports were published; Pemex, he promised, would take corrective action.

Over the next few years a multibillion-dollar cleanup plan was developed for Coatzacoalcos, which involved not only controlling emissions but also draining several swamp areas and refilling them with clean water. The plan was never carried out. In fact, no public accounting has been made. There is no record of exactly what Pemex is dumping into the atmosphere or the rivers, and the company does not release reports after an explosion; no studies have been made of the effects of pollution on public health.

This lack of information protects Pemex from legal redress, since residents lack the resources to undertake these kinds of studies on their own. The policy may come back to haunt the company in the near future. At the time of my visit in August 1995 the government had just announced a highly controversial plan to put Pemex's petrochemical division on the auction block. Eventually, all sixty-one petrochemical plants will be sold to the highest bidders.

After years of raiding Pemex to pay off its dollar debts, the petrochemical division, while profitable, is badly undercapitalized. The government has been trying to sell off the plants since 1992, but has not received much interest. This time it is doing things differently. It put the plants on the market at a time when the global demand for petrochemicals was strong. And it ordered Pemex to perform an environmental audit on all its petrochemical installations to be monitored by Profepa, the federal environmental prosecutor's office.

The audit was designed to assure foreign investors that the plants were operating in compliance with Mexican environmental law. No effort was made, however, to determine the extent of the damage that had already been done, or what would be required to remediate it. Héctor Ochoa López, Pemex's director of industrial and environmental protection in Coatzacoalcos, acknowledged only minor problems in the soil and subsoil. Pemex would allow me to visit only their most modern plant, Morelos. The other plants, which require such basic amenities as scrubbers and water treatment facilities to bring them up to code, were off limits, as was the Minatitlán refinery.

In the United States, when one company purchases another, a legal procedure called "due diligence" is carried out. Lawyers from the purchasing company go over the books of the company they are buying to make sure that it is operating in full compliance with the law and that there are no legal actions pending. In the case of Pemex, Mexican law is less than clear about who assumes the legal responsibility for any future claims stemming from environmental damage. For example, if in ten years a study were to reveal that there is a cancer cluster in Coatzacoalcos linked to the plants, it is unclear whether Pemex or the new owners would be responsible. Some experts I talked to insisted that Pemex would remain a minority partner in the new enterprises and would be responsible for all legal claims. Meanwhile, Antonio Azuela, Mexico's chief environmental prosecutor, told me that the audits were designed to serve as a basis for negotiation between Pemex and the companies buying the plants, and that once the sale was complete "the purchasing company assumes the responsibility." Because the audits determine only compliance and not any pending civil actions or long-term damage, investors have no way of knowing whether or not they are purchasing the equivalent of a Superfund site and, in a worst-case scenario, who would be responsible for the cleanup.

"Do you want to buy a whole bunch of problems?" said a high-ranking Pemex official when I asked him what kind of advice he would offer to investors interested in purchasing one of the petrochemical plants in Coatzacoalcos. "Nobody even knows what damage exists. Pemex has never worried about it because it knows that the state will both protect it and bail it out if it runs into any problems. But a private company, especially a foreign one, would not have those kinds of protections. If fishermen or peasants try to sue, they may win because it will no longer be Pemex."

The more optimistic analysis is that privatization will remove the nationalistic shield from the oil industry and tip the political balance toward campesinos and fishermen who complain of environmental damage. For Bozada, however, there is no correlation between the privatization and environmental enforcement. The problem, as he sees it, is a political culture that has allowed the oil industry to destroy the environment while bankrupting the country. Coatzacoalcos today is a sad place. The legacy of oil development is dirty air and a downwardly mobile work force. The neighborhoods built to house Pemex workers—suburban subdivisions reminiscent of Los Angeles—are being rapidly abandoned as jobs are cut. Bozada himself was let go from the local university when its budget was slashed, and he now teaches in a high school. Still, he feels it will be a sad day when the petrochemical plants are privatized. "During all these years that I was fighting I never lost faith that one day Pemex would be a clean company, with responsible executives—a patrimony of the nation," he said as we sat in his small office at the end of a long day. "Never in my wildest dreams did I think they would sell off the industry."

II

Despite the economic recession, Coatzacoalcos and Minatitlán remain company towns, and Pemex has been able to manage the political fallout from the environmental crisis. In the neighboring state of Tabasco, however, it has lost control. Since the mid-1970s, when Pemex first began producing in Tabasco, blocking roads and taking over wells have become favored pressure tactics of campesinos and fishermen in the region. By the middle 1980s, taking over wells had become a business. In many cases, according to a top state official, a Pemex manager will secretly notify local political operators, or caciques, about a spill that Pemex is trying to cover up. Later, the cacique will instruct campesinos to take over a well and demand compensation, declaring that the spill has destroyed their corn crop. The company is vulnerable because it never made the spill public in the first place. It is easier to pay off the campesinos than fight the takeover. The Pemex manager who disclosed the information takes a cut.

Pemex is responsible for enormous damage in the state of Tabasco. Dredging, dumping, and dams have completely altered the region's wetlands; oil spills have severely affected ocean fishing. Peasants throughout the state complain that acid rain is corroding their tin roofs and their barbed-wire fences; they say that it kills their corn, their tomatoes, their avocadoes. The pollution has killed wildlife and may be poisoning their children. Infant leukemia is reported to be on the rise in Tabasco. Then there are the explosions—in twenty years thirty explosions in Tabasco have left more than two hundred dead.

At the same time, Pemex is not responsible for every failed corn crop and every bad catch in the state. Yet everyone seems to want a piece of the company. When I spent an afternoon traveling around Lake Mecoacan near the Pemex marine terminal at El Paraíso, every village I visited had either received some sort of settlement or was organizing to demand one. Gabriel Ochoa Ferrera, a fisherman in Puerto Ceiba, told me he had discovered an underwater pipe dumping diesel into the ocean. He blamed Pemex for oil spills, chemical dumping, and dredging, which he said had destroyed his catch. He and the nearly one thousand members of various fishing cooperatives in the area had each received two thousand dollars from Pemex in 1993 in compensation. Heriberto Seguro Díaz from nearby Puerto Chiltepec told me he used to haul in a net dripping with oil; he also said acid rain had destroyed his coconut plantation. He was on his way to a meeting of local fishermen who were organizing to get Pemex to pay them for their losses. I asked if I could come along. "If you were Mexican, perhaps," he said.

Rámon Domínguez Sánchez, a fisherman in Jalapita, slapped mosquitos as he complained of oil spills that had ruined his nets, sewage that had produced algae, and a drop in coconut and orange production. In 1991 his twenty-five-person fishing cooperative received a one-time cash payment from Pemex.

I do not doubt that Pemex is responsible for the degradation of Lake Mecoacan and the decline of fishing in the region—the enormous marine terminal at El Paraíso is the source of numerous well-documented spills, and dredging undoubtedly disrupts breeding. But with no environmental impact studies and no scientific baseline there is no way to know what role overfishing has played. There are between fifteen hundred and two thousand fishermen working in Lake Mecoacan, according to state authorities.

The fact that Pemex has been forced to shell out money for damage it may be only partially responsible for is, of course, hardly a great injustice. But because no effort is being made to evaluate the claims scientifically, Pemex's payments are based on the amount of political pressure being applied rather than on evidence of real damage. This fact encourages well takeovers and civil disobedience and has enabled regional power brokers associated with the ruling PRI and the upstart PRD to make a living shaking down Pemex. Taking over wells and blocking roads has become a form of institutional protest in Tabasco—there were more than three hundred well takeovers in 1995. And the takeovers are used to draw national attention to all sorts of political disputes, some of which have nothing to do with Pemex. In the spring of 1995, for example, PRD supporters took over wells throughout the state to protest the victory of PRI gubernatorial candidate Roberto Madrazo over the PRD's Andrés Manuel López Obrador, a victory they claimed was based on fraud.

A year later, in February 1996, López Obrador was at it again. On the eve of internal elections for the presidency of the PRD for which López Obrador was a candidate, his supporters blocked sixty wells to protest environmental damage and electoral fraud in Tabasco. The army was sent in to dislodge the protestors. Scores were injured in the fracas, including López Obrador himself, and more than a hundred were carted off to jail. Yet the demonstrators refused to leave until the government agreed to formally discuss their grievances. President Zedillo declared, "No one has the right to use the country's resources to apply political pressure," while one of the government's top environmental officials argued that the damage done by Pemex was "reversible."

Paying out thousands of claims has cost Pemex hundreds of millions of dollars. But the real cost of the takeovers, which has not been calculated, is the loss of production. The two-week shutdown in February 1996 cost Pemex an estimated $10 million, and over the years the cost of closed wells, and of paying engineers to sit around and do nothing for months at a time, may well reach into the billions of dollars.

I saw just how politicized and corrupt the battle against Pemex had become when I spent a Sunday afternoon in the Chontal Indian town of Oxiacaque, located an hour from the state capital of Villahermosa, with Antonio de la Cruz. By the standards of Oxiacaque, de la Cruz's house is a palace. He owns two televisions. The small Sony is stacked on top of an enormous TV encased in a wooden cabinet. De la Cruz—who introduced himself with his full Christian name of José Antonio de la Cruz de la O—is a former mayor of the town and one of the few people living there who does not speak Chontal. He had supported the leftist opposition since it emerged in 1988 and had spent the previous six years "fighting against Pemex and the government."

In 1985 Pemex had begun exploration in the area around Oxiacaque. Within a few years it had perforated fifteen exploratory wells and installed a series of pipelines, which required digging up farmers' fields. Roads built to move equipment to the drill sites cut the flow of water through the wetlands and caused the flooding of cornfields. In 1989 de la Cruz led the first wave of protests. When the whole town shut down the road, five hundred police were sent in, and de la Cruz was hauled off to jail in a helicopter. But the protests continued, and in 1990 Pemex decided to pay up—about $75 every two months to farmers affected by the operations. In 1992, after another wave of protests, Pemex agreed to advance several years' worth of payments as one lump sum of $1,500 per person. "It was like winning the lottery," said de la Cruz. "There was a party every night." Other towns wanted in on the act, so they organized and blocked roads as well. Some of the leaders of the road closures were with the PRD, others with the PRI. Pemex made agreements with each community, but there was always another one that felt left out. Not one of the wells has ever been put into operation.

In the summer of 1994, soon after the state gubernatorial elections, de la Cruz and his followers received another payout. He showed me a copy of the handwritten agreement. Local people accused him of selling out to the PRI, and sure enough, soon after the agreement was signed, de la

Cruz went on the offensive against PRD gubernatorial candidate López Obrador, and Oxiacaque split into two camps—those with de la Cruz and those with another leader who continued to support the PRD. The PRD followers had shut down the road for twenty-five days in August 1995 and had reached a settlement with Pemex the Friday before my visit. De la Cruz and his followers were planning to close the road the following day, Monday. He needed to make sure his followers also got paid or he would lose power.

I asked de la Cruz to show me the Pemex drill site, and we jumped in his pickup truck and drove at breakneck speed with '70s funk blasting on his car stereo. The workers at the well clearly knew de la Cruz; they greeted him tentatively as we climbed the steep stairs to the drilling platform. From there we could see half a dozen other wells rising over the savannah like Mayan pyramids. De la Cruz shook the hand of the engineer in charge of the well, who was waiting for us at the bottom of the tower. "How's it going?" asked de la Cruz.

"Better, finally," said the engineer. "It looks like we'll finally be able to work starting tomorrow."

"I don't think so," said de la Cruz as he climbed back into his pickup truck. "We'll be out there bright and early."

A few days later I met ex–gubernatorial candidate and PRD leader Andrés Manuel López Obrador in his modest home in the state capital of Villahermosa. I asked him about de la Cruz. López Obrador was leaving in the morning for Mexico City, where he was hoping to receive a decision from the attorney general's office about the validity of the documents he had given them showing that the PRI candidate Roberto Madrazo had spent 70 million on his gubernatorial campaign, more than 60 times the legal limit and more than Bill Clinton spent on his presidential campaign.

"There are corrupt leaders, of course, but there are many people who have suffered damages and who have a different attitude," said López Obrador. Before his campaign for governor he had been the head of the National Indigenous Institute in Tabasco, and he knew the concerns of the villages well. "The way the government addresses the problem produces leaders who are always demanding that Pemex pay them money. It's a vicious circle. Pemex, instead of investing in a program of social development, pays people off, and this benefits the leaders. The corruption goes way up, because the money is channeled through the state government or the PRI.

"The problem with Antonio is that the state government gave him money for damages suffered by the campesinos, and he distributed a portion of the settlement and pocketed the rest. He is now on the side of the government, against our movement."

López Obrador argued that the real problem in the state was not strictly environmental; rather it was the way environmental damage had affected social well-being. "There is no environmental awareness, per se, but there is widespread concern about the material damage caused by environmental destruction," he said.

I asked if he thought there was any political advantage in being perceived as the "environmental candidate."

"Maybe in Europe, but not here," he said. "There is no push for conservation or defense of the environment for its own sake. It's an issue that doesn't matter to the people of this state."

III

The fact that "environmentalism" in the oil zone is focused on reparations should not be an impediment to the development of environmental controls on Pemex. Just the opposite—the strategy should be to develop ways to assess environmental damage from a purely monetary vantage point. The challenge of creating a framework for environmental accountability within a legal system that often acts arbitrarily or on the basis of political pressure is, of course, enormous, but there are strategies that could be effective.

Jorge Goñi, the general director of Tabasco's environmental office, is working on a new state environmental law that would require industries to post a bond to fund any eventual cleanup. Another alternative would be to create an independent environmental arbitration board to evaluate claims of environmental damage.

The point is that Pemex, and the country as a whole, must develop some mechanism for determining environmental damage and fair compensation. The experience of Pemex in Tabasco shows why environmental law is not a first world luxury but an essential part of any development strategy. Pemex lost billions of dollars because it failed to develop any strategy for mediation between the company and the local population. The lack of any way to force Pemex to pay for environmental damage has also caused wild distortions in Pemex's economic decisions. Pemex flares off enormous amounts of natural gas in the gulf because it has not developed the capacity to utilize this clean-burning fuel. It provides highly contaminating combustol fuel to the Federal Electricity Commission to burn in power plants (Pemex has enormous amounts of combustol warehoused because it does not know what to do with it). Once the environmental costs of burning heavier crude are factored in, developing natural gas is clearly a good investment. If Pemex ignores those costs, the decision may not look so obvious. Mexico does not even have an energy conservation strategy. In fact, government subsidies for gasoline encourage overconsumption in the belief that economic growth is sparked by increased energy use. "Once the cost of the health and environmental burdens and accompanying productivity losses associated with the burning of a liter of gasoline or fuel oil are taken into account, the true cost of petroleum products probably far exceeds the corresponding export price of fuel oil," noted Pemex analyst George Baker.

I had asked a Pemex official who ought to know if he would be willing to estimate the cost of the environmental damage caused by the company in the previous half-century. "How would you react to 5 billion dollars?" he said. "That's the best I can do off the top of my head."

Postscript: Mexico's federal attorney general's office determined that the documents submitted by López Obrador demonstrating that PRI gubernatorial candidate Roberto Madrazo spent $40 million on his election campaign were valid. However, it referred the case for prosecution to the PRI-controlled state authorities in Tabasco, which exonerated Madrazo of all wrongdoing. In July 1996, López Obrador was elected president of the PRD. Later that month, a series of devastating explosions at the Cactus natural gas refinery in Chiapas, just over the border from Tabasco, killed six workers, injured nine, and crippled Mexico's natural gas refining capabilities. The accident dampened the already limited interest in purchasing petrochemical plants with a history of industrial accidents and a legacy of environmental neglect. Confronting powerful opposition from the Pemex union and from within the PRI itself, the government cancelled the petrochemical privatization program in October 1996. Instead of selling the plants outright, the government proposed selling shares worth up to 49 percent of their value. The initial response from investors was less than enthusiastic.

—seven—

Trouble in Paradise

Thirty years ago Cancún island was inhabited by three fishermen and accessible only by boat. Then it was discovered by bankers in Mexico City, who thought they had found paradise. A crescent-shaped, white, sandy beach stretched along the narrow island. The ocean was turquoise, crystal clear, the temperature of bathwater. You could swim in January; the sun was out 330 days a year.

The bankers were not looking for the perfect place to take a vacation, however. They were after something more elusive. President Gustavo Díaz Ordaz had given them a mission: find dollars. Because of its trade deficit, Mexico badly needed foreign exchange. Maybe the bankers could not spin straw into gold, but they figured that with the right marketing plan they could turn sun and sand into cold cash.

The bankers soon hatched their scheme: they would build a new tourist utopia from scratch. One of the things they liked about Cancún was that it was virtually unpopulated. There would be no noisy protests when the bulldozers moved in, no campesinos or fishermen saying they wanted to keep things as they were. Cancún was conceived of as an ideal city, free of the urban blight and third-world chaos that was already scaring the tourists away from Acapulco. The planners wanted to avoid making Cancún overly urban; they left areas for parks and imposed height restrictions on buildings. They created public beaches—and they insisted that hotels not block shoreline access. On the mainland across from the hotel zone they planned a service city with broad, tree-lined avenues and banks, and offices, and housing for workers.

One of the great selling points of tourist development during the 1960s when Cancún was designed and built was that it was considered environmentally friendly. It was often described as a "an industry without smokestacks"; "Exploit the sun!" was its slogan. But from the bankers' point of view, protecting the environment meant avoiding pollution—industrial waste, smog, the garbage and sewage of the poor. Altering or destroying the natural habitat was not a concern.

The engineers who dredged the ocean to enlarge the beaches, who built a highway across the wetlands, cutting off the free circulation of water, and who dug enormous pits and used the earth to fill in the lagoon did not view any of these activities as environmentally harmful. They made no effort to hide the wounds they inflicted on the land; the enormous open pits from which the *saskab* (the Mayan name for the limestone earth) used to fill the lagoon was extracted line the main road into town.

Cancún residents divide their city's history into two phases—the utopian phase in which the city was planned and constructed, and the 1980s when that vision collapsed amidst the economic realpolitik. Mexico's vision in the 1960s and '70s when Cancún was planned and built was of a country moving irrevocably forward, a country in which the battle against poverty would soon be won. What the bankers and bureaucrats did not plan on was the "lost decade." The collapse of oil prices in 1981 forced a massive devaluation of the peso the following year. Under pressure from its international creditors, Mexico implemented a severe austerity program, cutting all social spending to the bone. In order to merely meet the interest payments on its unpayable international debt, Mexico retooled its economy, making the quest for dollars the driving principle of its entire economic policy. Tourism was one of the few bright spots on an otherwise bleak landscape.

In the name of foreign exchange, zoning restrictions were relaxed and hotels rose like a breakwater along the shore. Densities increased, shopping malls were built, beach access was blocked, and the utopian city succumbed to mediocrity. But the tourists kept coming, drawn by cheap package deals. By the mid-1980s, Cancún, once an exclusive resort, was drawing the spring-break crowd of rowdy college students. Drug money was being laundered through hotel construction, and the city soon became a favorite narco playground. Rafael Aguilar Guajardo, a drug lord from the border city of Ciudad Juárez, was gunned down in the Hyatt Cancún Caribe in April 1993.

Pollution became a growing problem. The slums spread northward toward Puerto Juárez. The sewage from the growing city backed up in the lagoon, causing algal blooms and creating a terrible stench. As Cancún lost its sheen, travelers began moving south down the coast, looking for a bit of unspoiled beach or a living reef.

By the time I arrived on a sweltering November morning in 1995, Cancún had reached truly massive proportions. The total population is officially around 200,000, though unofficial estimates put it 50 percent higher. Leaving the airport, we passed through a gauntlet of billboards: Burger King, McDonald's, Bowl Cancún, and the latest monstrosity of lowbrow celebrity hype, Planet Hollywood. As we raced toward downtown along the four-lane highway, I could make out the hotel zone on the other side of the lagoon. A fantastical skyline of luxury hotels rose into the blue-and-white sky: giant thatch huts, glass pyramids, seven-story Mediterranean villas. Like Muslims at Mecca, every one of them faced east.

Cancún was one of five beaches selected by the bankers to construct what Bob Shacochis described in *Harper's* as "an archipelago of artificial paradises"—Loreto and Cabo San Lucas in Baja California, Ixtapa near Acapulco, Huatulco on the Pacific coast of Oaxaca. But Cancún, with its white sand and calm waters, was always the star. In fact its very success begged a question. The city was designed in the 1960s with the specific goal of avoiding the kinds of environmental problems associated with cities like Acapulco, which had not been planned. But inevitably, Cancún began to suffer from the same kinds of problems—sewage and slums threatened to undermine its appeal. Was this the inevitable denouement of any mega-tourist project?

Some regional environmentalists in Cancún had coined a term to describe the phenomenon. They called the city a "zone of environmental sacrifice." Their argument is that Mexico's immediate economic and social concerns demand that the country exploit its beaches in the same way it exploits its minerals or its oil. They point out that Cancún still has its appeal—discos, beaches, sunny weather, cheap seafood. The development of the city has created not only thousands of jobs but real social mobility.

One of the standard arguments economists use to justify progrowth policies is that environmental problems spawned during the early phases of development will be corrected once income rises to the point where citizens are concerned about issues other than subsistence and governments can afford to invest in environmental protection. One Princeton University study, for example, found that sulfur dioxide emissions in cities rise until per capita income crests above the $4,000 per-person level and then falls precipitously as governments begin funding emission controls.

Indeed, Cancún's relative prosperity has spawned a small but vociferous environmental movement made up largely of hotel owners and small-business people. They realize that Cancún's attraction, and therefore their livelihood, depends to some degree on a healthy environment. The most visible force in Cancún's environmental movement is Araceli Domínguez, president of the Environmental Group of the Mayab (GEMA). I had booked a room in her small hotel.

I

Domínguez's hotel is called the Rey de Caribe—the King of the Caribbean. At twenty dollars a night it is the cheapest lodging in Cancún short of a bench at the bus station. But it's a pleasant enough place, with a small pool, a few hammocks, a garden, and a central location just a few blocks from city hall. Domínguez arrived just after I did. She was in a panic. "They're cutting down the tree!" she yelled to her husband Eduardo. "It can't be possible!"

Araceli and Eduardo ran out into the street, Eduardo in his bare feet. A pile of tree limbs was neatly stacked in front of an Italian restaurant called Paolo's. "Who gave you permission to cut down this tree?" Domínguez asked the proprietor. "This tree doesn't belong to you. It belongs to everyone."

"Señora, I do not do anything illegal," said Antonio Cerovolo, who spoke Spanish with a slight Italian accent. "I have permission from the environmental office. Believe me, it gives me great pain to cut down this tree," Cerovolo continued. By then a small crowd had arrived on the scene. "But I didn't have any choice. The tree is tearing up my restaurant."

Hemmed in by concrete, the tree had spread its roots in search of water. In the process it had ripped open the sidewalk, buckled the floor of the outdoor patio, and had started groping under the dining room floor. "You should tear up the patio instead of cutting down the tree," said Eduardo. "That tree has rights."

Back at the hotel, Domínguez called the city's Department of Ecology only to learn that it had in fact granted a permit to cut down the tree. "It can't be, it can't be," she sighed.

We sat down in her office, a room just off the lobby of the hotel. "I will always defend the trees," she told me. "Sometimes it makes me want to cry."

Among the people of Cancún and environmentalists in the region, Domínguez has earned a reputation for being extremely aggressive and sometimes alarmist. "Everyone in town knows who I am," she bragged. "Every day we get calls—they're cutting down a tree there, this hotel is destroying the beach. I have a very good relationship with the press. One phone call, and it's in the newspaper tomorrow.

"That's why the government is afraid of me," she continued. "Because I'm unpredictable. You never know in what moment, or precisely where, the bomb is going to go off."

Domínguez is like a one-person office of Greenpeace—her strategy is public protest, agitation, confrontation. She and her husband Eduardo are Mexico City natives who moved to Cancún in 1982 after he lost his job as an engineer in Coatzacoalcos, the superpolluted heart of Mexico's petrochemical industry. "We came here once and said, 'It's beautiful, we have to live here,'" recalled Domínguez. "We've always liked to live next to nature ever since we were first engaged. We wanted to work in a business in which we would have time to do what we like to do—fight for the environment."

Domínguez was one of the founders of GEMA in 1986. I had met another one, real estate developer José Campos, when I visited Cancún in 1992 (he has since moved to the United States). Aside from a few fishermen, Campos was about the closest thing Cancún had to a native inhabitant. His environmental concerns stemmed in part from a nostalgia for

Cancún as it used to be. "When I arrived here twenty years ago Cancún was a pristine area," he recalled. "There were eight hundred people here. You could see monkeys swinging in the trees near the airport."

Of course, if the monkeys were still in the trees, neither José Campos nor Araceli Domínguez would have been living in Cancún. They had been drawn by the tourist boom, by, to a greater or lesser degree, their ability to make money. The basis of their environmental critique was that development, the process that had made Cancún attractive to them in the first place, had gotten out of hand. "Sure everything in Cancún was planned," said Campos. "But with environmental values that are twenty years out of date."

Mobilizing against the environmental damage therefore has an economic logic. Campos, in fact, had tried to get the business community behind him. In 1988, in his capacity as president of the Business Center of Cancún, Campos cosigned a letter to the minister of tourism asking for brakes on further growth. "In the past few years the ideals that drove the first stages of our development have been lost and, in our opinion, replaced by a desire to obtain income at any price, without considering the consequences," the letter noted. "Mr. Minister, we are not ecologists, and, as businessmen, we do not oppose progress. But we find it hard to believe that the filling of fifty-four hectares of the lagoon system will not have effects on the ecology of the area."

GEMA's support comes largely from Cancún's thriving middle-class population of managers, small property owners, real estate agents, and service providers who understand that environmental destruction also means a loss in property values. "It's the anarchy, the violation of the existing rules, the corruption that is causing environmental deterioration," argued Domínguez. "The problem—for the environment and for everything else—is the lack of political will. Without a change in government we can't do anything, because there is impunity."

In this context, the battle over a tree becomes emblematic of the middle class's struggle for political representation and its fight to protect its economic interests. And it was because restaurant owner Antonio Cerovolo largely shares those values that he felt so indignant about being screamed at by Domínguez. "I'm an environmentalist too," he said when I stopped by the following day to get his side of the story.

Although Domínguez claimed that everyone in Cancún knew her, her neighbor had no idea who she was or that she claimed to represent Cancún's environmental consciousness. "Who is this woman to come and tell me I can't cut down the tree that is destroying my restaurant?" he asked. "There are people here who always want to blame the problem on someone else. The problem is not that we are cutting down one tree in the downtown. The problem is that there isn't a single tree in the slums. The problem is that they have cut down every palm tree on the beach."

II

If Araceli Domínguez believes in confrontation, Barbara MacKinnon Montes favors accommodation. "It's not that I'm against activists," she explained over coffee at the Cancún Howard Johnson hotel, next door to Domínguez's. "Activists get the attention. But in most cases they don't have the facts behind them. In Latin American countries they often do more damage than good because the pressure is so great to develop."

MacKinnon, who was born in the United States, has lived in Mexico for twenty-five years. Her husband, who died in 1987, was a native Yucatecan and a pioneer in the state's tourism industry. In the 1970s they spent their summers prowling the deserted coasts, driving down the back roads in search of rare birds. MacKinnon is an ornithologist, perhaps the leading expert on the birds of the Yucatán. "I could close my eyes and see how Cancún was, because I spent four years bird watching here before it was developed," said MacKinnon over the din of traffic on Avenida Uxmal. "We had woods, and deciduous forest on the back side of the dune. We had a pair of trogons that nested there in 1978."

MacKinnon knew Playa del Carmen when it was a small fishing village; she knew Isla Mujeres when it had only one hotel. Despite the transformation to which she has been witness, MacKinnon still has confidence that the process of development, which she sees as both inevitable and ultimately necessary in a country like Mexico, can be harnessed for environmental protection.

Cancún, she acknowledged, is not much of an example. By the early 1980s, with the city already losing its glow, developers began to sell the virtues of the sparsely populated coast south of the city, a place where you could still have the beach to yourself. A decade later, condos, time shares, golf courses, and marinas cover most of the hundred-mile stretch of coast between Cancún and the Mayan ruins at Tulum. In a few short years, Grupo Sidek, a Mexican developer, has transformed Playa del Carmen from a Bohemian backwater to a mini–Miami Beach.

MacKinnon, however, is hopeful that she can stop the overdevelopment in its tracks. South of Tulum, the paved highway cuts inland and a rutted jeep trail follows the coast. The jungle closes in, then gives way to wetlands and savannah where a weather-beaten wooden sign marks the entrance to the Sian Ka'an Biosphere Reserve. The reserve, only two hours south of Cancún, is a 1.6-million-acre (667,000-hectare) swath of largely undeveloped lagoons, mangroves, jungles, and beaches. It was created in 1986 at the initiative of Quintana Roo state governor Pedro Joaquín Coldwell. Because much of the coastal land inside the reserve was already in private hands, it would have been prohibitive for the government to expropriate the land and declare the whole region a national park. The UNESCO-sponsored Man and Biosphere Program is a much more flexible concept; it allows for "sustainable development" in the areas that have already been altered, while designating other, less disturbed regions, as "core" areas where all human activity except scientific research is forbidden. With funding from The Nature Conservancy and the World Wildlife Fund in the United States, MacKinnon founded a nonprofit organization called Amigos de Sian Ka'an to assist with the administration of the reserve. She was elected its first president.

MacKinnon is hopeful that managed development within the reserve will both protect the wild coast and provide a model for the whole region. "The principle we base our conservation efforts on is creating ownership of the natural resources," she explained. "You can't have the conservationists on one side and the developers on the other. You need to bring both sides together." MacKinnon is by nature a consensus builder; she put together a board that includes developers, politicians, and environmentalists and a list of benefactors that ranges from the Ford Foundation, to Greenpeace, to hotels in Cancún; even the PRI hard-liner Carlos Hank González is a contributor. Hank González is one of Mexico's richest men, a survivor of a long political career filled with allegations of corruption and embezzlement. He is reputed to have wide holdings in

Cancún and, according to a published report in the magazine *Proceso* on May 29, 1995, within the reserve itself.

MacKinnon's hope is to use development as a mechanism to give nature an economic value. In the 1960s, when Cancún was conceived of and built, tourists wanted sun and sea. By the 1980s a specialized but growing section of the market began demanding less luxury and more authenticity—places like Sian Ka'an. MacKinnon believes hotels that can tap this market will have an incentive to keep the natural environment pristine and prevent the reserve from becoming overdeveloped.

One idea being bandied about is to create a market in development rights in which each property owner in the reserve would be granted the right to develop only a limited number of hotel rooms. A property owner who chooses not to develop could sell the right to do so in an open market. In any case, the idea is to keep development small but find ways to ensure that property owners can turn a profit. "You have to develop the reserve," argued MacKinnon. "We just want it done right."

In 1992 I had seen the kind of ecotourism MacKinnon was talking about working south of Mexico, in the neighboring country of Belize. On Caye Caulker, a coral island off the coast of the small English-speaking country formerly known as British Honduras, I rented a room from an ex–lobster fisherman named George Jimenez. "Seventeen years ago, I was one of the first to see that tourism would be a new business on the island," Jimenez told me as we motored out to the nearby reef. For decades, Jimenez and the other residents of the small island had made a comfortable living selling their catch to Red Lobster, the U.S. restaurant chain. In the mid-1970s, the first tourists landed on the shores of Caye Caulker. As the tourist volume slowly increased, many families invested in guest rooms, restaurants, and services. Because none of the islanders sold their land to outside investors, development has been slow and limited. Nobody got rich, but the standard of living steadily rose. And the reef, though overfished, has not been damaged by the usual side effects of rapid overdevelopment. "Sometimes I think it would be good to make the whole reef a reserve," Jimenez concluded that afternoon as we headed back to the island after a day of snorkeling. "You don't come to kill the fish, you come to look at the fish. The fish should be valued not by the pound but by the seeing."

That was all fine and good. But I had my doubts that the same kind of success could be duplicated around Cancún, even within the reserve. What had limited tourist development in Belize was both a lack of capital and a labor shortage. Glenn Godfrey, who was at the time Belize's minister of tourism and the environment, explained his country's tourism philosophy to me a few days after I went snorkeling with Jimenez. "We made a deliberate decision not to be like Cancún," he said. "We didn't want to borrow millions of dollars to build big hotels. When you build large hotels you attract a lot of manpower and a lot of vested interests who want to keep on building. It's like a coke habit. Once you start building, you can't stop or all the construction workers will be unemployed. In the end, the only people who make money off the large hotels are the contractors."

Indeed, the little I had seen of supposed ecological tourism in the Cancún area did not make me feel optimistic. The two shallow reefs closest to Cancún have been stomped to death by throngs of tourists. Garrafón Reef, just offshore from Isla Mujeres, has been reduced to a pile of rocks by lotion-slathering sun worshippers who treat it like an underwater playground. About a thousand snorkelers visit the reef each day.

Meanwhile, a company called AguaWorld has installed a floating platform virtually on top of the reef at Punta Nizuc, just offshore from Cancún island, near the Club Med. Araceli Domínguez has been feuding with AguaWorld's owner, Germán Orozco, since he opened the platform in 1994. High-speed motorboats bring hundreds of tourists to the reef each day. Because they are on a platform, they tend to stay longer, and to use suntan lotion, which can damage the coral. The reef around the platform is badly trampled—much of the coral is dead. A marine biologist, David Gutiérrez, has conducted a survey of the offshore reef along the Quintana Roo coast; he told me that the platform had been built on top of some coral heads, which, blocked from the sun, had all died. In March 1995, a sightseeing submarine operated by AguaWorld slammed into the reef, bursting a window. "Water was coming in and there was total panic," Doreen McCann, a tourist from Rhode Island, told the local press.

When I visited Germán Orozco, the owner of AguaWorld, he insisted he was an environmentalist and employed the language of ecotourism to justify his operation. "We care for the reef, because our livelihood depends on it," he argued. "We provide a bathroom out there so people don't go on the reef, we tell them not to touch the coral." But from an economic standpoint, I am not sure that a live reef is worth much more than a dead one. Most of the first-time snorkelers—which is AguaWorld's market—do not know the difference. They see a few fish, they lie in the sun. It's just another day at the beach.

An even more cynical effort to exploit the environmental market is represented by Xcaret, a nature-oriented theme park an hour south of Cancún. Xcaret has dubbed itself "Nature's Sacred Paradise"; its billboards in Cancún exhort visitors to save the planet, conserve water, and put trash in its place. Xcaret's ad campaign seems to imply that the twenty-five-dollar entry fee buys more than admission to the park; it is also, somehow, a demonstration of environmental concern.

I spent an afternoon at Xcaret wandering through the aquarium, watching bored spider monkeys and listless jaguars, exploring the arboretum, and listening to the schmaltzy New Age soundtrack in the sparsely populated butterfly garden. Xcaret is a pleasant enough place—if theme parks are your thing—and the park has made some contributions to regional ecology, such as the sea turtle nursery. But Xcaret is no more ecotourism than the Bronx zoo. Its success does not increase the "economic value" of nature because all the animals are in cages. Nor does it contribute to the preservation and well-being of local culture. The "Mayan Village" at Xcaret features thatch huts, dugout canoes, and hemp hammocks, but not a single living Maya.

In fact, the construction of the theme park did significant environmental damage. A subterranean river was blasted open to provide a water ride through the earth; bulldozers were brought in to topple the jungle and build an artificial lagoon and a land spit into the sea. Araceli Domínguez has alleged that the construction of the spit damaged nearby patch reefs.

But the most sustained environmental protest has come over Xcaret's "Swim with the Dolphins" program, which is also its most popular attraction. For a hefty fee, park visitors can join the dolphins in their small pen. Opponents calls the conditions cruel, and even some visitors to the park agree. "If this is supposed to be a place with an ecological consciousness, we don't understand your attitude toward the dolphins," wrote some Argentinean visitors in the guest book near the aquarium. "Free the Dolphins!" added some Mexican visitors. A park employee getting ready to feed the crocodiles explained to me that the park is building a larger home for the dolphins. Besides, he added, "thirty thousand dolphins are killed each year by the fishing industry. The problem is not that Xcaret has ten."

But again this misses the point, because it conflates two different issues. Whether keeping dolphins in a small pen is cruel is separate from whether it constitutes ecotourism. If Xcaret were taking visitors out into the ocean to watch pods of dolphins in the wild, then it would be creating an economic incentive to protect them. By showing how to make money from penned dolphins, the park is instead raising the economic value of dolphins in captivity. In fact, "swim with the dolphins" programs have become the latest craze throughout the Caribbean.

Carlos Constandse, who designed and built Xcaret, bristles at the suggestion that he is not motivated by environmental idealism. His office in Cancún is decorated with a dolphin sculpture and quotes from Jacques Cousteau. Constandse, a Mexico City native, arrived in the Yucatán in the early 1970s. "I lived for a year on the beach and that's how I became connected to nature," he explained. Constandse made his fortune building hotels and condominiums in Cancún, but he is also a major supporter of the Sian Ka'an reserve. "In the developing world, you have an obligation not only to protect nature but to provide food for the people," he explained. "Any place that hopes to accommodate tourists has to make alterations."

After Xcaret was attacked in the local press for its environmental shortcomings, Constandse took out a full-page announcement to answer his detractors. In it, in three paragraphs, he traces the history of environmental thought since the humanists. The first generation of environmentalists, according to Constandse, were "The Fanatics," who are composed of all those among whom "ignorance and fear of change cause an unconscious paralysis and an insistence that we put nature before man. They prefer to have humanity ignorant, without work, and dying of hunger." Constandse calls the second generation "The Aware"; he describes this group as largely passive but concerned about environmental destruction. The third generation, among which Constandse clearly counts himself, is "The Actors"—"They have awareness and responsibility about the environment but put man, because he is a spiritual being, above nature. . . . They know that dignity is obtained through work and creativity, and with faith, hope, and courage, they overcome the fear that change can produce. . . . Those who believe in sustainable development can see the wisdom of this idea every day in Xcaret."

Instead of bolstering his environmental credentials, Constandse's self-righteous diatribe shows just how far Mexico is from harnessing tourism for environmental protection. If one of the most environmentally conscious developers in the country can argue that anyone who objects to keeping dolphins in pens is condemning all humans to misery in the name of environmental conservation; if he truly sees no contradiction between exhorting the citizenry to "put trash in its place" while Xcaret serves thousands of hamburgers a day in Styrofoam trays; then one can only imagine the extent to which most Mexican developers continue to view environmental regulations as meddling and counterproductive. That is why Barbara MacKinnon's work in Sian Ka'an has been so important. But it is also why finding an environmentally responsible formula for developing the Sian Ka'an reserve—and the rest of the Mexico's still untapped touristic resources—remains a truly daunting task.

III

Like every major industry in Mexico, tourism was developed from the top down. The country made its first forays into tourism after World War II, when Mexican consulates in the United States began a subdued campaign to attract vacationers. The effort was half-hearted because the government feared that an influx of foreigners would undermine the country's moral fiber. They pointed to Tijuana, where Hollywood celebrities flocked during Prohibition in search of legal booze and cheap sex, as an example.

By the end of the decade, Mexico was reconsidering. The postwar economic boom and the growth of commercial jet travel made the two-week foreign vacation a reality for the United States' growing middle class. With Mexico also undergoing a sustained boom, President Miguel Alemán began sprucing up Acapulco, a colonial-era port city on the coast of the dirt-poor state of Guerrero. Acapulco had already become a getaway for Mexico City's emerging elite.

Because tourist development was state directed, Alemán needed to find a way to link it to the project of nation building and modernization. He argued that instead of corrupting Mexico's moral character, international tourism would make the country more cosmopolitan. "The friendship of the people of one country and the people of another is as important as the friendship of one person to another," Alemán pointed out. Of course, he also had more personal motives for wanting to develop Acapulco. He set the standard for all subsequent tourist developments by buying up large amounts of land and then selling it back to developers as the tourist city spread.

By the 1960s Acapulco had caught on. It became the fantasy vacation spot, the prize that would provoke screaming pandemonium when it was awarded to a lucky contestant on an afternoon game show. Other destinations arose pell-mell along what became known as the Mexican Riviera—San Blas, Mazatlán, and Puerto Vallarta. From the beginning, however, tourism suffered from growing pains. The hotels boomed along the beach, sewage poured into the ocean, and the slums spread over the hills. The infrastructure backlog was not as great as in places like Mexico City and Monterrey, but the consequences were more serious because polluted beaches and the stench of sewage scared away the tourists.

By the mid-1960s the government had decided it was time to put things in order. The tourist industry was growing faster than exports, but the impending problems were clear. The government needed an integrated approach both to fully exploit tourism's potential and to limit the pollution problems associated with rapid growth. That is how the team of bankers appointed by President Díaz Ordaz came up with the idea of Cancún. They also realized that the Cuban Revolution in 1959 had closed the premiere Caribbean resort to U.S. vacationers. Cancún was aimed at capturing the wide-open East Coast market.

In 1969 the plan to build Cancún was approved. With loans from the International Development Bank, the government set up a trust called Fonatur (the National Tourism Fund) to develop and administer the new tourist cities. The plan was compared to the U.S. space program—a monumental effort that would bring enormous prestige to the emerging nation. Like Acapulco, Cancún acquired a political patron. President Luis Echeverría, whose wife's family hailed from the region, took a personal interest in the construction of the city. Like Alemán in Acapulco, he managed to acquire a prime beachfront lot, where he built a mansion. There were widespread reports that he secretly owned much more.

It is easy to understand how in an atmosphere in which the nation's most powerful politicians were personally backing the project, and in which the official rhetoric had raised the construction of a tourist city to a feat of heroic nationalism, little things like zoning and environmental regulations got lost in the shuffle. The problem was most severe in Cancún, especially when the Mexican economy hit the skids after the 1982 devaluation. But Huatulco, another Fonatur fantasy city, suffered a similar fate. Huatulco was born in 1983, when 50,000 acres (20,000 hectares) were expropriated along the rugged coast of Oaxaca. Progress came quickly to the backwater fishing village, which still lived without electricity or running water. Two thousand residents were relocated—many of them forcibly—to a squatter settlement just outside the proposed hotel zone. Wildlife, including several species of rare birds, was also disrupted as the jungle was cleared, hillsides were terraced, and hotels, most of them foreign chains, rose rapidly along a series of stunning bays. More than a decade later, even the authorities acknowledge that the project has been something of a disappointment. Huatulco has not drawn the sun-starved hordes in the numbers Fonatur anticipated, and the construction boom has slacked off. Meanwhile, the squatter settlement of La Crucecita has grown faster than anticipated. Sewage has spilled into the pristine bays, and land disputes remain unresolved. The worst blow to Huatulco's aspirations to becoming an international tourism center came after midnight on August 29, 1996, when 80 heavily armed guerrillas from a new rebel force calling itself the Popular Revolutionary Army (EPR) attacked the resort town, leaving 9 dead. Most of the EPR combatants were recruited from the miserably poor Zapotec Indian villages in the surrounding mountains.

During a 1992 visit to Cancún, I asked Fonatur representative Jorge Polanco whether he thought there was any risk that environmental problems could eventually undermine Cancún's appeal, the way they had in Acapulco. "I'm not an expert in ecology," he said. "But I think growth has to be controlled. There's a growing environmental consciousness here. There are problems—but they are manageable." Then he invited me to do the math. Cancún has more than twenty thousand hotel rooms; according to Fonatur calculations, each hotel room generates four permanent jobs, most of which pay above the minimum wage. Cancún receives more than 1.5 million visitors a year, and the city accounts for one-third of Mexico's $6.35 billion-a-year tourist industry. The government's total investment in the construction of Cancún, said Polanco, was approximately $3 billion. Each government dollar attracted ten times that amount in private investment. In 1991, Polanco claimed, the city raised $1 billion in tax revenues.

Nationally, tourism is the third biggest generator of foreign exchange after oil; it employs 604,000 people directly, and 2.1 million indirectly. That's 9 percent of the population. Even more significant, because it benefits from a weak peso, tourism stabilizes Mexico's volatile economy. In 1995, a year in which the Mexican economy contracted by 6.9 percent, the number of foreign visitors grew by more than 21 percent, and foreign exchange earnings from tourism, buoyed by the weak peso, were also up slightly. Of course, the government puts the best possible spin on the numbers. Much of the profit earned by the international hotels—between seventy and ninety cents on each dollar by some estimates—is sent out of the country. The revenues are also inflated because Mexico has failed to fully address the infrastructure backlog and repair the environmental damage in most tourist cities. In Cancún, for example, tens of thousands live without sewage service and running water. The government has pledged to clean up the contaminated Nichupté lagoon, which was once a nursery for lobsters and other commercial fish. Other damage can never be repaired—the destruction of the mangroves, the coastal dune system, and the loss of wildlife, for example.

But while megaprojects like Cancún may have made money for the federal government, they have also spawned a large-scale, capital-intensive style of development geared toward quick returns. They have institutionalized land speculation and fomented a tourist economy in which capital is highly concentrated, developers are used to thinking big, and power is concentrated in the hands of the federal bureaucracy.

Cancún's success was also due to economic and demographic conditions that are no longer prevalent. A generation of U. S. baby boomers with large disposable incomes created the perfect economic environment for mass tourism. But today the sun-and-fun market is saturated with warm weather destinations all over the world. Because it is used to thinking big, Mexico has had a hard time adapting to the new trends in travel such as nature tourism and adventure tourism, the fastest-growing segment of the market.

For example, in 1995 the Mexican government announced plans to develop the Xcalak peninsula, a largely unpopulated stretch of coast that extends from the midpoint of the Sian Ka'an reserve all the way to the border with Belize. The beaches along the last bit of wild coast are coarse and rocky, but the barrier reef, which extends from Cancún all the way to the southern tip of Belize, is one of the most spectacular in the world. Offshore is the Chinchorro banks, an atoll-like formation studded with sunken Spanish galleons. Adventurous scuba divers have been visiting for years, but the dirt road along the coast takes hours to navigate, and conditions in the few hotels are generally primitive. In the early 1990s a new trust was created to finance infrastructure development along what government planners have dubbed the "Costa Maya." The idea is to convert the Xcalak peninsula into an international mecca for ecotourism.

But the project got off to rocky start. When I visited Senator Benito Rosel from the right-center National Action Party (PAN) in his office in Mexico City, he insisted that the Costa Maya project is a scam to enrich a group of fat-cat politicians from the Yucatán. A good deal of the land on which the project is to be developed is owned by former Quintana Roo governor Jesús Martínez Ross. Even more alarming is an official decree signed by Yucatán governor and political godfather Víctor Cervera Pacheco on November 28, 1994, the day he left his post as minister of agrarian reform. In the decree, Cervera transferred title to nearly 100,000 acres (39,500 hectares) of federal land to the state of Quintana Roo, which happened to be governed by Cervera's close friend, Mario Villanueva Madrid. The transfer was supposed to facilitate the development of the Costa Maya project, but there was one major problem—a good chunk is within the Sian Ka'an Biosphere Reserve. Regional environmentalists have argued that the document signed by Cervera has no legal standing.

In fact the 180-mile barrier reef that shadows the Yucatán coast—the second longest in the world after Australia's Great Barrier Reef—remains the region's greatest unexploited natural resource. It is no less spectacular than Yosemite National Park or the Grand Canyon, but its true value, both in ecological and touristic terms, has never been fully appreciated. Since 1511, when the first European ship to visit the Yucatán sank on the reef (Hernán Cortés also lost a ship near Isla Mujeres in 1519), the reef had been more of a nuisance than a boon to development because it prevented large ships from finding safe harbor. Even the creators of Cancún bemoaned the lack of a deep harbor that could attract cruise ships.

That changed rapidly after 1974, when Jacques Cousteau visited the region. His ship, the *Calypso,* spent several months in the Yucatán filming two of Cousteau's most famous underwater documentaries—"The Incredible March of the Spiny Lobsters" and "Sleeping Sharks of the Yucatán." Even though the general public still viewed scuba diving as a dangerous sport suitable for only the stoutest adventurers, the diving world was starting to realize that recreational scuba diving required virtually no athletic skill and only a minimum of training. As early as 1953, after several of his companions were killed in diving accidents testing his innovations and probing the limits of human underwater activity, Cousteau himself noted with a certain irritation that, "Today, after our hesitant penetration of the one-hundred-and-thirty-foot zone, women and old men reach that depth on their third or fourth dive."

By the end of the 1970s, Cozumel island, across the channel from Cancún, had become one of the world's diving centers. Cozumel is ringed by some of the most spectacular reefs in the world—a wall of exploding colors and bizarre formations perched on top of a sea trench dropping 3,000 feet into an unknowable abyss. But the island also has the only deep harbor in the region. It quickly became a favorite cruise ship destination. The ships spawned gift shops and tacky tourist restaurants, which soon inundated the resort. Then, in the mid-1980s, the federal government decided it was time for a second pier on the island and granted the concession to a Mexican company, Consorcio H. The company announced a $230 million plan to build not only the pier, but also two hotels, a shopping mall, and a golf course.

Scuba divers and international environmentalists were aghast: the new pier was to be built virtually on top of Paradise Reef, one of the island's most famous dive sites. They demanded that the pier be moved to the northern part of the island where there was no reef, but Consorcio H would not budge. In 1994, Jean-Michel Cousteau, Jacques's son, came out against the project. He even took Quintana Roo governor Mario Villanueva snorkeling on Paradise Reef to persuade him to bar the new pier. In a nonbinding referendum held the following summer, 60 percent of Cozumel's population called for the dock to be relocated. In January

1996, with construction of the pier well under way, Mexican environmentalists petitioned the Commission on Environmental Cooperation (CEC) to evaluate the project. The commission, created under NAFTA, is empowered to investigate whether a signatory country is enforcing its own environmental laws. The Cozumel pier was the first case in Mexico brought under article 14, which allows citizens or nongovernmental groups to petition the CEC to investigate an allegation of noncompliance. In June 1996 the CEC recommended that the Mexican government open its files for inspection, a process known as a "factual record." Julia Carabias, Mexico's top environmental official, was not happy. "If there is a problem in the application of the law, then it should be the society and our government that determines it," she said. "I am not in favor of supranational organizations telling us how to govern."

Carabias lashed out at the environmental groups that had filed the complaint with the CEC and called Homero Aridjis, president of a leading environmental organization called the Group of 100, "a liar." Aridjis's concern with the Cozumel pier, Carabias alleged without offering any evidence, "was not ecological but economic."

Directly across the channel from Cozumel I got an underwater view of some of the worst destruction along the whole reef system. In 1986 a company called Calica, a joint venture between Ica of Mexico and Vulcan of Alabama, opened a limestone quarry on the mainland just south of Playa del Carmen. The pulverized rock is shipped back to the United States for road construction. In order for large ships to pick up the cargo, the company created a deep harbor. While company officials swore to me they had not damaged the reef, when I hired a boat to scuba dive in the deep channel I saw thousands of broken corals and sea fans littering the muddy sea trench the company had opened. There was not a single, solitary fish—only a lobster, which had taken refuge in an enormous truck tire that had settled on the bottom.

Such destruction is especially distressing because, in the three decades since Jacques Cousteau explored the Yucatán's reef system, much has been learned about reefs and the crucial role they play in the world's ecology. Reefs, which take thousands of years to build, are made up of the calcified skeletons of billions of tiny coral polyps. Scientists are just beginning to explore their startling biological wealth. Because corals defend themselves against predators by emitting toxins, they have a huge potential for biomedical research. An estimated twelve hundred medical compounds have already been synthesized from corals, including anti-inflammatory drugs that have shown promise in the treatment of AIDS and cancer.

Reefs protect shorelines around the world from erosion. They are the key link in a large and complex marine food chain on which millions of people depend. Finally, some scientists suggest that reefs are a barometer of the planet's overall environmental health—a dead reef could be an augur of a greater ecological peril.

Like the tropical rain forest to which they are often compared, reefs are extremely fragile, and their continued health depends on the preservation of precise conditions that are often altered by tourist development. Silt from the construction of roads, hotels, and artificial beaches can flow into the ocean, blocking the sun and damaging the reef. The dumping of untreated sewage, rich in organic nutrients, produces seaweed and algal growth that can smother coral. A single touch can kill a coral polyp, and trampling by overzealous tourists has all but destroyed a number of shallow reefs. Dive boats have smashed coral colonies with poorly thrown anchors. A boom in commercial fishing has also depleted certain species and altered the ecological balance regionwide. Caribbean lobster in particular has been heavily exploited and sold mostly to U.S. restaurant chains because it can be frozen and later thawed.

Most of the damage so far has been localized. The Yucatán reef is still healthier than other reef systems in the Philippines and the Caribbean islands. In recent years, new zoning laws have been implemented and marine reserves created. But Cancún developers still do not see the reef as an economic asset; they view any attempt to limit development as a threat to their bottom line. There is therefore enormous pressure to keep building even after development has reached the point at which further growth diminishes the value of the original investment. Instead of slowing down and shifting to smaller projects, Cancún may be heating up. In the summer of 1996, the Mexican government appeared to be on the brink of legalizing gambling in Cancún. Gambling could bring another wave of runaway development, tipping the balance and completing the cycle of Acapulcoization. Given the role that both the jungle and the coral reef play in regulating the world's environment, their further destruction would be a tragedy of global proportion. But with the peso struggling, the government believes it has few options but to provide jobs and attract capital, even if it has to sacrifice a reef or a lagoon to do it.

IV

Although the environmental cost of Cancún seems high from a global perspective, the view is very different up close. Certainly Samuel Mezo, a fisherman just down the coast was willing to pay it. After all, Cancún made him a millionaire.

I met Mezo on the beach at Xpu-Há on a breezy November afternoon in 1995. He was framing windows in a two-story hotel he was building, the muscles in his arm rippling with each hammer stroke. Trailers full of gringos were scattered about the palm-studded beach that arched along a turquoise bay. I asked Mezo when he had seen his first tourist, and I was surprised that he remembered exactly. It was 1952, at four in the afternoon. Mezo was sixteen. He looked down the beach where we were now sitting and saw a strange figure trudging slowly toward him. The man was tall and very light skinned. He was carrying a knapsack and a military-style canteen. His name was Peter Lembo, an American. He stayed with the Mezo family for two months, helping them fish in return for his keep. "He wasn't a great deal of help," recalled Mezo. "But it wouldn't have occurred to us to charge him."

Mezo could not have known it at the time, but his life was about to change forever. For thirteen years, ever since his father, Anastasio, sailed from Cozumel and settled in Xpu-Há, the Mezos had lived a simple but comfortable existence as fishermen. The Mezos, in fact, were part of the first wave of mestizos to resettle the Yucatán coast. In 1847 the Maya Indians rose up and drove all the foreigners from the peninsula. The reconquest of the forgotten corner of the Mexican republic was arduous and bloody. In 1901 the Maya were defeated, but not until the 1930s were the last revolts put down. In 1939, when the Mezo family arrived at Xpu-Há, there were two families up the coast in Paamul, three families in Playa del Carmen, and six families in Tulum. Cancún island was deserted. There were no roads, no radios. The only warning that a hurricane was about to hit the coast came from Anastasio Mezo, who would survey the clouds gathering over the open ocean.

Like the handful of other families on the coast, the Mezos lived from fishing and, later, from their coconut planation. They sold the fish to the rubber camps, where hundreds of Maya were press-ganged into gathering chicle from trees in the jungle. They also ate a lot of lobster, mostly when nothing else decent was available. The crustaceans were as plentiful as insects; Mezo recalled hunting them on the beach at night with a machete.

In 1964 Mezo joined the merchant marine and sailed around the world. He did not return home until 1973, when Anastasio Mezo passed away. The beach he knew was largely unchanged, but he kept hearing on the radio that the government was planning to build a whole tourist city up the coast on Cancún island.

By the mid-1970s tourists were arriving with some regularity at Xpu-Há, and the five Mezo children who still shared the beach took their machetes and widened the trail so that cars could pass. By the end of the decade, they had built *palapas* (small bungalows made from palm thatch and mud) and began charging the tourists, mostly American hippies, to spend the night in them. In the winter of 1982 the whole beach was full of campers.

In 1993 the Mezo brothers caught a big break. They sold a piece of their land to a German developer called Robinson's Club for $1 million. Samuel invested his share of the money in building more bungalows.

Samuel Mezo knows that the days of hunting lobsters on the beach with a machete are long gone. He thinks Cancún is overbuilt and ugly. He also has many friends who sold out too early and made a pittance on land that was worth millions. But when he thinks about the changes, when he compares his life now to how it was then, he thinks that, on balance, tourism has been a positive force.

"Fishing for me was a beautiful life," said Mezo, as he put down his hammer. "Tourism was a change. But I think it was a change for the better."

Of course, it was hardly surprising that Mezo, who had made a pretty penny in the tourism boom, was generally supportive of the industry. So in order to get another perspective I decided to visit the slums of Cancún. I hopped on a city bus and rode out to the shantytowns. Ten minutes north of downtown, the tourist strip gave way to a bustling working-class shopping district. Stores selling T-shirts, packaged tours, and newspapers were replaced by others selling hardware, shoes, and clothing. The houses were made of cinderblock, with clothes drying on lines strung across the yards. Rusted rebar poked through the roofs like weeds in an unkempt garden. To those who do not understand its function, the rebar is ugly, an eyesore. To the poor, it represents faith in the future, a belief that with time and hard work they will save enough money to someday build a second story.

As we left the center behind, the potholes grew bigger and then the paved street turned to dust. Roof dogs, a fixture of Mexican shanties, snarled at us as we drove by. Smoke from garbage fires filled the air. At the very edge of the city, houses of roughly hewn trees lashed together with rope and covered with cardboard stood in open lots. The utopian city had deteriorated into apparent chaos.

But like many slums I have visited in Mexico, I found Zone 103 in Cancún to be a neighborhood of upwardly mobile migrants who saw in their surroundings not misery but the promise of a better life. Manuel, a storekeeper I met at the bus turnaround, had migrated from a town near Merida four years earlier. He and his wife, who hailed from Tabasco, had saved up three thousand dollars to buy a plot of land and open a small store. They told stories of success and achievement, and they believed in Cancún with a faith that had probably not been seen since the days of the bankers. A cousin, Manuel told me, had started cleaning rooms in one of the large hotels and was now a supervisor. "If you work hard and save your money, in Cancún you get ahead," said Manuel, sounding like a brochure or a politician. "There are many opportunities."

In the eroding hills of Oaxaca and on the fringes of the Tabasco oil fields, I met many poor people who were concerned about environmental problems because they directly affected their well-being. But to the residents of the shanties of Cancún, the relationship between environmental deterioration and social welfare is abstract at best. They are perfectly willing to see the tourists trample the reef to death if it means a better life for their children.

That is why the defense of the environment is largely a middle-class concern in Cancún. The creation of a class of property owners who feel protective of what might be called "a quality of life" is the backbone of the city's environmental movement. But the middle class has not always been able to prevail in a political system controlled by the federal bureaucracy, beholden to the interests of large capital, and under enormous pressure to provide basic employment. The second brake on development in Cancún is the growing international awareness that the reef, the jungle, and the whole tropical ecosystem play an enormous role in regulating the global environment. That is why international environmental groups have taken an interest in the region. Those interests are represented by Barbara MacKinnon and the Amigos de Sian Ka'an. Because Araceli Domínguez's battle for environmental protection is inextricably linked to a larger struggle for political representation and enfranchisement, she feels justified in being confrontational, aggressive, and not completely constrained by the facts. MacKinnon is looking for results, not political power, and therefore pragmatism wins out over confrontation, scientific rigor over alarmism.

Because environmental protection is not a grass-roots issue in Cancún, increased environmental protection may well depend on increased prosperity. The contradiction is that the growth needed to propel more people into the middle class, unless is it carefully managed and controlled, could continue to undermine the city's appeal as a tourist haven.

What has already been lost? One hundred miles south, inside the Sian Ka'an reserve, a series of lagoons, barrier islands, wetlands, and mangroves closely parallel the original landscape on which Cancún was built. I had spent a day there, riding in a motorboat across a turquoise lagoon. I saw a crocodile, a lanky white ibis perched in a tree, a kingfisher, a yellow-headed vulture, and countless other birds I could not identify. I swam in a river that meandered through the wetlands; I drifted past the ruins of an ancient Mayan city.

It was a remarkable journey through a unique landscape, but one I also realize would hold little appeal for Manuel, even if he were fortunate enough to someday see it. Comparing Sian Ka'an with Cancún made me deeply sad, but I took some solace in the knowledge that the transformation had in some clumsy and imperfect way benefited people like Manuel. It also helped to keep things in perspective, something that is not always easy when you are standing in the middle of the slums. When I boarded the bus back into town, I passed the same roof dogs; I saw the same day-care center, the clotheslines, the cement homes. The pavement returned, then the stores, and then I was deposited downtown. I walked to Araceli Domínguez's hotel, picked up my bags, and said good-bye. I caught a cab to the airport, once again watching the billboards flash by, staring at the strange skyline of the tourist city looming across the lagoon like a set from a science-fiction movie. My plane took off over a large expanse of unbroken jungle, then banked and doubled back to the sea. I could make out the barrier reef dividing the shallow turquoise water from the darker blue of the open ocean. Cancún, the enormous fantasy city, grew rapidly smaller until it appeared for a final moment as a black speck, a single dot in an enormous landscape of green and blue extending to the hazy horizon.

−eight−

Dumping on the Border

In the early 1990s, when I first began to visit Tijuana regularly, the famously squalid city just over the border from San Diego was experiencing a sustained boom. *Maquiladoras,* or foreign-owned assembly plants, were sprouting throughout the city like desert scrub after a spring rain. Civic leaders proudly described their city as the new Hong Kong of North America, but they closed their eyes to the downside of the industrial boom: pollution.

Wages in the maquiladoras, though less than five dollars a day, were still higher than what desperate families could earn in the eroding countryside, and so a steady stream of migrants from the interior poured into Tijuana. They came on the second-class buses and moved into a cousin's house until they could stake out a plot of land in the scrubby hills. The city's infrastructure was completely overwhelmed, not only by the new migrants but by the factories themselves. The maquiladoras dumped toxic chemicals down the drain and buried sludge-filled drums in the desert.

No neighborhood suffered more from Tijuana's runaway development than Ejido Chilpancingo. Chilpancingo was established in 1974, at the same time that the Mexican federal government expropriated land from a collective farm and created the Otay Mesa industrial park on a two-hundred-foot bluff overlooking the Alomar River. The express purpose of Ejido Chilpancingo was to provide a place for the factory workers to live.

The neighborhood lives in the shadow of the city's largest industrial park, and every morning you can see lines of people slowly climbing the stairs that have been built in the bluff to get to their jobs at the factories. After two decades, Chilpancingo (since the area was urbanized, "Ejido" is often dropped) has become relatively prosperous by Tijuana standards; there are cinderblock homes and electricity, and most of the 770 property owners no longer work in the factories. Instead they have moved into the service sector, investing in taxis, buses, and small stores, or commuting to better jobs in downtown Tijuana. About two thousand factory workers— mostly young men and women who have migrated from Mexico's poorer interior states—still live in cramped boarding houses within Chilpancingo. Tens of thousands more have settled in the hills on the other side of the Alomar River, many in tin and cardboard shacks without water, sewage service, or electricity.

I first visited Chilpancingo in January 1992. Like every squatter colony in Mexico, Chilpancingo has a "leader," an unelected, de facto mayor who serves as a liaison between the neighborhood and city authorities. In Chilpancingo, Maurilio Sánchez Pachuca had moved beyond the usual battles to get the municipal government to bring water, electricity, and sewage lines to the community. He had also launched a crusade against the polluting factories.

The directions I had been given to Sánchez Pachuca's house were typical for the unmarked slums: take the new road to Tecate, make a right after you pass the last factory, and keep going downhill until the road turns to dirt. As soon as you cross the creek, just ask the first person you see— everybody knows who he is. I found the house, a green and white cinderblock building with a wrought-iron gate in front, without trouble, but his wife told me that her husband had gone into the hills to meet with the squatters. His son offered to help me find him, however, so we jumped in the car and drove off through the town's muddy streets.

As we drove across the shallow Alomar River (the bridge washed away long ago), the ordered grid of Chilpancingo's streets degenerated into a crisscrossing network of dirt roads that snaked through the hillsides. We found Sánchez Pachuca in the Loma Bonita neighborhood talking to a group of *colonos,* as the neighborhood residents are known, about his efforts to get a water line for the community. In the meantime, he suggested to a group of about forty people who had gathered in a covered courtyard, everyone can save water and improve the neighborhood by using leftover, sudsy dishwater to water trees and plants.

Sánchez Pachuca interrupted his lecture to greet me. He is a round man except for his face, which is square and heavy. His head is covered in thick black hair with a streak of gray above the part. A bushy mustache hangs slightly over his upper lip. He was dressed in a white shirt, dress slacks, loafers, and a cardigan against the morning chill. Sánchez Pachuca walked quickly toward me, his pace, energy, and mobility surprising because of his bulk. He asked me to sit for a few more minutes while he finished up his meeting and then offered to cancel the rest of his morning activities so he could take me on a tour of the industrial park.

In 1965 the Mexican government inaugurated its Border Industrialization Plan and invited U.S. factories to establish maquiladoras, or assembly plants, in Mexico. Under a 1962 U.S. customs regulation, U.S. companies are allowed to export materials from the United States to another country, assemble the materials there, and reimport the finished product into the United States, paying duty only on the value added.

The Mexican program got off to a slow start, but by 1982 it was booming, although not for the reasons the Mexican government had hoped. The collapse of international oil prices had forced Mexico to devalue the peso in order to service the $80 billion international debt it had rung up by borrowing against future oil earnings. The devaluation reduced the dollar value of Mexico's minimum wage by 66 percent, to around five dollars a day. Suddenly labor in Mexico was a better deal than in Korea, Taiwan, or Singapore, where most assembly work was being done. Today, there are more than 2,000 maquiladoras along the length of the U.S.–Mexico border, 550 in Tijuana alone.

Sánchez Pachuca and I drove down the hillside from Loma Bonita and back across the river. He told me that when he arrived in 1982 the Alomar ran clear and cool down from the mountains near Tecate. Its bank, lined with poplar trees and watered by periodic flooding, was a popular picnic spot and a perfect vantage point for watching the eagles soar above the desolate brown mountains on both sides of the Cañon del Padre. In the spring and fall, great squawking flocks of Canadian ducks flapped overhead on their journey along the Pacific Flyway.

Now, jagged rows of workers' shacks rose up to the crest of the hillside behind me, and I could see a line of factories perched on the bluff half a mile away. The Alomar ran orange and sudsy; the rocks in the streambed were stained red. Piled up along the bank were discarded oil drums and mounds of what looked like industrial waste.

The Tijuana city government never connected the factories to the municipal drainage system. Whatever the factories washed down the drain ran into an open spillway, formed a toxic creek in Chilpancingo's main street, and drained into the Alomar. The problem would have been bad enough if the factories were dumping normal wastewater. But because they were largely unsupervised, they disposed of toxic waste like used industrial solvents by simply pouring them down the drain. The toxic creek ran right past a kindergarten, leaving behind shimmering green and yellow puddles that enticed curious children. Because the Alomar is a tributary of the Tijuana River, everything dumped into it is eventually carried across the border into the United States and out to the river's terminus at Imperial Beach, just south of San Diego.

We left my car in front of Sánchez Pachuca's house and took his brown Dodge Dart up to the cement drainage canal, which sloped down the steep hillside. The factories, Sánchez Pachuca explained, wait for rainy days to dump their waste down the drain so that mixed with the normal effluent their dumping will be less obvious.

"As soon as a few drops fall from the sky this canal fills up with a liquid so bad it makes your eyes sting," he said, as he stood over the dry canal, which looked like a toboggan run headed straight for Chilpancingo's main street.

There are more than two hundred factories in the Otay Mesa industrial park—from American and Japanese giants like Panasonic, Maxell, and Johnson and Johnson to smaller American and Mexican companies. Because many share the same sewage line, it is impossible to tell which companies are responsible for the dumping. But when we visited the industrial park on a Sunday morning we found several companies flagrantly violating environmental laws when they figured no one would be around. Workers from a Mexican company called Felpa were burning some sort of waste in an open pit—the black smoke made my throat tingle and my eyes burn. I scaled a fence nearby to look in on Metales y Derivados, a San Diego–based company that extracted lead from car batteries, melted it down into ingots, and shipped it back across the border into the United States. Sitting in the lot was a twenty-foot mound of lead sulfate, a highly toxic byproduct of the reclamation process.

Under Mexican law and international treaty, the lead waste should have been returned to the United States for proper disposal, but instead, according to Sánchez Pachuca, trucks often dumped it on the banks of the Alomar River. (On several occasions I had seen mounds of what looked like the same stuff along the riverbank.)

What impact were the factories having on the community? Almost everyone I talked to during several visits over the next two years was suffering from some sort of minor or not-so-minor environmental illness— from itching, to boils, to infections and diarrhea. (A 1990 government study reported that 16.4 percent of the population had some sort of skin disease, and 8.5 percent were suffering from respiratory illness.) Farmland around the factories had been ruined by the toxic runoff, animals had died, and the groundwater was so contaminated that the government was forced finally to condemn all the town's wells. An analysis of creek water near the factories done by a Mexican university in 1990 revealed levels of lead 3,400 percent higher than the U.S. federal standard and cadmium levels 1,230 percent higher.

Sánchez Pachuca introduced me to an eleven-year-old boy named Juan José who lived up the block from him and seemed to be suffering from a host of pollution-related ailments. His skin was covered with red blotches, his hair was falling out by the handful, he was lethargic, and he had lost ten pounds.

"I don't know," he said, when I asked him why he didn't want to eat. "I guess I'm just not hungry."

"We're not against the factories," insisted Sánchez Pachuca, as we completed the tour and headed down the road into the canyon. "We just want them to do things right.

"They don't treat people like this in San Diego or El Segundo," he added, referring to a Los Angeles suburb. "Well, we're human beings too."

I

In the summer of 1990, Mexican President Carlos Salinas de Gortari traveled to Europe to promote investment in Mexico. Since taking office at the end of 1988, Salinas had implemented a series of economic reforms designed to make Mexico more attractive to foreign investors. The Europeans were not biting. They had their hands full with Eastern Europe, which was experiencing a similar metamorphosis after the fall of communism. Salinas returned to Mexico empty-handed. The best hope for attracting capital, Salinas realized, was to cut a deal with the gringos. He suddenly threw his weight behind an idea Washington had been quietly pushing for years—a continentwide free-trade agreement.

Salinas's decision set the gears in motion for what would eventually become the North American Free Trade Agreement, or NAFTA. By late 1990, Washington, Mexico City, and Ottawa were touting an agreement that would link 360 million consumers in a $6 trillion regional economy. In the United States, the battle over NAFTA became one of the most widespread and wrenching public policy debates in recent history. Wrapped up in a seemingly dry trade issue were fundamental questions about economic nationalism in an age of global competition—the new rights of capital versus the old rights of labor. "In the final analysis," said Craig Merrilees, who directed the anti-NAFTA Fair Trade Campaign, "the question is how to hold on to U.S. environmental policies and labor standards, all of which are slipping away. If we continue to allow companies to escape the rules and regulations of national governments we will have an era of unregulated laissez faire."

The United States was split largely along class lines. Big business backed the treaty, arguing that it needed to find ways to lower the cost of manufacturing in order to compete with low-cost Asian imports. Unions universally opposed it, arguing that the flight of manufacturing to Mexico had already cost hundreds of thousands of well-paid jobs. The middle class was divided, but many environmental groups, large and small, were in the opposition camp. Free trade with Mexico, environmentalists argued, would drag down U.S. environmental standards as companies flocked to Mexico to avoid more stringent environmental regulations. The buzzword became "downward harmonization."

Suddenly, conditions in the Mexican maquiladoras, which had been the focus of a few regional activists, became a national concern and a symbol of everything that was wrong with NAFTA. Chilpancingo was the classic example—a horribly polluted neighborhood where Mexican workers who held jobs that would have earned union-scale wages in the United States took home less than five dollars a day.

For the duration of the three-year NAFTA debate, the border environmental crisis was in the news. In July 1990, the *New York Times Magazine* published a feature entitled "The Border Boom: Hope and Heartbreak," by Sandy Tolan. The story, which focused on the Nogales area, chronicled the lives of maquiladora workers who lived in crowded shanties, took home fifty-five cents an hour, drank water stored in chemical drums, and refused to relinquish their dreams of a better life. In Matamoros, across from Brownsville, Texas, the stories were even more alarming. The ninety-three maquiladoras in the city had an abysmal safety record. There had been explosions at a company called Retzloff Chemicals in 1983 and 1990; another company, Preservation Products, suffered an explosion in 1989. Stockpiled in front of the Quimica Fluor plant, which manufactures hydrofluoric acid (and is owned partially by Du Pont) were thousands of tons of waste; when farmers in nearby fields complained that their sorghum plants were shriveled, the company paid them off. In 1991 former workers at the Mallory Capacitors plant filed a lawsuit alleging that exposure to dangerous chemicals during pregnancy had caused a slew of miscarriages and birth defects.

In May 1991 the National Toxic Campaign Fund published a report called "Border Trouble: Rivers in Peril," which described the border region as a "2,000-mile-long Love Canal." A third of the sites the group tested for toxic discharge were found to contain levels of toxins 20 to 215,000 times higher than those permitted under U.S. law. Among the worst examples were samples taken near the Ford plant in Nuevo Laredo and the General Motors plant in Matamoros.

Mexico's pollution problem, it was repeatedly pointed out, was also the United States' problem. The Tijuana River carries human and industrial waste across the border and through farmers' fields outside San Diego before emptying into the Pacific. U.S. government officials warned of possible outbreaks of malaria, cholera, and encephalitis along the U.S. portion of the river. Further east, sewage and industrial waste from Mexicali drains into the New River, which empties into the Salton Sea, California's largest lake and a national wildlife refuge. Dumping from factories in Nogales, Mexico, has contaminated groundwater on both sides of the border and may have contributed to a cancer cluster across the border in Nogales, Arizona. The Rio Grande, which runs along the Texas border from El Paso to Brownsville, is choked with sewage and industrial waste. All told, more than 100 million gallons a year of Mexican raw sewage are dumped into border rivers that flow into the United States.

Other reports focused on the toxic waste generated by the maquiladoras, or the air pollution, or industrial accidents. In Tijuana, for example, the city's main gas facility is in one of the most densely populated residential zones in the city. Police chief Luis Octavio Ortega Ramírez noted in a memo to the city's mayor that an explosion at the plant—like the one that killed hundreds, perhaps thousands, at the San Juanico facility near Mexico City in 1984—could rupture chlorine tanks at the nearby water purification plant. Such a scenario, the memo noted, would instantly kill thousands of people.

Emergency procedures were also clearly inadequate. In January 1992 an accident at a Mexican-owned fertilizer company called Qomsa in Mexicali caused the release of a cloud of hydrochloric acid and forced the evacuation of more than one hundred thousand nearby residents. Under a joint agreement, U.S. authorities should have been notified of the spill at the Qomsa plant so that they could have conducted the necessary evacuations on the U.S side, but EPA (Environmental Protection Agency) officials did not even hear about the toxic leak until two days after it happened.

The environmental uproar came as a surprise to President George Bush and the NAFTA boosters. They had expected NAFTA to be widely popular with the American public. It was a key part of Bush's economic policy, and later a key point in his reelection campaign. The president had anticipated that Congress would jump on board and grant him "fast-track" approval for the treaty. Under fast-track procedures, Congress would vote up or down on the entire, unamended treaty within sixty days of its submission. Government negotiators from the three countries would not even come to the table without the fast-track procedure in place because without it their work could be undone by a factious Congress.

In the end, Bush won the battle for fast-track approval, but not without some arm twisting. The environmental outcry forced Bush to soften his initial position, that environmental issues had no place in a trade agreement. In late 1991 Presidents Bush and Salinas promised to work toward a parallel environmental plan. In February 1992 the U.S. government released the Integrated Border Environmental Plan (IBEP), which called for several hundred million dollars in joint U.S.–Mexican investment to clean up the border. Environmentalists called the IBEP "a plan to plan," a vague program that lacked financial commitments and promised only "informal exchanges" and "cooperation" between the United States and Mexico. The IBEP was also roundly criticized for failing to deal with the potential for further growth under NAFTA.

As NAFTA gained steam, U.S. environmental groups began to gear up for a fight. The Sierra Club and Friends of the Earth filed suit to force the government to conduct a review of the environmental impact of the treaty. Along the border, the Bisbee, Arizona–based Border Ecology Project began to mobilize a coalition of U.S. and Mexican environmental groups. Emboldened by visits from journalists and U.S. activists, poor Mexican communities began to call on the government to rein in the factories.

But opposition to NAFTA in Mexico was always marginal, even in the most polluted neighborhoods. For most people, the promise of jobs outweighed the pitfalls of pollution. Salinas never bothered to sell NAFTA in Mexico because its approval by the PRI-controlled Congress was a foregone conclusion. Instead he spent all his time pitching NAFTA in the United States—he promised U.S. audiences that NAFTA would curb illegal immigration, turn Mexico into a prosperous first world trading partner, and fund a major environmental cleanup.

The Mexican government's case for NAFTA was made by Tijuana industrialist Enrique Mier y Terán, whom I met in his downtown office. He argued that his city's environmental problems had been greatly exaggerated and that the best solution in any case was the new growth promised by free trade. NAFTA would provide a new framework to regulate and monitor a relationship that had previously been haphazard, he said.

Tijuana's business elite envisioned that their city would one day become the new industrial hub of North America, comparable to Chicago or Detroit earlier in the century. Tijuana, they pointed out, is where cheap

Mexican labor meets efficient U.S. infrastructure. And Mier y Terán pooh-poohed the environmental danger of rapid growth. "This is the start of a new industrial age," he said. "Tijuana factories are going to supply all of North America." Under NAFTA, Mier y Terán argued, Tijuana would become a global manufacturing center, attracting not only U.S. and Canadian companies hoping to reduce labor costs, but also European, Asian, and Latin American companies looking for access to the North American market. Eventually, Mier y Terán envisions that products manufactured in Tijuana will reach markets from Alaska to Tierra del Fuego. The environment would take care of itself.

But ironically, it is Mexico's economic and environmental crisis that has transformed Tijuana from a bawdy border town, which enticed American tourists with lax liquor laws and officially tolerated prostitution, into an international manufacturing center. After the devaluation of the peso in 1982, the Mexican government instituted a series of austerity measures in order to meet payments on the debt. One of the most inefficient and subsidized sectors of the Mexican economy is the peasantry—corn farmers on small plots who were more likely to use hoes than tractors to sow their fields. By the end of the 1980s, the Mexican government had cut price subsidies on corn, tightened credit, and begun importing tons of lower-priced American corn grown on huge mechanized farms in Iowa and Nebraska.

The end of subsidies exposed the long-term environmental problems in the Mexican countryside, and corn farmers from Oaxaca to Michoacán found they could no longer survive. Millions of peasants gave up and left for the United States, Mexico City, or the border.

Felipe Martínez was one of them. When his older brother inherited the small family plot, Martínez left his hometown of Rancho Ochoa in Sonora State in 1988 at the age of eighteen. He found a job in Tijuana at the Lamkin factory, a San Diego–based golf club maker, where he earns five dollars a day. He spends most of it on a small room in a boarding house in Chilpancingo and sends the rest home to his wife.

Martínez was sitting in a chair in front of his room on a sunny Sunday morning when I stopped by. "In Tijuana there's always work," he said, referring to the "help wanted" signs in front of almost every factory. "But you can never get ahead."

Martínez seemed tired and worn down, but he had lots of dreams. He wanted to build a house on the scrub land on the other side of the Alomar River, bring his wife up from Rancho Ochoa, and start a family. Better yet, he wanted to cross the border into the United States. "Someday, I'm going to try my luck," he said.

Tijuana's factories and shanty towns are filled with people like Martínez—recent arrivals with shallow roots and a desire to improve their lot. Indeed, the city's industrial growth would not have been possible without a corresponding downturn in the Mexican countryside, because towns like Rancho Ochoa feed the large labor pool that keeps factory wages low despite the high turnover.

II

I first heard about the disaster at the Alco Pacific plant from Carmen Vázquez, the former director of Tijuana's Office of Civil Protection. Vázquez's leather briefcase was full of information about impending environmental disasters in Tijuana. For example, in the Revolución district south of downtown, flames poured continuously from sewer grates. A recent sewer explosion had sent manhole covers twenty feet into the air. Vázquez also had photographs of a U.S.–owned maquiladora that was burning telephone cables in a remote canyon outside Tijuana in order to extract lead and copper. Children were sick, she told me, and over a hundred dairy cows around the plant had died from inhaling the toxic fumes.

Vázquez had grown up in the arid state of Coahuila. When she was a child, her father took her horseback riding in the desert. They collected flowers, rode down the dry arroyos, and were welcomed in the homes of the humble people. But what drove her to tackle the city's worst environmental problems was not so much a love of nature as a sense of righteous indignation. It was tragic, she believed, that the government did not take responsibility for protecting its own people.

Vázquez had almost no experience in public safety matters when she was offered the post of running Tijuana's Office of Civil Protection in 1990. Her only qualification was organizing the safety drills in her daughter's school. But newly elected mayor Carlos Montejo Favela from the opposition National Action Party (PAN) offered her the post as thanks for her support of the party. He did not expect her to do anything. Her "office" was a chair, a desk, and a manual typewriter stashed in an empty room. Her "job" was to collect her salary and go home.

But Vázquez had other ideas. She hired a secretary and paid her out of her own salary. She used her own money to buy a two-way radio. She went back over old complaints that had never been acted upon. She visited Chilpancingo and other polluted neighborhoods like the Cañon de Pato, the Cañon de Sáenz, and Jardines de la Mesa. In January 1991 she learned from the head of the federal environmental protection agency, at the time known as Sedue (the Secretariat of Urban Development and Ecology), that a U.S.–owned maquiladora that had been extracting lead from car batteries had been abandoned and that tons of toxic waste had been left behind. The name of the plant was Alco Pacific.

"At its peak, the Alco plant was operating twenty-four hours a day," Vázquez said. "The whole area was covered in dust. One study found that cows from the ranch next door had a high level of lead in their blood, and many pregnant cows had spontaneously aborted or given birth to deformed calves, which soon died."

The day after I talked to Vázquez I drove out to the abandoned plant. The settlement of El Florido (also called Ojo de Agua) is a former cattle ranch at the outer reaches of Tijuana's growing urban sprawl. As in Chilpancingo, many of the houses are made of wood and tar paper. The better cinderblock homes have picket fences made of scrapwood, maybe a small vegetable garden, and an old Chevy with U. S. plates parked out front. Some of the residents still work at nearby ranches; others work at the factories that line the lightly traveled old highway to Tecate; still others commute an hour by bus to their jobs in downtown Tijuana.

The fifty-foot yellow smelter that towers over the community is a network of ducts and tubes visible from half a mile away. It was built by a Mexican company called Amezco in 1980 and purchased by an American named Morris Kirk in 1987. Metal recycling, especially when it involves lead, is highly regulated in California. State and federal laws mandate expensive emission-control equipment, respirators for workers, and proper disposal of all toxic waste. It is not surprising that Alco Pacific was one of at least four southern California–based metal recyclers to move their operations to Tijuana during the 1980s.

No one was at the plant the day I visited, so I walked along the corrugated aluminum fence looking for an opening. I found one around the back side near the dairy ranch and stepped into what seemed like a lunar landscape. Greasy gray and brown dirt was spread out over acres; mounds of lead slag were piled so high they looked like sand dunes. Inside the abandoned smelter, open drums full of solvents and other chemicals—plus some yellowish, powdery waste—were scattered about on the dirt floor.

Former workers told me that the car batteries delivered by truck each day from the United States were cracked open in the yard, and that battery acid was sometimes neutralized, sometimes just dumped on the ground. The lead was then extracted and melted in the huge furnace without emission control.

Workers did not wear respirators, but their blood was tested regularly for lead. Juan Agustín, a former worker, was told on several occasions that the lead level in his blood was high and that he should take some time off and drink lots of milk. Rubén Flores Velázquez, another worker, was also told to take time off because of high lead levels. In an accident in 1988, a furnace exploded and splattered him with hot lead, severely injuring an eye.

Still, Flores Velázquez said, he had nothing against the company. "In Mexico it's different from in the United States," he told me as we sat on a wooden bench in his front yard. His left eye waggled aimlessly as he explained how the social security hospital had performed several unsuccessful operations to repair his vision. "We know the risks of this kind of work when we take the job," Flores Velázquez concluded. "And we accept them."

In 1989 Alco Pacific entered into a contract with RSR-Quemetco, America's largest lead recycler, based in Dallas. Under the commercial agreement, Alco was paid a fee to process 30 million tons of lead slag provided by RSR's facility in City of Industry, near Los Angeles. Even though RSR had decided it could not profitably extract further lead itself, it believed that Alco would be able to do so in Mexico. The lead was transported across the border to Tijuana, where it was stored in Alco's open yard.

In January 1991 Morris Kirk concluded that he had miscalculated: he did not have the ability to extract any more lead from the stockpiled slag. But rather than return the lead waste to the United States to be disposed of properly, he decided to close down the Tijuana factory and skip town. He did not even bother to pay the workers severance pay.

For six months, the four thousand tons of lead waste that Kirk had left behind cooked in the Tijuana sun. Sometimes an easterly wind blew from the mountains around Tecate and lead dust billowed through the streets of El Florido. A pool that collected inside the abandoned plant drained onto a nearby dairy farm. In 1990 fourteen cows died after jumping wildly in the air and foaming at the mouth.

Then the rains came, initiating a series of complex chemical reactions. Sulfuric acid that had soaked into the ground was ignited, and the fire spread underground. By January 1992 the fumaroles that had been rising above the waste became a full-fledged fire. That is when Vázquez, in her capacity as head of Tijuana's Civil Protection Office, took over. She mobilized the fire department, health officials, police, and even the Mexican army. Fire fighters wearing respirators and special protective gear struggled for a month to bring the blaze under control. When they turned over the soil, the earth billowed away in a silvery brown cloud.

The scene at the Alco Pacific site made Vázquez furious. For a decade the factory had been operating with the full knowledge of Mexican environmental officials. They had done nothing to stop it, even though cows that provided milk to Tijuana residents had died of apparent lead poisoning.

"If the Mexican government did not supervise Alco adequately, then they share responsibility for what happened there," Vázquez said. Lead is highly toxic, and even trace amounts can hinder mental development in children. Vázquez ordered that blood tests be performed on all local residents.

After the fire at the Alco plant, Vázquez became almost reckless in her denunciations of the ineptitude of environmental authorities. She called for the relocation of the natural gas facility and began sending letters to Maurilio Sánchez Pachuca, promising to do her best to help resolve Chilpancingo's problems. In January 1992 she learned that factories had been clandestinely disposing of toxic waste in a squatter colony, Jardines de la Mesa. Mayor Montejo ordered Vázquez to publicly declare that the neighborhood was inundated not with toxic waste but with domestic garbage. The mayor and the top federal environmental official, Rubén Castro Bojorquez, called a press conference to announce that they would send out a brigade to pick up the trash and invited the people in the neighborhood to help out. Meanwhile, Vázquez had secretly supplied a local journalist with photos of the drums filled with industrial waste. "Excuse me, Sir," said the journalist to an embarrassed Sedue official. "But what do you call these drums?"

Vázquez was picking a fight. Mexico's federal government is controlled by the PRI, which until the 1988 election of Ernesto Ruffo in Baja California Norte in 1988, had never lost a governorship. Ruffo was a member of the conservative PAN party, to which Vázquez also belonged.

Permitting the Ruffo victory garnered international legitimacy for the PRI and helped Salinas portray himself as an enlightened democrat, despite the fact that his own presidential victory was tainted by allegations of fraud. (In fact it was Salinas's heir apparent, Luis Donaldo Colosio, then president of the PRI, who recognized the Ruffo victory and thereby incurred the wrath of PRI officials in Baja California and hard-liners throughout Mexico.) But it was quite another thing for a municipal bureaucrat to upstage the mighty PRI-appointed director of the federal environmental protection agency in Tijuana. The final straw came when Vázquez went public with the news that flames were pouring from sewer grates near downtown. The day after a story on the sewers appeared in the *San Diego Union,* Vázquez was fired. On March 12, 1992, under pressure from the federal government, an assistant to Mayor Montejo called Vázquez into his office. "You are very undisciplined," he said. "The mayor is very tired of having problems aired in public. These are issues which should be addressed internally."

A few days after being fired, Vázquez went to brief her replacement, José Luis Ortega, on the cases she was working on. "Don't bother," he said. "I'm not planning to follow up."

III

In September 1991, six months before she was fired, Carmen Vázquez sent a letter to Maurilio Sánchez Pachuca, inviting him to an October 2 meeting about the pollution in Chilpancingo. "I personally visited the Alomar Creek . . . on the 19th of September with the representatives of the three levels of government [municipal, state, federal]," she wrote in the letter. "The purpose of this meeting will be to discuss . . . solutions . . . to the problems."

For a decade, Sánchez Pachuca had been sending letters to local officials, congressmen, senators, and even the president. "Once again we are asking for your valuable help because we have read in the newspaper how you are concerned about improving the environment," wrote Sánchez Pachuca in a letter to President Salinas on September 26, 1991. "We have faith in you, Mr. President. Help us to restore the Cañon del Padre, to build pavilions so that experts can come give ecological talks for the whole population, so that our children's future will be different from what we are now suffering. We want plants to recycle toxic waste water, and we want the factories to return all waste to the point of origin. . . . [We want to present] a good appearance for the signing of the trilateral free-trade treaty that you have so aptly negotiated." The letter to Salinas is indicative of Sánchez Pachuca's political skill—it is a petition, not a demand, which appeals not to the law but to the moral stature of the president. It is signed by representatives of the various communities affected by the pollution, each one organized into a neighborhood association.

Traditionally, political power in Mexico derives not from individual voters but from their representatives, who broker votes in exchange for political patronage. While the Mexican constitution of 1917 guarantees individual rights, the corporatist tradition of group rights remains the stronger political current. Because neither the judiciary nor the legislative branches of government have true independent authority, petitions for social redress are generally made directly to the president who, for obvious political reasons, is more apt to respond to an organized group than to an aggrieved individual.

Sánchez Pachuca worked the system like a veteran politician. He demonstrated his authority in the community by organizing protest marches and demonstrations. He ratcheted up the political pressure by sending appeals to people high up in the political bureaucracy (the governor, the head of environmental protection in Tijuana, the chief environmental prosecutor in Mexico City). He also mixed deference and flattery with bold threats and exploited the rivalry between state, municipal, and federal authorities in Tijuana.

In late 1992 Sánchez Pachuca went to the press with his latest allegation: the pollution in Chilpancingo was responsible for a spate of brain-damaged babies. For Josefina Morales, fifty-four-years old and a nine-year resident of Chilpancingo, the death of her granddaughter was only the latest in what she believes is a long history of pollution-related maladies and deaths. Everyone in her family suffered from itching and boils, she told me as we sat in the kitchen of her modest house just below the factory-lined bluff. A doctor in Guadalajara had told her that the scaly sore on her hand that would not heal was the result of hand-washing clothing in the polluted water. Her son Martín, who worked at the Sanyo plant, complained of itching and rashes. Over the years, eight family dogs had lost their hair, gotten sick, and died.

Morales recognized that the factories offered her family a stable, if modest, income. By pooling the pay from several children who worked in the factories, she was able to acquire a refrigerator, a stove, and a television. Perhaps that is why talking about the pollution made her more depressed than angry. Her voice faded in and out as she explained that, the year before, her daughter Blanca Estela had given birth to a child with anencephaly, a rare and fatal birth defect in which the baby is born with an open skull and undeveloped brain. "She had a face like an angel, but her head was like a water balloon," said Morales. "She made three little cries—ei, ei, ei. Like a little kitten. That was all."

At least three other children in Chilpancingo—and perhaps as many as six—had been born with anencephaly or a related nonfatal defect called hydrocephaly in the previous three years. In Matamoros and across the border in Brownsville, eighty children were born with anencephaly between 1986 and 1991. After six anencephalic babies were born during a five-week period in 1991 in Brownsville, the Texas Department of Health commissioned a study to look at the possible causes. In 1991 there were thirteen anencephalic births in Brownsville, more than six times the expected norm. "Members of the community believe that this apparent cluster may be caused by environmental exposure in the area, such as the use of pesticides, and the growing maquiladora industry in Mexico," the report noted.

By the summer of 1992, with free-trade negotiations in full swing, Chilpancingo began to get some attention. Sánchez Pachuca was in the local press almost weekly and was frequently featured in the international press as well (the *Wall Street Journal* and the MacNeil-Lehrer News Hour both did stories on the neighborhood). Sánchez Pachuca, a former state

Judicial Police officer, used his new stature to strengthen his control over the community. He mobilized street protests, threatened maquiladoras, and got city officials on the phone. With free trade in the balance, even President Salinas began to take notice.

In 1991 the state government of Baja California began developing statewide environmental laws to supplement the 1988 Federal Law of Ecological Equilibrium. Biologist Jorge Barroso, who helped write the new law, was appointed head of the new agency, called the State Ecology Office.

Barroso made the Chilpancingo problem one of his priorities. Using new scientific equipment, he was able to identify fourteen companies in the Otay Mesa industrial park that were dumping toxic waste, including lead, down the drain. Among the companies, which were either closed or ordered to install waste treatment facilities, were American Optical, Hooking International, and many smaller Mexican-owned factories.

Meanwhile, the threat of prosecution from a Los Angeles deputy district attorney named David Eng forced San Diego–based Metales y Derivados to agree to clean up its act. Like Alco Pacific, Metales y Derivados extracted lead from car batteries, and like Alco Pacific it had left behind a sizable mess. Under a U.S. court order, Metales was required to install new equipment, store the lead properly, and clean up its facility.

In January 1993 a series of winter storms stacked up over the Pacific and inundated Tijuana with more than eight inches of rain. The storm buckled sidewalks, flooded downtown stores, toppled power lines, and destroyed at least twelve hundred homes across the city. It also claimed thirty-one lives, mostly in neighborhoods like Chilpancingo, where squatters had built shanties on riverbanks, canyons, or steep hillsides. Because the rain had been light for most of the decade, few realized the danger.

Antonio Campos González, who came to Chilpancingo from a village in Michoacán in 1989 and found a job in a factory, lived with his family in a wooden hut along the Alomar River. When I visited him the day after the rains stopped, he was standing outside his mud-caked home in disbelief. The Alomar had been transformed from a small creek into a raging torrent, and many ramshackle homes had been carried off downstream. Bobbing on the surface of the river were seat cushions, splintered plywood, and pieces of foam rubber. For three days, Campos's house had been completely submerged, and his few possessions had been swept away.

Still, Campos considered himself lucky. He told me of watching in horror as some neighbors struggled to cross the raging river so they would not miss a day's work at the factories.

"Every day they would pass by on their way to work," he said. "One day last week we saw them go into the river; then they went under. They came up once more and then they went under and I didn't see them again after that."

At least five would-be immigrants attempting to cross the Tijuana River into the United States were swept away and presumed drowned.

But for Chilpancingo, at least, the flood also had a silver lining. On the night of January 12, a few days after the rains stopped, Sánchez Pachuca's phone rang at two in the morning. The call was from a man claiming to be President Salinas's personal secretary. At the time, Salinas was in Tijuana inspecting the flood damage. Sánchez Pachuca yelled at the man for playing such an obvious joke on him and hung up. A moment later the phone rang again; this time it was a personal friend of Sánchez Pachuca's, who assured him that Salinas was on his way to Chilpancingo. Sánchez Pachuca rushed out to meet him.

Salinas was coming to Chilpancingo not because he was personally moved by the plight of the people there—many other neighborhoods are much worse off. But the surprise victory of Bill Clinton in the U.S. elections had made passing NAFTA even more complicated and places like Chilpancingo even more important.

A few months earlier, in August 1992, negotiators from Mexico, Canada, and the United States had holed themselves up in a Washington hotel room and worked around the clock to finish a draft of the treaty. President Bush, lagging badly in the polls, wanted to be able to make a big announcement at the Republican National Convention, only days away.

As it turned out, the completion of NAFTA did not give the Bush campaign much of a boost. While Bush insisted that NAFTA would mean more trade and more jobs, public opinion surveys taken at the time suggested that most Americans associated it with U.S. factories moving to Mexico.

Shortly after the convention, Bush began challenging Bill Clinton to take a position on NAFTA. Clinton kept deferring, saying he had not had a chance to read the two-thousand-page document. Because labor and environmental groups were the strongest and most organized opponents of the treaty, Clinton knew that if he rejected NAFTA outright he would

be vulnerable to charges that he was still in the pocket of the "special interests." But though he was campaigning as a New Democrat who would
stand up to that kind of pressure, he could not afford to completely alien-
ate two core constituencies of his party. In typical Clinton fashion, he com-
promised. The candidate announced he would support NAFTA as long as
he was able to successfully negotiate parallel agreements dealing with labor
and the environment. The strategy seemed to work. Many labor and environmental groups mobilized behind Clinton during the campaign.

The Clinton victory was a major setback for Salinas. He had a close
personal relationship with Bush, and they had planned NAFTA together.
Bush and Salinas had concurred that environmental issues had no place
in a trade agreement. Now with Clinton in debt to environmental and
labor groups and the pressure against the treaty mounting, Salinas would
have to scramble. Sánchez Pachuca had made a nuisance of himself. In the
best Mexican tradition, it was time to buy him off.

Salinas's limousine could not get across the creek leading into Chilpancingo because the bridge was washed out; so the president and his small
entourage met with Sánchez Pachuca in the middle of the muddy road.
At three in the morning, the two men talked briefly and then Salinas left.
Officially, nothing was promised. But the message was clear: federal officials in Tijuana would know that the president himself had taken an interest in Chilpancingo's pollution problem. Within a few months, the streets
of Chilpancingo were being dug up and a sewer system was finally being
installed. It was part of a $300 million plan to turn Chilpancingo around.
With funding provided by the World Bank and private Mexican investors,
the government planned to build a cement canal for the river, along with
bridges, roads, and other infrastructure that would attract housing, shops,
and light industry. Sánchez Pachuca's gambit had paid off; things were
looking up for one of Mexico's most polluted neighborhood, and he
deserved a good deal of the credit.

IV

Meanwhile, the case against Alco Pacific was also advancing, but for entirely different reasons. David Eng, the deputy district attorney in Los
Angeles who had reached a settlement with Metales y Derivados, was also

investigating Morris Kirk and Alco Pacific for illegally transporting hazardous waste through Los Angeles county. Eng, a Chinese American from rural Washington State who spoke no Spanish and had no experience with Mexico, seemed an unlikely candidate to become a leading prosecutor in transnational dumping cases. But the U.S. attorney's office had already determined that Alco had not violated any federal laws, so it was left to Eng to bring Kirk in on a state count.

Although existing U.S. federal and state laws make it extremely difficult to pursue U.S. companies that pollute in Mexico, Eng determined that Kirk had violated a California statute barring the transportation of hazardous waste within the state. The case had come to Eng's attention after U.S. customs inspectors located a small amount of lead waste in a truck returning from Tijuana and traced it to a lead recycling facility in City of Industry near Los Angeles. It turned out the facility belonged to RSR-Quemetco. In September 1992 Eng obtained a search warrant for RSR's Dallas headquarters. During the search he found documents suggesting that RSR knew that the waste had been taken to Mexico and abandoned.

When he began his investigation, Eng got a less-than-enthusiastic response from Mexican environmental officials. Ramiro Zaragoza, who headed the Sedue office in Tijuana, and Antonio Sandoval, who was the top environmental official in the state capital of Mexicali, both told Eng to get lost. "They made it clear," said Eng. "We don't need you here. This is Mexico. You can't come down here and tell us what to do."

But the foot dragging turned into enthusiastic cooperation once Mexico's top environmental prosecutor, Santiago Oñate, began to take an interest in the Alco case. Not once did Oñate, according to Eng, mention the political significance of the Alco case, but he must have been aware of the implications. Oñate was extremely close to President Salinas and was directly involved in negotiating the environmental side agreement to NAFTA in Ottawa, Canada. Meanwhile, NAFTA opponents began pointing to the Alco case as an example of how the treaty would only encourage environmental renegades to cross the border. Dozens of U.S. delegations visited the abandoned Alco site and continued to keep the pressure on. Among them was a March 1993 group that included then–House Majority Leader Richard Gephardt (D-Mo.). The mess, in fact, was too much for at least one member of the congressional delegation, who said that after touring the plant he could not support NAFTA. "I call myself a free trader," said Representative Ron Wyden (D-Ore.), "but I can't vote for it." (Wyden later changed his mind.)

In early May 1993—as Eng was getting ready to take the case to the grand jury—RSR agreed to a settlement. It called for $2 million to be given to the Mexican government to defray the cleanup costs; $200,000 in fines; and $300,000 to be donated for medical assistance along the border to treat victims of the pollution. "The North American Free Trade Agreement, under siege in Congress, is about to get a big lift from a Los Angeles prosecutor who once feared the trade pact would create an environmental 'nightmare,'" crowed the *Wall Street Journal*. Oñate flew from Ottawa, where he had been negotiating the environmental side-agreement, to Los Angeles to announce the settlement in a joint press conference with Eng.

Negotiations on the side-agreements were entering the final phase, and the political dynamic was rapidly changing. Many major environmental groups—among them the Environmental Defense Fund and the World Wildlife Fund—had climbed on board. Other groups, such as the Sierra Club, Friends of the Earth, and various regional organizations, continued to oppose the pact. (Unions were also not satisfied with the labor side-agreement and mobilized against the treaty.) By promising to negotiate side-agreements and thereby garnering the support of at least some environmental groups, Clinton created a political dilemma. While Democrats in Congress were saying they would back NAFTA only if Clinton came up with strong side-agreements, the Republican members who already supported the deal were threatening to back out if the side agreements added too many new regulations. Getting NAFTA passed under those conditions required an extraordinary difficult balancing act. Clinton had to come up with mechanisms that looked good on paper—thereby placating the Democrats—but that lacked teeth, thereby pleasing the Republicans.

The result of that kind of compromise was the creation of the trinational (Canada, the United States, and Mexico) Commission on Environmental Cooperation (CEC), NAFTA's environmental enforcement body. The commission, based in Montreal, Canada, is empowered to investigate whether a signatory of the treaty is engaged in a "persistent and sustained pattern" of nonenforcement of its own environmental laws. The CEC's only real weapon, however, is the "public shame factor," as one CEC official put it. The commission has no real punitive authority; only in certain limited instances is it empowered to recommend sanctions against the offending nation. Critics of the side agreement also pointed out that the process for bringing an environmental grievance was so cumbersome (it was estimated that it would take two to three years for a claim to wind its way through the review procedure), and there are so many exclusions (natural resource extraction, for example) that the CEC's authority was likely to be limited.

(In fact, although the CEC has handled only two investigations involving Mexico in its first two and a half years of existence, it has received praise from environmental groups for its even-handed approach to the Cozumel pier dispute. Rather than taking two to three years, the review process is expected to be completed in less than a year.)

While Clinton was touting the side-agreement as a milestone in transnational environmental enforcement, a number of U.S. trade journals were quietly publishing articles explaining why the CEC would have little authority. A background paper published by the conservative Heritage Foundation noted, "The U.S. negotiating team had to settle for a face-saving agreement that contained little or no power of enforcement. The side agreements are largely meaningless." Jaime Serra Puche, the Mexican commerce secretary who negotiated the NAFTA deal, was quoted as assuring a group of Mexican business people that it was "highly improbable that the sanction stage could ever be reached."

The other environmental agency created under NAFTA was the Border Environment Cooperation Commission (BECC), a binational (the United States and Mexico) agency based in Ciudad Juárez, Mexico, and empowered to evaluate funding for environmental infrastructure projects along the border. Projects approved by the BECC are eligible to receive low-interest loans from the North American Development Bank, a lending institution also created under the free-trade accord, which has its offices in San Antonio, Texas. But critics of the side accord were quick to point out that the bank was not authorized to loan money for cleanup projects. Because the NADBank was designed to be self-financed, it can only loan money for commercially viable projects like sewage treatment plants and landfill projects, which represent only a small portion of the border's environmental backlog.

Settling for a weak side-agreement was not the only compromise Clinton had to make to get NAFTA passed by a skeptical U.S. Congress. NAFTA is the law today not because of broad political support but because Clinton used arm twisting, horse trading, and promises of pork to get legislators to back the treaty. The original reason the treaty was completed in two years was for the political boost a quick deal would provide Bush and Salinas. By the time NAFTA was sent to Congress, expectations were so high that Salinas could argue with some justification that a "no" vote would trigger an anti-American backlash in Mexico. Clinton, meanwhile, suggested that a defeat would send a protectionist message, undermine his position in trying to wrestle trade liberalization from Japan, and jeopardize all future trading relationships.

Although Bush's plan to use the treaty as a springboard to reelection did not work out, Salinas did benefit politically from NAFTA, at least initially. Salinas was anxious to get NAFTA approved before he left office in 1994 because the Mexican political system, with its complete lack of checks and balances, is so notoriously unpredictable. Salinas successfully used NAFTA to undermine Mexico's leftist opposition, since the left's whole platform—nationalization of key industries, protectionist policies, and price supports for small farmers—would violate the treaty. Today, even though Salinas has been excoriated as the culprit in Mexico's current economic debacle, even though he has been whispered to be involved in political assassinations, and even though he was effectively expelled from the country, his economic program is largely intact. That is due in large part to NAFTA.

The push to implement NAFTA quickly, which served narrow political interests in both the United States and Mexico, also meant squandering a unique chance to make some headway against the border environmental crisis. Some border environmental groups have estimated that the cost of cleanup could be as high as $20 billion, an impossible amount in an era of budget tightening.

In an effort to sell NAFTA to a skeptical U.S. public, both Bush and Clinton whitewashed the Mexican government. U.S. embassy officials in Mexico City and State Department sources in Washington praised Mexico's economic and political reforms, its advances in fighting drugs and corruption, and its newfound commitment to the environment. The facade came tumbling down the same day NAFTA went into effect, as the Zapatista rebels mobilized throughout Chiapas. Over the next few months a series of political assassinations, including the murder of presidential candidate Luis Donaldo Colosio at a Tijuana campaign rally in March 1994, further destabilized the government until, in December 1994, it was forced to resort to a massive devaluation of the peso.

But even before the devaluation, Mexico had reverted to its old practices almost immediately after the NAFTA spotlight was turned off. In December 1993, a month after NAFTA was passed, Eng netted a conviction against Morris Kirk, who pleaded no contest to a felony count of illegal transportation. He was fined $2.5 million and sentenced to eighteen months in state prison. With NAFTA in the bag, Oñate had left his post as attorney general in charge of the environment to serve in the campaign of Luis Donaldo Colosio in December 1993. By that time, Eng's relationship with Mexican environmental officials had been deteriorating for months. A few months after NAFTA passed, Mexican officials asked Eng's investigator Pete Martinez to leave the premises of a U.S.–owned company in Tecate that was suspected of illegally transporting waste from Los Angeles.

In January 1994 Eng received a call from Antonio Sandoval, the top federal environmental official in Baja California, asking him to transfer the $2 million settlement that RSR "owed" to Mexico. Eng called Sandoval's office and explained that he was under no obligation to release the funds and that, in any case, he would have to go before a U.S. judge with a specific project in order to get the money released. A week later he got another call from Sandoval asking for $100,000 to build a fence around the Alco site. Eng immediately became suspicious because until then he had been dealing exclusively with Oñate. Besides, he reasoned, "no damn fence in Mexico is going to cost $100,000." Eng asked for concrete plans and a contract. He never heard a peep from Sandoval until May, when he got another call asking for $250,000 to put a plastic tarp over the fourteen-acre site. Eng asked for a contract he could take into court and present before the judge. He never heard from Sandoval again. "I don't think at that point they had any intention of cleaning up the site," said Eng.

The Mexican government did hire a number of U.S. environmental consultants to estimate the cost of remediation. They came back with figures ranging from $5 million to $32 million. Oñate had promised to match the $2 million settlement. "Whatever it takes," he had said. But the money never materialized. Two years after the settlement, lead waste that Kirk left behind at his Tijuana factory still sat in huge mounds out in the open, and lead dust blew through the streets of El Florido. In 1994 Eng was frustrated and discouraged. He told me he felt used.

V

When I dropped in on Maurilio Sánchez Pachuca in December 1993, he proudly announced that he had lost some of his paunch. "I've never been thin," he explained. "But all that stuff before, that wasn't fat—it was caused by a worm. The worm made my stomach swell up like this." He made a little semicircle with his arms out in front of his stomach.

It was not just losing weight that had put Sánchez Pachuca in a good mood. NAFTA had been passed, Tijuana was anticipating a glorious future, and Sánchez Pachuca was planning to get a piece of the action. Ground was being broken on a new development project, and Sánchez Pachuca was handling the real estate sales of some local farmers. If everything fell into place, he stood to make a lot of money.

The fact that Sánchez Pachuca was looking to cash out did not make me think any less of his environmental crusade. He had played Mexican politics like a pro, and I certainly did not expect him to abandon the endgame.

But I always suspected that all the talk about eagles and Canadian ducks was for the benefit of people like me—the press, the U. S. environmentalists. Sánchez Pachuca liked to talk about vistas, clean air, and biodiversity as we drove around Chilpancingo in his brown Dart, but one day, as we sat at the Formica desk in his office, I asked him why he had become an environmentalist. An American might talk about going camping in the Rockies, or seeing a gray whale spout off the Pacific coast, but the first thing Sánchez Pachuca mentioned was a terrible flood in 1982, which destroyed his house and carried off everything he owned. He also talked about his childhood experience planting corn with his father in the mountains of Oaxaca.

As with many Mexican environmentalists I have talked to, especially those from a humble background, what motivated Sánchez Pachuca was his belief that polluting the land was like throwing away perfectly good food—it was wasteful. Land is valued for what it produces, what it gives people—not the beauty of its trees or its wildlife. In Chilpancingo, saving birds had little local appeal.

Of course, Sánchez Pachuca was still concerned about the long-term impact of a decade of dumping. He worried that there could be cancer clusters or more cases of anencephaly. And he acknowledged that Chilpancingo's victory was not necessarily a victory for all of Tijuana. The waste from the factories was probably just being dumped in some other neighborhood.

In 1993, Sedesol (the federal environmental protection agency that had replaced Sedue) announced that 30 percent of all waste generated by the maquiladoras was being returned to the United States for proper disposal, up from 18 percent the year before. That meant that 70 percent of the waste was not being returned. "You just take the drums out in the desert and no one will bother you," said Sánchez Pachuca.

But for a family that must struggle to find clean drinking water and take care to avoid infection from household waste, the health problems caused by the pollution from the factories, while real, are not the most pressing issue in their lives. In my visits to Chilpancingo, I have met only a few people who expressed a desire to seek revenge against the factories for all the years of pollution. Most of the complaints I heard were about the low wages, which condemned the workers to persistent poverty.

Even for those who no longer work in the factories, the economic opportunities represented by living next door to the industrial park seem to outweigh the costs. After meeting with Sánchez Pachuca, I went to see what had become of Antonio Campos González, the factory worker from Michoacán who lost his house in the 1992 flood. On the bank of the Alomar River I ran into a man named Isidoro García relaxing under a poplar tree. García told me that the houses along the bank had been condemned and that the people had been relocated. He said he was looking forward to the new development.

In fact, García was just plain bullish on Chilpancingo. After twenty years of working as a construction worker in the United States, he had decided to return home to Mexico the year before, when work became scarce during the U.S. recession. He had spent months scouting Tijuana looking for the best location to build a dream house with the $65,000 nest egg he had saved up. He settled on Chilpancingo, convinced that the proximity to the factories would give the community an economic boost. He also built a twelve-room boarding house for workers.

Then, as he was putting the finishing touches on his new house, he smelled something funny coming from the vent outside the bathroom. When he lit a match to investigate, suddenly a huge, orange fireball leapt through the grate—leaving him with singed eyebrows and Chilpancingo's new sewer system with thousands of dollars in damage. The following week, an associate of former Panamanian general Manuel Noriega who had opened an illegal steroids factory in the industrial park was arrested for dumping more than a hundred drums of solvent down the drain.

García dismissed the whole incident with a shrug, arguing that an occasional sewer explosion is simply the price of progress. "The factories are 100 percent good for Mexico," he insisted. "Pollution is just a side effect."

A few days after Isidoro García's bold predictions, the mood in Chilpancingo, along the border, and throughout Mexico changed radically. On January 1, 1994, the very day that NAFTA went into effect, masked Zapatista rebels took over towns in the southern state of Chiapas. The rebels were a dramatic reminder that Mexico had a long way to go to reach the kind of stability and economic growth promised by NAFTA. "I was getting calls from all over the world," said Tijuana industrialist Enrique Mier y Terán. "Investors were panicked until I told them to look at a map, and they saw how far Tijuana is from Chiapas."

Three months later, however, Mexico's burgeoning political crisis came to Tijuana when PRI presidential candidate Luis Donaldo Colosio was gunned down at a campaign rally near the airport. Although a lone gunman was arrested at the scene, there were widespread rumors of a conspiracy reaching high levels of the government. When PRI party secretary Francisco Ruiz Massieu was shot on the street in Mexico City six months later, investors began pulling their money out of the Mexican stock market. By depleting its hard-currency reserves the Mexican government was able to halt the run and gain control of the peso for a few more months.

Then in December 1994, soon after newly elected President Ernesto Zedillo took office, the Zapatista rebels "mobilized" throughout the Chiapas highlands. The military maneuver turned out to be inconsequential, but it was enough to send the already badly battered Mexican peso plummeting. The government attempt to halt the hemorrhaging through a limited devaluation failed to restore confidence; in a single day the peso lost 40 percent of its value. Mexico would have defaulted on its international obligations if not for a U.S.–led $48 billion bailout.

By the middle of 1995 President Zedillo had shown himself unable to halt the slide. The arrest of Raúl Salinas, the ex-president's brother, for the murder of PRI secretary Ruiz Massieu in February 1995 did little to restore credibility, especially after it was later revealed that Salinas had stashed away nearly $100 million in accounts in Switzerland, London, and the Cayman Islands. The money was rumored to be payoffs from business people who won lucrative government concessions during the Salinas administration; there were other well-substantiated reports that some of the funds were paid to Raúl Salinas by the Mexican drug cartels in exchange for protection. The much-praised Salinas privatization program that had brought investors streaming into Mexico was revealed as a massive transfer of state assets to a handful of friends and business associates of the former president. The Mexican economy continued to deteriorate, slumping 6.9 percent in 1995, the worst single-year decline since the Great Depression.

The economic collapse had an enormous impact on every aspect of Mexican life, including the border environmental crisis. Instead of the promised prosperity, which was supposed to generate the revenue to fund a border cleanup, badly strapped border cities had to cancel infrastructure projects. Several major projects were dropped, including a water treatment plant in Ciudad Juárez, and the United States was forced to pick up the tab for water treatment facilities in Texas and California when the Mexican government was unable to meet its financial commitments. The ambitious plans for the NADBank were scaled back when Mexican border cities decided they could not afford to take out loans for infrastructure projects that would have to be repaid in dollars.

Instead of the expected boom, Chilpancingo found itself once again trying to accommodate a flood of new migrants drawn from the countryside and increasingly from the slums of Mexico City and Guadalajara who were forced north by the stagnant economy. The infrastructure backlog continued to mount, and the plan to develop the area along the Alamo

River was postponed indefinitely. Like millions of other Mexicans, Maurilio Sánchez Pachuca saw his dream of prosperity crushed by the crisis.

That is not to say that NAFTA—or more properly the public spotlight focused on the border by the debate over the treaty—has not helped to limit some of the worst abuses. In 1995 forty maquiladoras based in Matamoros, including General Motors, paid a $17 million settlement to sixteen mothers in the Texas border town of Brownsville, whose children had been born with either anencephaly or spina bifida, a related defect. The lawsuit alleged that the birth defects were caused by plant emissions that had wafted across the border. In the aftermath, many of the maquiladoras in the Matamoros area began returning their waste to the United States for proper disposal instead of illegally discarding it at the Matamoros municipal dump. Several large maquiladoras in Matamoros also constructed wastewater treatment plants.

Meanwhile, the BECC, after getting off to a slow start (it took a year for the new agency even to acquire a director) approved half a dozen projects in 1996. Among them was a $1 million plan to install a wastewater treatment facility in the FINSA industrial park in Matamoros where, in 1990, U.S. activists recorded levels of methylene chloride, an industrial solvent, 215,000 times higher than permissible under U.S. law. Domingo González, an environmental activist who has seen his hometown of Brownsville grow from a border backwater to an industrial boomtown, acknowledged that NAFTA has encouraged the worst polluters to clean up their act. "But the changes are never dramatic," he said. "They happen very, very slowly."

In Tijuana, as well, lawsuits and increased public awareness have had a noticeable impact. In June 1996 the Los Angeles district attorney's office and PROFEPA, the Mexican federal environmental prosecutors office, held a joint press conference to announce a plan to finally clean up the Alco site. Gil Garcetti, the L.A. County district attorney whose grandparents immigrated to the United States from Mexico, promised in halting Spanish to aggressively pursue any U.S. company that dared to pollute in Mexico; Antonio Azuela, Mexico's top environmental prosecutor, spoke of his great satisfaction in "guaranteeing public health"; Antonio Sandoval, the environmental delegate in Mexicali who had asked for $100,000 to build a fence around the Alco site, outlined his office's efforts to prosecute Alco without once mentioning that it was David Eng and the Los Angeles district attorney's office that had brought the company to justice. Eng, on the other hand, took a diplomatic approach, praising Mexican authorities for the close cooperation in the Alco prosecution, which had led to $2.5 million in fines and a sixteen-month jail sentence for Morris Kirk, the company's CEO.

"I doubt companies will commit these kinds of crimes so blatantly in the future," Eng said. He vowed to continue to prosecute cross-border dumping cases "as long as I'm welcomed in Mexico.

"I will respect the sovereignty of Mexico and the will of its people," he promised. "We can disagree on a lot of things, but not on the environment."

There was also good news from engineers at Geomatrix, the Newport Beach, California, company that had won the contract to do the remediation work. Since the lead had not migrated into the water table, the company's plan to contain the waste by capping it at the site would provide sufficient protection for the surrounding community.

The Alco prosecution, the civil lawsuit in Brownsville, the increased media scrutiny, and the creation of the BECC, the NADBank, and the CEC have all contributed to an increased awareness of the border's environmental woes. But the progress is in no way proportional to the depth of the crisis and the threat to public health on both sides of the border. The participants in the Alco press conference were reminded of that fact by Maurilio Sánchez Pachuca, who showed up uninvited and unannounced. During the question-and-answer period he took the microphone to protest that Chilpancingo had not received the attention or treatment that the Alco site had. "We have a similar problem," he pointed out. "According to a survey we've done, 99 percent of the population is suffering from some sort of illness."

Perhaps it was, in part, the hopes and expectations created by NAFTA that had left Sánchez Pachuca so deeply disappointed. Despite the promises, the attention, and the visit from President Salinas, Sánchez Pachuca was still fighting the same fights and making the same speeches. "Governments come and go and nothing ever changes," he said bitterly.

–nine–

The Political Environment

Environmentalism in Mexico has shallow roots. Aside from Miguel Angel de Quevedo, Mexico's most famous tree hugger, the country can point to only a handful of conservationists of any consequence. During the 1960s, when environmentalism took hold in Europe and the United States, Mexico was too caught up in the promise of development to question its results.

President Luis Echeverría, who took office in 1970, seemed to view environmentalism or conservation as part of a conspiracy by "multinationals" who hoped to preserve resources in the underdeveloped world so that they themselves could one day exploit them. José López Portillo, who succeed Echeverría, called concerns about pollution "hysterical exaggeration. Man has the genius to both grow and preserve the environment," he claimed.

But there was one point on which Mexican authorities could not be so smugly dismissive: the spectacular growth of Mexico City was causing obvious social problems. As the city expanded, water, air, and urban space became increasingly scarce. The birth of the country's environmental bureaucracy therefore responded more to the explosive growth of Mexico City than to international trends. In 1972 Echeverría created the first environmental agency: the Subsecretariat of Environmental Improvement (SMA), which was under the Secretariat of Health.

By the end of the decade responsibility for the environment (or "urban ecology," as it was called) had been transferred to the Housing Secretariat; from there it went to Urban Development, and finally to Social Development (Sedesol). It was only when environmental protection became a make-or-break issue in the NAFTA debate that President Salinas created two specialized environmental institutions within Sedesol—an environmental prosecutor's office (PROFEPA) and the National Ecology Institute (INE), charged with reviewing environmental impact statements and granting permits.

No one was quite sure what to think when newly elected President Ernesto Zedillo named Julia Carabias, one of Mexico's leading environmentalists, as the secretary of fisheries within days of taking office in December 1994. Carabias was clearly not a political appointee, and she had no particular knowledge of the fishing industry. In the next few days, however, Zedillo's strategy became clear. He began to dismantle Sedesol, whose primary function had been to administer Salinas's highly politicized and controversial social works program, Solidaridad. INE and PROFEPA were plucked from Sedesol and transferred to Fisheries; responsibility for water and forests was transferred from the Secretariat of Agriculture. The Secretariat of Environment, Natural Resources, and Fisheries—the new environmental superministry—was born.

A year after Carabias was appointed, I visited her in her wood-paneled office in the south of Mexico City. It was the largest office I had ever seen—as big as my entire apartment. In the middle was a conference table large enough to seat every environmentalist in Mexico. Outside an enormous picture window the Ajusco volcano rose steadily above the urban chaos into a clear blue sky. Everything about the office screamed power, but Carabias seemed not to hear. She was sitting quietly behind a desk reading when I entered. She shook my hand and offered me a seat at a corner of the massive table. A photographer snapped away, recording the event for posterity.

The environmental officials who came before Carabias were bureaucrats who were more interested in the view from the office than the office itself. Carabias, by contrast, is a biologist who has spent most of her professional life in the academy. Her life's work is investigating sustainable development in extremely poor rural communities. No one who knows Carabias personally or has read her work doubts her commitment to the Mexican environment. But her effectiveness as an administrator has been called into question.

In a country ruled by an insular group of bureaucrats, Carabias is an outsider. She is not a member of any political party, but her political sympathies point more toward the leftist PRD than the PRI. Because she is not a part of the system, Carabias must battle not only the entrenched interests, which see any environmental restriction as meddling and counterproductive, but also a political culture in which, as a leftist and a woman, she is at an extreme disadvantage.

In her first year in office Carabias succeeded in changing the rhetoric of environmental protection. Unlike her self-congratulatory predecessors, who claimed one environmental victory after another, she sounded the alarm cautiously. At a ceremony in which President Zedillo spouted the usual platitudes about creating "an environmental culture" and "balancing environmental protection with economic growth," Carabias pointed out that "we must keep in mind that it will not be possible to reverse the environmental deterioration in the short term. We are talking about a process that has been going on for a long time and will require a long time to resolve."

When a TV newscaster asked her when Mexico could expect to see the return of the great forests that once covered the country, Carabias said, "Let's not kid ourselves. That would be utopian."

"In terms of environmental degradation we've reached a critical point," she told me when I asked her to assess Mexico's current situation. Carabias seems to have a permanently mournful expression on her face, and no wonder. "We have extremely high levels of deforestation—the highest in Latin America," she continued. "Every one of our watersheds is contaminated. All the large cities have air pollution. We are rapidly losing our biodiversity; it's a loss that has not even been evaluated." (Since that interview, Mexico has moved into first place worldwide in deforestation—2.5 million acres [1 million hectares] of forest are lost each year.) As she went on, she looked down distractedly at the pad that was rapidly filling with doodles. She had covered two pages with arrows and lines, squiggles, circles, numbers, and geometric shapes.

"The first big problem is development." She drew the letter "D" (for *desarrollo*) and underlined it. "That is being hampered by the environmental deterioration. There is also a health problem." She drew an "S" for *salud*. "There is a problem of natural regeneration." She drew an "N" for *naturaleza*. "The situation is grave."

In her role as Mexico's top environmental authority Carabias sees a bleak picture. But in her role as manager of the country's natural resources Carabias finds room for hope. Despite the centuries of deterioration, "the country still has a tremendous amount of natural resources." Carabias continued: "We have enormous diversity. With the exception of the extremes, all the world's ecosystems are represented in Mexico. The potential is enormous—and the resources are not exhausted, not even close. We can still use our own natural resources to develop this country."

Combining environmental protection with the responsibility for developing the country's natural resources is a new experiment in Mexico, and an especially important one because implicit in the arrangement is a recognition that those resources are finite. In the past, the job of various ministers charged with natural resource development was to get the job done as quickly as possible. Environmental protection was not a sought-after post.

The creation of Semarnap (the forgettable Spanish acronym by which the new environmental ministry is known) and the appointment of Carabias as its head are important steps forward in what Mexican political scientists often call "institution building." Since Article 27 of the constitution calls on the state to manage the country's natural resources in the public interest, and since this is the legal basis for the state's authority to intervene to protect the environment, it makes sense to combine environmental protection and natural resource development in the same ministry. With a growing body of environmental law, particularly the comprehensive General Law of Ecological Equilibrium passed in 1988, Mexico has made enormous strides since the 1980s in developing a legal and institutional framework for environmental protection. "Sustainable development" has entered the official lexicon.

But since the law is applied with a great deal of discretion in Mexico, it costs the government nothing to demonstrate its new commitment to the environment by periodically passing new legislation. New law does not necessarily translate into action; often there is no funding for enforcement. No environmental dispute has ever been litigated in Mexico; there are literally only a handful of environmental lawyers in the whole country.

The normal practice is to handle environmental disputes administratively and to resolve them through internal negotiations. The credo of Mexican environmental protection was perhaps best stated by Ecology

Director Alicia Barcena in 1984. "We do not want closed industries," said Barcena. "We are managers of the environment, but even so we are obligated to approach a solution with industrial firms by means of credits, incentives, and the training of personnel."

Environmental enforcement has become more aggressive since then, but negotiated settlement rather than punitive action remains the guiding philosophy. For example, in the summer of 1995, Semarnap supervised environmental audits of Pemex, the state oil company. "The idea is to determine what the company is sending into the air and into the water," explained Carabias. "The obligation of the company is to correct [the emissions] within a certain time frame. The goal is to get the company to operate without pollution; the audit does not include any remediation. How could we ask them to remediate everything? No, they'd have to remediate the whole country and we wouldn't accomplish anything."

This is a pragmatic position that ignores the fact that if Pemex is violating the law by polluting the air and the water, then it should be subject to fines and prosecution. By asking Pemex only to avoid pollution in the future, Semarnap sends an extremely weak message about the consequences of violating the country's environmental laws. The other apparent weakness of using administrative sanctions rather than criminal prosecution is that disputes are resolved away from any public scrutiny, so there is always the possibility of bribery. Mexican environmental inspectors have the authority to close down a factory for polluting without requesting any sort of judicial review. They also earn a salary of about $150 a month. The temptation is enormous on both sides. Several factory owners have told me that bribery is routine.

Despite these vulnerabilities, Carabias is wary about moving environmental enforcement away from administrative sanctions and into the courts. "I worry that the courts could start granting stays [amparos] against our enforcement actions without sufficient institutional capacity," she explained. "There is too much leeway in our laws."

Critics allege that because the agency's enforcement actions are based on negotiated agreements, personal relationships and political influence often play a role in Semarnap's actions. Carabias, according to her detractors, does not have the political backing to stand up to the power brokers who often push for approval on big projects.

One environmental controversy in the summer of 1995 was over the approval of a salt-mining project in Baja California Sur, which critics claimed would disrupt the breeding of the gray whales that migrate through the region each spring. Homero Aridjis, a well-known poet and the president of Mexico's best-known environmental organization, the Group of 100, alleged that Carabias was buckling to intense pressure to approve the project because Herminio Blanco, the secretary of commerce, was representing the government on the company's board of directors. ESSA, the salt-mining company, is a joint venture between Mexican capital and the Mitsubishi Corporation of Japan. In February 1995 the National Ecology Institute (INE) rejected the company's environmental impact statement but later sent a letter to the company offering advice on how it could be improved.

Carabias insisted that decisions are based on scientific evaluation and not political pressure. "Right now the debate is between poets and artists and technicians and bureaucrats," she said. "We need to let the experts speak."

Political connections, however, and not scientific analysis also seem to explain why the government granted a concession to develop one of the nation's natural treasures to a reputed con artist. In April 1995 INE president Gabriel Quadri signed a concession that permitted Canadian businessman Barry Sendel to develop the Caves of Cacahuamilpa in Guerrero State. Cacahuamilpa is Mexico's version of Carlsbad Caverns—an immense network of colorful stalactite-covered underground passages. Sendel promised to clean the place up, to build a hotel and a restaurant, and to channel a part of the revenues to the state government in Guerrero. Sendel also wanted to build robotic dinosaurs and laser shows inside the caves; he apparently has a thing for giant reptiles. His previous scheme was to install a "Dinosaurium" theme park in Montreal. Creditors there claimed he skipped town owing them millions of dollars. That was not the first time Sendel had gotten into financial trouble. In 1979 he served time in a U.S. federal prison for participating in a check-kiting scheme. Sendel never told the Mexican government any of this. "I didn't think it was necessary," he said when I finally got him on his cell phone. But he said he did tell them about his plans for the dinosaurs. "We gave them the plans at the beginning."

Quadri did not perform even a basic background check on Sendel. He said it was not his job. But was there another reason why Sendel, despite his checkered past and his bizarre plans to put a laser show inside a natural wonder, was not scrutinized? Quadri defended his actions by noting that Sendel and his project had been recommended by Guerrero Governor Rubén Figueroa, a powerful PRI hard-liner with an unsavory reputation. (Figueroa later resigned in disgrace after being accused of covering up the murder of seventeen campesinos by state authorities.) Sendel himself told me the project would never have gotten off the ground without Figueroa's backing. "He introduced me to people in the federal government—the right people who make the decisions."

The day after Sendel's past was revealed in press reports, his wife was arrested for cashing $40,000 in bad checks. Then a warrant was issued for Sendel himself on fraud charges. A few days later the cave concession was withdrawn on "technical grounds" that allegedly had nothing to do with the scandal.

A project that may have received less-than-careful scrutiny because it had a powerful backer had been canceled without so much as a hearing or a clear explanation. Carabias's conclusion? "There's an important lesson here," she said. "The law has many safeguards. We are following the letter of the law."

Suddenly she sounded like a politician.

I

A few months after I met with Carabias I got a phone call from Homero Aridjis. The day before, January 30, 1995, a freak snowstorm had dumped several feet of snow in the mountains that ring Mexico City. The sky over the city was dark blue and depthless, as if had been scrubbed and polished. From the balcony of my apartment I could see that the city was encircled by snowy mountains. Popocatepetl appeared in the eastern sky as a massive white pyramid that seemed to hover, detached, above the valley floor.

The snow that had cleaned Mexico City's air, Aridjis wanted me to know, had also fallen in the mountains of Michoacán, where monarch butterflies take refuge each winter. As many as a third of the butterflies had been killed. I decided to drive out to Michoacán to survey the damage.

The monarch sanctuaries scattered through the rugged Chincua mountains may be Mexico's best-known natural wonder. They were "discovered" in 1975 when a Mexican peasant named Rafael Sánchez led Canadian scientist Fred Urquhart to a quiet grove in the fir-covered mountains of Michoacán. For four decades Urquhart had been searching for the wintering ground of the orange and black monarchs that migrate south from the northern United State and Canada each fall. When Urquhart saw millions of monarchs clinging to the trees and hanging off the branches like clusters of fruit, he burst into tears.

A decade later, in 1986, five separate areas where the monarchs were known to congregate were made part of a protected reserve. Aridjis, who hails from Michoacán, was instrumental in goading President Miguel de la Madrid to issue the protection decree. The 40,000-acre (16,000-hectare) monarch butterfly biosphere reserve was created amid widespread optimism, with promises of funding from international environmental groups and the Canadian government. Peasants, fearful that the reserve would end the logging industry on which they depended, were assured that an ecotourism boom would make up for the shortfall.

A decade later hope had dissolved amid reciprocal accusation. The snowstorm brought the rift between international environmentalists and local peasants out into the open. Aridjis was a hated man in Angangueo, the super-depressed capital of the regional logging industry. Manuel Mendoza Cruz, the mayor of a nearby community called Los Rendones, told me logging had dropped 50 percent in the decade since the reserve was created. Monarca A.C., an internationally financed environmental group that provided a smattering of jobs in the desperately poor region, folded in 1995 amidst allegations of corruption. Tourism, meanwhile, has been a trickle rather a flood. "We're not against the butterflies," Mendoza insisted. "But the government needs to take our needs into account."

Those needs were simple: Mendoza told me he was organizing a protest march for the following weekend to petition the government to lift restrictions on logging within the reserve. "The forest belongs to us," Mendoza said. What was left it of it, he might have added. Half a century of logging has reduced the once extensive fir and pine forest to a few stands perched on shaved hillsides.

Quite simply, said Lincoln Brower, an entomologist at the University of Florida and a leading expert on the monarchs, there is not enough forest left to accommodate both logging and butterflies. The monarchs, Brower explained, require extremely precise conditions in order to form colonies—they nest only on southeastern slopes, and only in fir trees, and they require a balance of sun and shade. Those conditions are fast disappearing as clandestine logging slowly eats away at the last remaining forest. Fewer trees mean greater temperature extremes. Thinning the tree cover also dramatically increases the monarch's vulnerability to inclement weather—rain, high winds, and snow, all of which periodically hit the Chincua range. "The forest is like a blanket which protects the butterflies," said Brower. "Right now it has a lot of holes in it."

At the current rate of destruction, Brower predicted that the monarch sanctuaries—and one of the most remarkable natural migrations on the planet—would be destroyed within a decade. "The people in the region are blaming the butterflies for their poverty," added Aridjis. "But it is not the butterflies' responsibility to raise everyone's standard of living. It's an insect, not an industry."

The battle over the butterflies seemed to bring together many of the issues I had been looking at for several years. In one sense it was a classic environmental stalemate—people who wanted to exploit resources on one side, those who wanted to conserve them on the other. But what made the controversy uniquely Mexican was that the dialogue was taking place across an economic chasm. Mexico is one of the most economically divided societies on the planet, and the enviromental movement—such as it is—is caught on both sides of a chasm.

The part of Mexico that is highly developed, the first world Mexico, supports a small but highly influential group of environmentalists who are concerned about air pollution and urban transportation, but who also worry about global issues like climate change and loss of biodiversity. The Group of 100, of which Aridjis is the head, is the most visible of these groups. Greenpeace has also been more and more active in recent years especially in the areas of air pollution and toxic waste, while the Centro de Derecho Ambiental (Environmental Law Center) has been working hard on legal reform. There is a small academic community that is less public but highly influential in formulating policy; there are a number of important regional groups; there is a small and marginal Green Party; and here and there you will find a conscientious local official like Carmen Vázquez. But there is no mass membership organization or political movement associated with environmentalism in Mexico; by and large it remains an elite issue.

Environmentalism is also a concern on the other side of the economic gulf, but it is much more narrowly defined. The most urgent battles are for clean water, drainage, paved streets, a piece of land, and a way to make it produce. In many poor communities—certainly in Angangueo—the term "enviromentalism" has acquired a negative connotation. Environmentalists invariably come from outside the community, and they usually want to restrict access to some basic resource on which the community depends.

The mistrust is mutual. For many first world environmentalists, it is demands for basic resources made by the poor that are putting the strain on Mexico's—and the world's—environment. Mexico's growing poor population, they argue, is cutting down the forests to plant its corn, crowding the cities, and contributing to its own misery by having too many children. They point out that Mexico's population has nearly quadrupled in the second half of the twentieth century, from 25 million in 1945 to 90 million today.

There is no doubt that demographic growth has contributed to environmental destruction; it has caused peasant farmers to intensify production on their plots and cut down the woods in order to survive. Even though Mexico has reduced its birthrate from 3.5 in 1960 to 1.8 today, the country's population is expected to top 100 million by the year 2000. That will mean further demands on land and resources. But the correlation between Mexico's (and the world's) growing population and its growing environmental deterioration is far from exact. More important than the size of the population is how resources are managed. For example, the greatest environmental calamity in Mexico's history took place in the aftermath of the Spanish Conquest, when the country's population declined by as much as 90 percent. Mining and ranching did far more damage to the environment than 20 million corn farmers. In modern times, the distribution of marginal farmland, the growing dependence on fertilizers, the cycle of debt, and the collapse of corn prices have had as much to with rural to urban migration as population growth. It is simplistic therefore to blame the explosive growth of Mexico City or the destruction of the last of the monarchs' winter sanctuaries on poor families with too many children.

The more fundamental—and more complex—cause of Mexico's environmental crisis is the limitations of "development." This is why what is happening in Mexico is so critical for the whole planet. For every Korea that has made the transition from a traditional economy to a modern one, there are three Mexicos, countries that experienced years of growth but where development eventually stalled. This is true in both the socialist and the nonsocialist world (during the cold war the United States and the Soviet Union agreed on little aside from the promise of development). Mexico's situation is therefore not dissimilar from that of Brazil, India, and Egypt, or even Hungary, Romania, and the former Soviet Union. All of these countries consumed enormous amounts of resources attempting to build a modern economy, and now, to one degree or another, each is confronting a legacy of severe environmental damage. Mismanagement—or nonmanagement—of natural resources has ruined whole areas of Mexico before they could even be developed. The forestry industry is one example; the nation has received only short-term, marginal economic benefit from the destruction of its forests and jungles.

In Mexico, and around the world, policy makers did not worry that development often steamrolled traditional economies. Peasants displaced by these enormous economic changes were encouraged to head to the cities where they would find work in the factories. No one worried that the rivers were filling with sewage. No one worried about the jungle that was being cut down or the oil spills fouling the coast. No one even got too upset about industrial explosions. These were described as "the cost of development." It was assumed that once the process was completed, the countries would have the resources to clean up the mess.

Only when development slowed did Mexico begin to feel the effect of decades of environmental neglect. Suddenly there was no money left to prop up the countryside—thousands of villages that had always been poor but were once self-sufficient could not produce enough to eat. The infrastructure backlog in the cities continued to spiral out of control; the bill for environmental damage by the state-owned oil industry is billions of dollars. As Carabias herself pointed out, the damage is so severe that environmental destruction is threatening to undermine future growth. Far from generating the revenues to finance an environmental cleanup, the process of development has created enormous social problems that must be attended to immediately.

In the era of vanishing borders, these social problems will have continentwide implications. That is why the way U.S. policy makers deal with the Mexican environmental crisis will set an important precedent. So far, the United States has responded to Mexico's far-reaching economic, social, and environmental problems with the North American Free Trade Agreement and increased border enforcement. The rationale behind NAFTA is simply to fine-tune the failed developmentalist approach. The economic growth spawned by NAFTA, so the treaty's supporters promised, would slow illegal immigration, undermine the appeal of drug trafficking, and fund an environmental cleanup along the border. Despite the hoopla and the wrenching debate over its passage in the United States, NAFTA has become almost irrelevant. With the Mexican economy in a shambles, the boom that was supposed to fund the environmental cleanup has failed to materialize. Once again, development failed to live up to its promise, and leaving the environmental problems for later proved shortsighted and counterproductive.

It is also simplistic to see Mexican immigration to the United States as a function of underdevelopment. In fact, the environmental and economic disruption that comes with development is generally what triggers migration; new roads, telephones, money orders, fax machines, cheap airfares, and television encourage it. Putting up fences along the border might win votes for U.S. politicians, but spending time with the U.S. Border Patrol and talking to the migrants waiting to cross has convinced me that the border is too vast and the migrants too determined for enforcement to have more than a limited effect. The call for greater enforcement is largely a knee-jerk response to a complex process of integration and makes certain elements of the U.S. population uncomfortable. The fact is that the cultural and economic melding is far too advanced to be stopped by some miraculous economic takeoff or a strong border. The integration between the developed and developing world is not unique to the United States and Mexico. It is part of a global trend.

That is why the United States needs to take a greater interest in Mexico's environmental crisis. The few institutions created under NAFTA to deal with environmental disputes are clearly inadequate. The bureaucratic procedures for using NAFTA's Commission on Environmental Cooperation (CEC) are so cumbersome that its role will be extremely limited. These institutions need to be strengthened. Solid environmental management will help mitigate the disruptions in Mexico as it struggles to come to terms with the limitations of development.

International environmentalists also need to examine their reaction to Mexico's environmental crisis. Global warming, the depletion of the ozone layer, and the loss of biodiversity are among the most visible and compelling concerns. But environmentalists in Mexico and around the world should not focus on the potential for environmental cataclysm at the expense of the more fundamental but less dramatic environmental issues that affect daily life. Living in Mexico City—a place that has already suffered a kind of ecological collapse—has convinced me that the most crucial environmental struggle in the coming decades will be providing water, food, and clean air, and ensuring basic human health in a world where resources are more and more limited. The most compelling work for environmentalists—and for the planet—should be to develop a dialogue across the economic divide.

The first step in planning for this future is to acknowledge that development is selective and erratic. Many people are left behind; others elect not to participate. Uniform, global progress is not the world's destiny. The challenge is to create mechanisms that will allow the "developed," the "developing," and the "undeveloped" sectors of human society to more equitably share the world's resources and to coexist in a world in which each is assured certain rights. The challenge of the next century will be to find ways for fishermen and petrochemical plants to share the same river.

One battle in which grassroots and elite environmentalists were able to find common cause was the year-long struggle to block the construction of a golf course in Tepoztlán, a charming backwater an hour south of Mexico City in the mountains of Morelos. Claiming that a planned $300 million luxury development that included an eighteen-hole golf course would change the character of the town and use enormous amounts of its scarce water, campesino protestors stormed city hall, took municipal authorities hostage, forced environmental authorities to review the permit, and eventually ousted the town's PRI mayor. Environmental groups in Mexico City and Washington, D.C., supported the protesters by writing letters, speaking out on their behalf, and offering advice.

The fight over the golf course, however, was not so much an environmental struggle as a battle over local control of resources and political power (the protesters were allied with the PRD). This is a historical demand in Mexico, from the colonial era through the revolution and into the present. These kinds of political battles will heat up in the coming decades as Mexican central authority begins to crack and communities begin to perceive that the federal bureaucracy has mismanaged their resources. But the type of natural alliance with international environmentalists that took place in Tepoztlán will not always be so easy, because once local communities gain control of their resources they may choose to exploit them. Indigenous and peasant communities are complex, and they come down on both sides of the development debate. The Tarahumara, for example, are wary of roads, towns, and even doctors. The Zapatista rebels have picked up guns to fight for these same things.

The ability to look for a pragmatic solution when conservation clashes with indigenous or peasant rights depends on one's analysis of the depth of the world's environmental crisis. In the case of the monarch butterfly reserve, a major ecological phenomenon with continentwide implications hangs in the balance. The landscape is so degraded that there simply is not a lot of room to maneuver. In the aftermath of the snowstorm, Homero Aridjis, Lincoln Brower, and Duke University Professor Laura Snook got together to hammer out a last-minute proposal to save the forest. In order to stem illegal logging, they proposed creating a fund to buy the reserve's core areas outright, compensating the peasant communities. They proposed paying an annual rent in addition. Finally, they suggested greater investment in ecotourism development. The funds would come from the governments of the United States, Canada, and Mexico and be augmented by donations from environmental organizations. It was a good plan, but one I doubted the peasants of Angangueo would accept. They had heard it all in 1986 when the reserve was created. But the money had never arrived, and ecotourism had proved to be disappointing at best. The only sure thing for them is the trees; the peasants have learned they can rely on no one else.

As I drove through the eroded landscape near the monarch reserve, I found myself thinking of Aztec prophecies of environmental doom. The fragile earth had been abused; it seemed like just a matter of time before it lashed out violently, taking human society down with it. But nature, like hope, does not die so easily.

At ten in the morning I climbed the twisty mountain road above Angangueo and entered the Chincua reserve. At the ranger station, I met two Mexican biologists, Eduardo Rendón and Eneida Montesinos, who were doing research for Lincoln Brower. They offered to guide me to the monarch colonies.

After twenty minutes of walking we reached 8,000 feet, and the snow appeared in white blotches. As we pushed on over a ridge it grew deeper, crunching below our feet as we sank to our shins. We skirted a ridge and then climbed a steep hill to a quiet grove called Mojerena Alta, which hosts the largest known colony of monarchs in the world. We were the first to visit it since the storm hit.

I took in the scene with a mixture of awe and horror. Millions of monarchs covered every inch of every tree in the grove; they dripped from the branches like sap and flew gently in swirling pockets of sun. Then I looked down. The snow-covered ground was carpeted with dead butterflies; I could not walk without stepping on them. The biologists shook their heads and then began a census of the dead. I found a perch on a rock and watched them work. As the morning turned to afternoon, the sun crested the ridge and began to shine into the grove. Then something amazing happened. I looked at the ground and saw the butterflies slowly fluttering their wings. "They're not dead," realized Rendón. "They're only stunned. They're moving their wings in order to raise their body temperature so they can fly again."

Soon the meadow of monarchs was in motion, rising slowly into the air, swirling like leaves, and then alighting gently on the fir trees, once again finding sanctuary from the harsh world.

Notes

Introduction

Biodiversity statistics are from T. P. Ramamoorthy, Robert Bye, Antonio Lot, and John Fa, eds., *Biological Diversity of Mexico: Origins and Distribution* (Oxford, Eng.: Oxford University Press, 1993).

Chapter One

The Aztecs called themselves Mexica (pronounced me-shi-ca), from which the name of the modern country is derived. The term *Aztec* refers to the mythical homeland of Aztlan and was not widely used until the eighteenth century. Most scholars prefer Mexica, but since the bulk of this book is about the modern country of Mexico, I use the term *Aztec* to avoid confusion.

There are many Aztec creation myths, but they all drive home the same point: The earth was created in violence, and the gods must be nourished by human blood in order to forestall imminent doom.

The opening section on the Aztecs and land is based on Eric Wolf's *Sons of the Shaking Earth,* which, almost forty years after publication, remains the most comprehensive analysis linking the formation of Mesoamerican society to the land itself. *The Basin of Mexico* by Sanders, Parsons, and Santley offers a wonderfully detailed account of the human adaptations to the unique environment in the Valley of Mexico.

For Aztec life and religion I relied on Burr Cartwright Brundage's *Rain of Darts;* R. C. Padden's *The Hummingbird and the Hawk;* Jonathan Kandell's *La Capital;* Hugh Thomas's *Conquest;* and especially Jacques Soustelle's *Daily Life of the*

Aztecs. There is wide debate about the population of Tenochtitlan. The figure I use—500,000—is the low end of Soustelle's estimate.

The view that the Aztecs consolidated their power by gaining control over water was developed by Marxist anthropologist Angel Palerm, who applied the theory of social formation developed in Karl Wittfogel's *Oriental Despotism* (New Haven, Conn.: Yale University Press, 1957) to the Valley of Mexico. See *Obras hidráulicas prehispánicas en el sistema lacustre del Valle de México* (Mexico City: INAH, 1973).

Most scholars continue to believe that environmental factors played some role in the demise of Mesoamerica's pre-Columbian cultures, although in the case of the Maya recent research has focused on the role of warfare. See Arthur A. Demarest, "The Violent Saga of a Maya Kingdom" (*National Geographic,* February 1993, pp. 94–111). Even less is known about why Teotihuacan and Tula collapsed. Kandell provides an environmental explanation for the demise of Teotihuacan (*La Capital,* pp. 22–23); Richard A. Diehl attributes the collapse of Tula to military attacks on the drought-weakened city. See *Tula: The Toltec Capital of Ancient Mexico* (London: Thames and Hudson, 1983).

The extent of and the reasons for Aztec sacrifice are still widely debated. Some scholars believe the Spaniards exaggerated the number of victims in order to justify their own brutality. In a controversial 1977 paper, Michael Harner of the New School for Social Research argued that Aztec sacrifice was an ecological adaptation to a lack of domestic animals. The Aztecs, his argument goes, slaughtered humans because they had no cattle. Sacrifice and cannibalism, according to Harner, were even more widespread than commonly supposed—250,000 people, as much as 1 percent of the population, may have been eaten in a given year. Human sacrifice became a sort of feedback mechanism that would kick in during times of famine; if the rains were late, for example, it must have been because the gods were angry, and the only way to appease them was to offer more sacrifices. The sacrifices themselves both controlled population growth and provided meat in times of scarcity—like driving cattle to the slaughterhouse during a drought. The failure to consider the nutritional benefits of institutional cannibalism, Harner argues, may "represent European ethnocentrism . . . , a natural product of a continent that had relatively abundant livestock for milk and meat" (in "The Ecological Basis of Aztec Sacrifice," *American Ethnologist* 4, pp. 117–35).

The discussion of the ecological and biological impact of the conquest is taken largely from Alfred Crosby's groundbreaking work on the subject, *Germs, Seeds, and Animals; Ecological Imperialism;* and *The Columbian Exchange.* Charles Gibson, in his comprehensive *Aztecs under Spanish Rule,* offers a detailed account of the ecological forces that transformed the Valley of Mexico after the conquest—grazing, erosion, deforestation, and disease. For the impact of grazing and the phenomenal growth of the herds, I relied on Crosby and on François Chevalier's *Land and Society in Colonial Mexico.* Lesley Byrd Simpson mentions the destruction of forests in the colonial era, including the Indians' complaint about deforestation near Taxco in *Many Mexicos* (New York: G. P. Putnam, 1941). For a comprehensive overview of the great debate over the New World demographics see Thomas's *Conquest,* Appendix I, pp. 609–14.

The account of sheep in the Mezquital Valley is taken from Elinor G. K. Melville's *Plague of Sheep.*

For the Spanish view of land I relied on a number of primary sources, including Cortés's *Letters from Mexico;* Bernal Díaz's *Conquest of New Spain* (New York: Penguin Books, 1963); Sahagún's *Historia general de las cosas de Nueva España;* and Cabeza de Vaca's *The Account.* The Cabeza de Vaca expedition landed in Florida in 1528 but soon lost contact with the boats and was stranded in the wilderness. His description of his arduous eight-year journey across Texas and northern Mexico is not only full of wonderful ethnographic and natural detail but also gives real insight into the Spanish understanding of wilderness. See also Anthony Pagden's *Fall of Natural Man;* D. A. Brading's *First America;* and Chevalier's *Land and Society in Colonial Mexico.*

The description of how a temporary abundance of land changed indigenous farming practices and eventually fueled agrarian revolt comes from Gibson's *Aztecs under Spanish Rule;* John Tutino's *From Insurrection to Revolution in Mexico;* Eric Van Young's "Moving toward Revolt: Agrarian Origins of the Hidalgo Rebellion in the Guadalajara Region," in *Riot, Rebellion, Revolution,* ed. Friedrich Katz (Princeton, N.J.: Princeton University Press, 1988), pp. 176–204; and Brading's *First America.*

The account of the centennial celebration is from Mauricio Tenorio's "1910: Mexico City and El Centenario" (unpublished paper). John Womack's authoritative *Zapata and the Revolution* and Arturo Warman's *We Come to Object* were my two main sources on the revolution.

Chapter Two

The account of San Juan Mixtepec is based on two visits to the community, the first in September 1993 and the second in March 1996. I also consulted Jutta K. Blauert's doctoral dissertation, "Autochtonous Approaches to Rural Environmental Problems: The Mixteca Alta, Oaxaca, Mexico," which she thoughtfully deposited in the San Juan Mixtepec library. I reported on the transformation of the Mixteco region in an article for Pacific News Service, "NAFTA or Not,

Mixteco Indians Form New Hybrid Economy with U.S.," October 6, 1993. Special thanks go to Carlos Rincón for sharing his original research on the historical roots of environmental destruction in the Mixteca region with me; also to Leo Schibli and the staff of Serbo in Oaxaca for advice, guidance, and the use of their extensive library.

The history of erosion is taken from these interviews and Serbo documents. Raul García-Barrios argues that there has been a second wave of accelerated erosion in the Mixteco region over the past few decades. See Raúl García-Barrios and Luis García-Barrios, "Environmental and Technological Degradation in Peasant Agriculture: A Consequence of Development in Mexico," in *World Development* 18, no. 11, pp. 1569–85.

Statistics on land reform under Cárdenas and ejido production in the 1940s are from Whetten's *Rural Mexico.*

Angus Wright's *Death of Ramón González* was an essential source in the preparation of this chapter. The statistics on erosion in the Mixteco region, the history of the Green Revolution in Mexico, and the anecdote about the use of DDT at Jones Beach are all from Wright.

The excerpt from Juan Rulfo's "They Gave Us the Land" is translated by George D. Schade.

Other sources on the Green Revolution and agricultural policy generally include *Distorted Development* by David Barkin (Boulder, Colo.: Westview Press, 1990) (which also provided the statistics on meat consumption in Mexico) and *Defending the Land of the Jaguar* by Lane Simonian. The effects of the Green Revolution in Morelos were chronicled by Arturo Warman in *We Come to Object.* Ironically, Warman, who wrote the definitive critique of agrarian reform, is currently the head of the agrarian bureaucracy. But in a further Kafkaesque twist, agrarian reform was declared over two years before Warman was named the secretary of agrarian reform in 1994. Warman is not empowered to give away land. His role seems more to provide a bit of comfort to the dying.

Pesticide abuse in Mexico was first documented in Mexico by Lilia Albert in the late 1970s; see *Plaguicidas, el ambiente, y la salud* (Mexico City: Centro de Ecodesarrollo, 1990). See also Esther Schrader, "A Giant Spraying Sound," *Mother Jones,* January/February 1995, and Lane Simonian, "Pesticide Use in Mexico: Decades of Abuse," *Ecologist* 18, no. 2/3..

Facts and figures on desertification and erosion are compiled from the following sources: *Informe de la situación general en materia de equibrio ecológico y protección al ambiente 1993–1994* (Mexico City: SEDESOL-INI, 1994); Victor M. Toledo, "Ecología y nueva ley agraria en México," and Julia Carabias and Enrique Prevencio, "Hacia un modelo de desarrollo agrícola sustentable," both in José Luis

Calva, ed., *Alternativas para el campo mexicano,* Vol. 2 (Mexico City: Fundación Friedrich Ebert, 1993). Statements from state authorities in Guanajuato about the aquifer were printed in the Mexico City daily *The News,* December 14, 1994. On water shortages in the Sonora area, see José Luis Moreno, "El agua en Sonora: escasa, mal utilizada, y contaminada," in *Agua, salud, y derechos humanos* (Mexico City: Comisión Nacional de Derechos Humanos, 1995). On salinization, see *Informe de la situación general.*

Statistics on arable land are taken from a Banrural report cited in *Mexico: A Country Guide* (Albuquerque, N.M.: Inter-Hemispheric Education Resource Center, 1992). For a critique of Salinas's agricultural policies, see David Barkin, "Agrarian Counter-Reform in Mexico," *New Solutions,* Summer 1993. For a summary of the different theories on the impact of NAFTA on rural migration, see Philip L. Martin, *Trade and Migration: NAFTA and Agriculture* (Washington, D.C.: Institute for International Economics, 1993).

Chapter Three

The anecdote about the Mexico City sinkhole is from Mark Fineman, "In Mexico, Survival Is a Group Effort," *Los Angeles Times,* July 23, 1996. I spoke with Alfonso Martínez Baca at his office in Mexico City on August 3, 1995. He provided the figures on the amount of water lost to leaks (30 percent) and the amount of energy needed to provide Mexico City's water. Additional information was provided in a written statement from Luís Antonio Ramírez Valadés, a spokesperson for the Gerencia Regional de Aguas de Valle de México (the regional water administration for the Valley of Mexico) in January 1995. Half a dozen agencies oversee water in Mexico City, and they seldom agree on figures, much less policy. Where possible, I have tried to corroborate figures with those cited in *El agua y la Ciudad de México* (Mexico City: Consejo Nacional de Investigación in collaboration with the National Academy of Sciences, 1995), the most complete study to date of the city's water crisis. The book provided most of the statistics for water use and the rate of sinking, but in some instances its conclusions were disputed by government officials. For example, Martínez Baca disagreed with the study's finding that "in Mexico City, only 10 cents is recovered for every cubic meter of water despite the fact that the estimated cost is $1.00 per cubic meter" (p. 38). He also disagreed with the conclusion that "in Mexico City, the annual deficit to provide water and drainage is $1 billion " (p. 259). He claimed that the annual deficit for providing water in the city is $125 million.

Luis Manuel Guerra, president of Inaine, an environmental consulting firm in Mexico City, supplied me with the figures on electricity use. Guerra and Judith

Mora are the coauthors of a 1988 study called "Agua y energía en la Ciudad de México: Perspectivas del año 2000" (Mexico City: Fundación Friedrich Ebert, 1988). Martínez Baca disagreed with Guerra's numbers. He claimed that Mexico City uses 529.4 million kilowatt-hours a year for its water needs, an amount that is only 5 percent of the nation's energy output. The figure, however, is only half what the government acknowledges it uses merely to pump water from the neighboring valleys.

On pollution of the aquifer, see Marisa Mazari and Douglas M. Mackay, "Potential for Groundwater Contamination in Mexico City," *Environmental Science and Technology* 27, no. 5, pp. 794–802.

Sources for the section on the history of water in Mexico City include Alain Musset, *El agua en el Valle de México: Siglos XVI–XVIII* (Mexico City: Pórtico de la Ciudad de México and Centro de Estudios Mexicanos y Centroamericanos, 1992); Michael Mathes, "To Save a City: The Desagüe of Mexico-Huehuetoca, 1607," *Americas* 26, April 1970, pp. 419–30; Fernando Benítez, *La Ciudad de México, 1325–1980,* Vol. 3 (Barcelona: Salvat, 1982); *Memoria de las obras del sistema de drenaje profundo de Distrito Federal* (Mexico City: DDF, 1975); and Kandell, Palerm, Gibson, and Soustelle, *Daily Life of the Aztecs.* Soustelle mentions the prohibition on two-story homes in Tenochtitlan except for the elite (p. 11); the figure of 30,000 Indians killed in the 1629–1635 flood is from Kandell (p. 200). I want to thank Roberto Melville of CIESAS in Mexico City for pointing out the parallel between Tenochtitlan's and modern Mexico City's use of water from other regions—and for all his help with this chapter.

The history of the Lerma Valley is based on "Tules y sirenas: El impacto cultural de la industricalzición en Alto Lerma" by Beatriz Andrea Albores Zarate (Mexico City: El Colegio Mexiquense, A.C., 1995). See also "Los problemas del valle de México," by Adolfo Orive Alba, in *Ingenieria hidráulico en Mexico* 6, Spring 1952.

When I visited the Mezquital Valley during the 1991 cholera epidemic, the government had banned the farmers from using wastewater to cultivate any vegetable that is eaten raw. The prohibition was widely ignored; farmers I talked to told me that given the small size of their plots they needed to grow vegetables to survive; see "Mexico's Black Waters: A Life-and-Death Resource," *San Francisco Examiner,* November 24, 1991. See also "Prevention of Water Pollution by Agriculture and Related Activities," FAO Expert Consultation, Santiago, Chile, 1992, pp. 20–23. At the time of this writing, the Gran Canal is being covered as far as the Mexico State line.

The history of the Lake Texcoco project is from Gerardo Cruickshank García, "Proyecto Lago de Texcoco," in *Agua, salud y derechos humanos,* ed. Iván Restrepo (Mexico City: Comisión Nacional de Derechos Humanos, 1995).

For air pollution I relied on Iván Restrepo, ed., *La contaminación atmosférica en México* (Mexico City: Comisión Nacional de Derechos Humanos, 1992). Particularly useful was "La contaminación atmosférica en la Ciudad de México," by Jorge Legorreta and Ángeles Flores. Other sources include Marjorie Miller, "Can Mexico Clean Up Its Air?" *International Wildlife,* March/April 1993; Charles O. Collins and Steven L. Scott, "Air Pollution in the Valley of Mexico," *Geographical Review* 83, no. 2, pp. 119–33; "99% de los capitalinos con problemas en vías respiratorias," *Proceso,* February 6, 1995; Pete Hamill, "Where the Air Was Clear," *Audubon,* January-February 1993; and Simonian, *Defending the Land of the Jaguar.* The research, which found similar levels of nitrogen dioxide and hydrocarbons in Mexico City and New York's Lincoln Tunnel, was conductd by U.S. toxicologist Tom Dydek in 1987 and cited in Simonian (p. 204). On the carcinogenic effects of ozone, see Rob Edwards, "Ozone Alert Follows Cancer Warning," *New Scientist,* May 27, 1995. Luis Manuel Guerra, a chemist and president of a Mexico City–based environmental research firm called Inaine, was also an invaluable source on air pollution.

Information on the Cutzamala system is from *Sistema Cutzamala* (Mexico City: Comisión Nacional de Agua, 1994). According to the National Water Commission, Mexico has invested $100 million in infrastructure for each cubic meter of water the Cutzamala system brings to Mexico City.

On the 1985 earthquake, I relied on Elena Poniatowska, *Nada, Nadie* (Mexico City: Ediciones Era, 1988).

Chapter Four

Most of the information on the Zapatista conflict, the settlement of the Lacandón, and jungle agriculture is based on personal interviews over the course of several years. I first visited the Chiapas jungle in 1990, while researching my master's thesis on the Guatemalan refugees. I also spent a considerable amount of time in the Ixcán region, the continuation of the Lacandón jungle just across the border in Guatemala, talking to peasants there about making the jungle produce ("The Rise and Fall of Guatemala's Ixcán Cooperatives: 1965–1989," master's thesis, Stanford University, 1989). In the aftermath of the Zapatista revolt I visited Chiapas in March 1994, January 1995, and September 1995. Among the many people who assisted me during those visits are Jan de Vos, Andrés Aubry, Will Hoffman, Porfirio Camacho, Ronald Nigh, and Ignacio March.

Chiapas history is from Thomas Benjamin, *A Rich Land, A Poor People: Politics and Society in Modern Chiapas* (Albuquerque: University of New Mexico Press, 1989). For background on Chiapas and the Zapatistas, see John Ross, *Rebellion from the Roots* (Monroe, Maine: Common Courage Press, 1995); George Collier, *Basta!*

(Oakland, Calif.: Institute for Food and Development Policy, 1994); and Alma Guillermoprieto, "Zapata's Heirs," *New Yorker,* May 16, 1994. Carlos Tello Díaz, *La rebelión de las Cañadas* (Mexico City: Cal y Arena, 1995), provides a detailed and well-written account of the Zapatista's origins, but the book was widely criticized by the Mexican left because it seems to rely on government security documents for its account of the uprising. *La guerra de Año Nuevo* (Mexico City: Editorial Praxis, 1994) is a compilation of newspaper articles from the first days of the fighting and is the source for the account of the battle of Ocosingo.

On oil, see "El petróleo, detrás de la degradación social y ecológica en Chiapas," *Proceso,* no. 970, June 5, 1995.

The Zapatista demands are from *Compromisos por la paz,* the document the Zapatista rebels prepared in preparation for the February 1994 peace talks. It was published in *La Jornada,* March 3, 1994.

On the Lacandón Indians, see Perera and Bruce, *The Last Lords of Palenque.* Perera also reported on a joint Mexican-Guatemalan government plan to dam the Lacandón River to provide electric power (see *The Nation,* April 20, 1992, pp. 508–9). Facing intense international pressure, the Salinas government backed down. With the current strife in the Lacandón region it is unlikely the project will get off the ground anytime soon. Still, it remains one of the myriad environmental threats facing the dwindling jungle.

On environmental history, see James D. Nations, "The Ecology of the Zapatista Revolt," *Cultural Survival,* Spring 1994; see also Jan de Vos, "Una selva herida de muerte, historia reciente de la selva Lacandona," in *Reserva de la Biosfera Montes Azules, Selva Lacandona: Investigación para su conservación,* and Jan de Vos, *Viajes al Desierto de la Soledad* (Mexico City: Secretaría de Educación Pública, 1988). Cuauhtémoc González Pacheco, *Capital extranjero en la selva de Chiapas: 1863–1982* (Mexico City: UNAM, 1983), provided a history of logging; Xochitl Leyva and Gabriel Ascencio, "Lacandonia al filo de agua" (unpublished manuscript), was an invaluable source of local history and also provided statistics on grazing land conversion. The description of productive reforestation is based on a personal interview with Ronald Nigh in September 1995.

Chapter Five

Most of this chapter is based on firsthand reporting, specifically a ten-day trip to the Sierra Madre in June 1995 and a second shorter trip in March 1996. Two articles provided background: Alan Weisman, "The Deadly Harvest of the Sierra Madre," *Los Angeles Times Magazine,* January 9, 1994, and Alex Shoumatoff, "Trouble in the Land of Muy Verde," *Outside,* March 1995.

Randy Gringich's master's thesis, "The Political Ecology of Deforestation in the Sierra Madre Occidental of Chihuahua" (University of Arizona, 1992), was an excellent source of local history.

Sources for the short history section include Simonian, *Defending the Land of the Jaguar;* Martin D. Crocker, "The Evolution of Mexican Forest Policy and Its Influence upon Forest Reserves," Ph.D. diss., Oregon State University, 1973; Lázaro Mejía Fernández, "La política forestal en el dessarrollo de la administración pública forestal," Seminario de Titulación (master's thesis), Universidad Autonoma de Chapingo, 1988; Starker Leopold, *Wildlife of Mexico;* William Vogt, *Los recursos naturales de México* (Mexico City: Sociedad Mexicana de Geografía y Estadística, 1965); and Enrique Beltrán, *La batalla forestal* (Mexico City: publisher unknown, 1964).

On traditional medicine in the Sierra Madre, see Francisco Cardenal, *Remedios y practicas curativos en la Sierra Tarahumara* (Mexico City: Editorial Camino, 1993).

Chapter Six

The account of the San Juanico explosion is from Carlos Monisiváis, *Entrada libre: Antología de la sociedad que se organiza* (Mexico City: Ediciones Era, 1987). For background on Pemex, see *Oil and Mexican Foreign Policy* (Pittsburgh, Penn.: University of Pittsburgh Press, 1988) and *The Politics of Mexican Oil* (Pittsburgh, Penn.: University of Pittsburgh Press, 1980), both by George W. Grayson; see also Jonathan C. Brown and Alan Knight, eds., *The Mexican Petroleum Industry in the Twentieth Century* (Austin: University of Texas Press, 1992). Alan Riding's *Distant Neighbors* has an authoritative chapter on the petroleum industry.

Most of the firsthand reporting for this chapter was conducted during a ten-day visit to Veracruz and Tabasco in August 1995. The amount of damage paid out by Pemex in 1992–93 is taken from Mark Stevenson, "The Black Tide," *Insight,* November 20, 1994. On environmental damage in Tabasco I relied on José Eduardo Beltrán Hernández, "Los impactos de petróleo," and Edilberto Cervantes Galván, "Prioridades nacionales y intereses locales: La explotación del petróleo en Tabasco," both in Vol. 3 of *Tabasco: Realidad y perspectivas* (Mexico City: Miguel Angel Purrúa, 1993). A fifteen-volume series on environmental destruction in Coatzacoalcos was published by the Centro de Ecodesarrollo and the Universidad Veracruzana in 1987. Particularly useful was Vol.15, *Energía, ambiente y desarrollo.* On the February 1996 well takeovers in Tabasco, see Andrew Downie, "Tabasco Farmers Block Pemex Facilities in Pollution Fight," *Houston Chronicle,* February 11, 1996, and Alvaro Delgado, Gerardo Albarrán de Alba, and Armando Guzmán, "Explosiones, aguas infestadas, tierras ensalitradas, desaparición de cultivos, comunidades invadidas, costo del paso de Pemex por Tabasco," *Proceso,* February 19, 1996.

John Ross's story, "Dangers in Paradise" in the July/August 1992 issue of *Sierra,* provided background on Coatzacoalcos. For a more recent look at the area's air pollution problem, see Humberto Bravo, Rodolfo Sosa Echeverría, and Ricardo Torres Jardón, "La calidad del aire en la conurbación industrial de Coatzacoalcos-Minatitlán," in *La Contaminación atmosférica en México* (Mexico City: CNDH, 1992).

On Laguna Verde, see Dimitris Stevis and Stephen P. Mumme, "Nuclear Power, Technological Autonomy, and the State in Mexico," *Latin American Research Review* 26, no. 3, pp. 55–82. See also Octavio Miramontes, "Wooing Mexico to Nuclear Power," *Bulletin of Atomic Scientists,* July/August 1989, pp. 36–38.

Chapter Seven

The reporting for this chapter is based on two trips to Cancún, the first in January 1992 on assignment for *Condé Nast Traveler,* the second in November 1995. On the Princeton study, see Jonathan Marshall, "How Ecology Is Tied to Trade Pact," *San Francisco Chronicle,* February 25, 1992. The history of Cancún is from Fernando Martí, *Cancún: A Fantasy of Bankers* (Publisher unknown, 1990). See also a report by Luz del Carmen Colmenero Rolón, José de Jesús Antonio Palma Gutiérrez, and Armando Ferreira Nuño, *Medio Ambiente y Desarrollo en Quintana Roo,* published in collaboration with Grupo Ecologista de Mayab, A.C. (GEMA) and CANTE, A.C., January 1990. History and statistics on visitors come from Jens Sorensen and David Gutiérrez, *Cancún: The Visions and the Realities in the Planning and Development of an International Coastal Tourism Center,* a case study prepared for the Professional Training Project of the International Coastal Management Program at the University of Rhode Island, February 5, 1993 (draft). Information on Acapulco, Huatulco, and Fonatur was taken from Bob Shacochis, "In Deepest Gringolandia," *Harper's,* July 1989. On Huatulco, see also John Ross in *Sierra;* Francisco Ortiz Pinchetti, "Embargo contra Fonatur en Huatulco por negarse a pagar el impuesto predial," *Proceso,* no. 951, January 23, 1995. On politics in Quintana Roo and the Costa Maya project, see Gerardo Albarrán de Alba and Martín Morita, "El 'estilo selvático' de gobernar ha convertido a Quintana Roo en paraíso de narcos y coto de la violencia y la venganza criminal y política," and the related sidebar, "A dos dias de dejar la reforma agraria, Cervera Pacheco 'cedió' a Villanueva Madrid, de manera ilegal, tierras de la reserva de biosfera de Sian Ka'an para un proyecto turístico," both in *Proceso,* no. 967, May

15, 1995. On the Cozumel pier, see Julia Preston, "Where Cruise Liners Intrude, Nafta Tests Waters," *New York Times,* February 26, 1996. Carlos Constandse's open letter defending Xcaret's environmental record was published in *Por Esto! de Quintana Roo,* December 3, 1994.

The Mexican government has not been forthcoming about the size of its total investment in Cancún, but Jorge Polanco's $3 billion is in line with figures reported in Sorensen and Gutiérrez. However, Polanco's estimate of annual tax revenues struck me as very high. The primary federal tax has been a 10 percent value-added tax, which was raised to 15 percent in 1995. The estimated size of Cancún's economy is $2 billion per year. That would mean the government would more likely collect between $250 million and $500 million in total revenues. All other tourism statistics are from the Secretariat of Tourism, *El Turismo en México: Aspectos Relevantes,* November 27, 1995.

Chapter Eight

This chapter is based on firsthand reporting done between 1992 and 1994 in Tijuana, San Diego, and Los Angeles. Stories I wrote about Chilpancingo and the Alco Pacific plant appeared in the *SF Weekly,* April 1, 1992; the *San Francisco Examiner,* November 8, 1992; *The Nation,* November 30, 1992; *California Lawyer,* February 1993; the *Daily Journal,* July 7, 1993; and Pacific News Service, December 27, 1993. See also Stryker Meyer, "Visitors Chilly on 'Maquila' Conditions," *San Diego Union-Tribune,* March 6, 1993; Diane Lindquist, "Pollution Leaves Faint Tracks," *San Diego Union-Tribune,* April 6, 1993; Randy Loftis, "A Pile of Trouble," *Dallas Morning News,* November 1, 1992; and Bob Davis, "Nafta May Get Lift from Pact on Toxic Site," *Wall Street Journal,* June 15, 1993. On the problems with the environmental side-agreement, see Allen R. Myerson, "Trade Pact's Environmental Efforts Falter," *New York Times,* October 17, 1994; Robert Collier, "Cleanup along the Border Still a Dream," *San Francisco Chronicle,* September 26, 1995; and Nancy Nusser, "Economic Crisis Guts Environmental Projects," *Atlanta Journal and Constitution,* April 2, 1995. On anencephaly in Matamoros, see "An Investigation of a Cluster of Neural Tube Defects in Cameron County, Texas," a report by the Texas Department of Health with technical assistance from the Centers for Disease Control, July 1, 1992. See also Ana Arana, "The Wasteland," *San Francisco Examiner, Image Magazine,* August 30, 1992.

I reported on maquiladora conditions in Matamoros for the *Los Angeles Times* (see Mark Fineman, "Environmental Nightmare on U.S.–Mexican Border Abates," *Los Angeles Times,* March 12, 1996).

Chapter Nine

I interviewed Julia Carabias at her office on July 24, 1995. The brief history of Mexican environmentalism is from Simonian, *Defending the Land of the Jaguar* (as are the quotations from Echeverría and López Portillo), and from Stephen P. Mumme, C. Richard Bath, and Valerie J. Assetto, "Political Development and Environmental Policy in Mexico," *Latin American Research Review* 23, no. 1 (the quotation from Barcena was taken from this article).

I reported on Barry Sendel and the Caves of Cacahuamilpa for the *Los Angeles Times;* see "Mexico's 'Case of the Caves' Shows Perils of Privatization" by Mark Fineman, July 16, 1995.

I wrote about the butterfly die-off for the *San Francisco Chronicle;* see "Cold Blow to Monarch Butterflies," January 6, 1996. See also John Ross in *Sierra;* Laura Snook, "Conservation of the Monarch Butterfly Reserves in Mexico: Focus on the Forest," *Biology and Conservation of the Monarch Butterfly,* Science Series of the Natural History Museum of Los Angeles County, no. 38, 1993; Lincoln Brower is the leading expert on the monarch migration, but his publications on the subject are too numerous to cite here.

Selected Bibliography

Given the enormous amount of scholarship on Mexico, there is surprisingly little on either environmental history or contemporary environmental problems. Here I have compiled a bibliography on the Mexican environment for the general reader. Most of the government reports and academic studies used in the preparation of this book are cited in the chapter notes. Where possible, I have provided English translations of the Spanish works.

Berlandier, Jean Louis. *Journey to Mexico during the Years 1826–1834* (2 vols.). Translated by Sheila M. Ohlendorf. Austin: Texas Historical Association, 1980.

Brading, D. A. *The First America: The Spanish Monarchy, Creole Patriots and the Liberal State, 1492–1867*. Cambridge: Cambridge University Press, 1991.

Brundage, Burr Cartwright. *A Rain of Darts: The Mexican Aztecs*. Austin: University of Texas Press, 1972.

Cabeza de Vaca, Àlvar Núñez. *The Account: Àlvar Núñez Cabeza de Vaca's Relación*. Translated by Martin A. Favata and José B. Fernández. Houston: Arte Público Press, 1993.

Chevalier, François. *Land and Society in Colonial Mexico: The Great Hacienda*. Translated by Alvin Eustis. Berkeley: University of California Press, 1963.

Collier, George. *Fields of Tzotzil: The Ecological Bases of Tradition in Highland Chiapas*. Austin: University of Texas Press, 1975.

Collier, George, with Elizabeth Lowery Quaratiello. *Basta! Land and the Zapatista Rebellion in Chiapas*. Oakland, Calif.: Institute for Food and Development Policy, 1994.

Cortés, Hernán. *Letters from Mexico*. Translated by A. R. Pagden. New York: Grossman Publishers, 1971.

Crosby, Alfred W., Jr. *The Columbian Exchange: The Biological and Cultural Conse-quences of 1492.* Westport, Conn.: Greenwood Press, 1973.

————. *Ecological Imperialism: The Biological Expansion of Europe, 900–1900.* Cam-bridge: Cambridge University Press, 1986.

————. *Germs, Seeds, and Animals: Studies in Ecological History.* New York: M. E. Sharpe, 1994.

Díaz del Castillo, Bernal. *The Conquest of New Spain.* Translated by J. M. Cohen. New York: Penguin Books, 1963.

Gibson, Charles. *The Aztecs under Spanish Rule.* Stanford, Calif.: Stanford Uni-versity Press, 1964.

González, Luis. *San Jose de Gracia: Mexican Village in Transition.* Translated by John Upton. Austin: University of Texas Press, 1979.

Humboldt, Alexander von. *Political Essay on the Kingdom of New Spain.* Translated by John Black. New York: Alfred A. Knopf, 1972.

Kandell, Jonathan. *La Capital.* New York: Henry Holt, 1988.

Landa, Diego de. *Yucatan before and after the Conquest.* Translated by William Gates. New York: Dover Publications, 1978.

Leopold, A. Starker. *Wildlife of Mexico.* Berkeley: University of California Press, 1959.

Melville, Elinor G. K. *A Plague of Sheep: Environmental Consequences of the Con-quest of Mexico.* Cambridge: Cambridge University Press, 1994.

Musset, Alain. *El Agua en el Valle de México: Siglos XVI–XVIII.* Mexico City: Por-tico de la Ciudad de México, 1992.

Ortiz Monasterio, Fernando. *Tierra profanada: Historia ambiental de México.* Mex-ico City: INAH, 1987.

Padden, R. C. *The Hummingbird and the Hawk: Conquest and Sovereignty in the Val-ley of Mexico: 1503–1541.* Columbus: Ohio State University Press, 1967.

Pagden, Anthony. *The Fall of Natural Man: The American Indian and Origins of Com-parative Ethnology.* Cambridge: Cambridge University Press, 1982.

Perera, Victor, and Robert D. Bruce. *The Last Lords of Palenque: The Lacandón Mayas of the Mexican Rain Forest.* Boston: Little, Brown, 1982.

Riding, Alan. *Distant Neighbors.* New York: Alfred A. Knopf, 1985.

Ross, John. *Rebellion from the Roots.* Monroe, Maine: Common Courage Press, 1995.

Rulfo, Juan. *The Burning Plain and Other Stories.* Translated by George D. Schade. Austin: University of Texas Press, 1973.

Sahagún, Bernardino de. *Historia general de las cosas de Nueva España.* Mexico City: Editorial Porrúa, 1975.

Sanders, William T., Jeffrey R. Parsons, and Robert S. Santley. *The Basin of Mexico: Ecological Processes in the Evolution of a Civilization.* New York: Academic Press, 1979.

Schele, Linda, and David A. Freidel. *A Forest of Kings.* New York: William Morrow, 1990.

Simonian, Lane. *Defending the Land of the Jaguar: A History of Conservation in Mexico.* Austin: University of Texas Press, 1995.

Soustelle, Jacques. *Daily Life of the Aztecs on the Eve of the Spanish Conquest.* Translated by Patrick O'Brian. Stanford, Calif.: Stanford University Press, 1961.

Thomas, Hugh. *Conquest.* New York: Simon and Schuster, 1993.

Todorov, Tzvetan. *The Conquest of America.* Translated by Richard Howard. New York: Harper & Row, 1984.

Traven, B. *The Rebellion of the Hanged.* New York: Alfred A. Knopf, 1952.

Tutino, John. *From Insurrection to Revolution in Mexico.* Princeton, N.J.: Princeton University Press, 1986

Warman, Arturo. *"We Come to Object": The Peasants of Morelos and the National State.* Translated by Stephen K. Ault. Baltimore, Md.: Johns Hopkins University Press, 1980.

Weber, David J. *The Mexican Frontier, 1821–1846: The American Southwest under Mexico.* Albuquerque: University of New Mexico Press, 1982.

———. *The Spanish Frontier in North America.* New Haven, Conn.: Yale University Press, 1992.

Whetten, Nathan L. *Rural Mexico.* Chicago: University of Chicago Press, 1948.

Wolf, Eric R. *Sons of the Shaking Earth.* Chicago: University of Chicago Press, 1959.

Womack, John, Jr. *Zapata and the Mexican Revolution.* New York: Alfred A. Knopf, 1968.

Wright, Angus. *The Death of Ramón González.* Austin: University of Texas Press, 1990.

Index